ONE L

ONE LOVE

The Reggae Boyz:
An Incredible Soccer Journey

Robbie Earle and Daniel Davies

ANDRE DEUTSCH

First published in 1998 by André Deutsch Ltd
This edition published in 1999
by André Deutsch Ltd
76 Dean Street
London WIV 5HA
www.vci.co.uk

A catalogue record for this book is available from the British Library

ISBN 0 23399 450 5

Typeset by Derek Doyle & Associates
Mold, Flintshire
Printed and bound in the UK

1 3 5 7 9 10 8 6 4 2

Front Cover Photo © Mark Leech

CONTENTS

To Nev – this one's for you, kid.

ACKNOWLEDGEMENTS

Robbie Earle

Thank you to Sandra, Otis and Saffie; Mum and Dad; my sisters Steph, Yvonne and Winsome; Rene Simoes and Carl Brown; Captain Burrell – for having the dream; Horace Reid; Brian Sparrow, Joe Kinnear and Sam Hammam; The Super Dons; Spider, Peter and Boopie; Garth Crooks; John Barnes; Bob Hazel; Peter Miller; Stevie Allen for the physio; Dr Marcos and Dr Rosanne; Denise Nicholls and Dr Rose; Alfredo and Mr Gartell; Derek Haven – the Jamaican High Commissioner; the staff at the Wydham Hotel; David Watt; Mark Bright; John Rudge.

Daniel Davies

Thank you: Mum, Dad and Huw; Robbie; Brian Sparrow; Hannah MacDonald; Terry Parris; Rose, Melanie and Christine at Air Jamaica; Suzanne McManus at Super Club Hotels; Devon Chin; Audley Boyd and the RJR Sports Club scrimmage crew; Nodley Wright; Evon 'Man-trol' Hewitt; Earl Bailey; Alan 'Skill' Cole; John Barnes; Dave Cottrell and all at the late, lamented *Goal Magazine*; Stephanie Jones for the translation; Ryan Herman for holding the fort; all at Zone; Rene Simoes, Peter Cargill, 'Spider' Lawrence; Colin Levy at Barclay Stratton; Will Hyde at ZfL; Rosemary Carty at the Pegasus Hotel, Kingston for the signed Pele shirt; Laurent Retord and all in Pierrevert and Manosque; Pete Stanton and Simon Buckley; Derry; Olivia; and last but not least, Mr Green.

Half the proceeds from the royalties for *One Love* will be donated to Father Hulong's Orphanage in Jamaica.

FOREWORD BY JOHN BARNES

First of all I have to say what a wonderful achievement it was for Jamaica to qualify for the World Cup. In the sporting context, the Caribbean is best known for cricket and athletics but football has always been an established sport in Jamaica and Jamaicans have felt that they should be at the World Cup. That is the nature of the people.

My father, a former Jamaican football captain, wanted me to be a swimmer but I remember sloping off to 'play ball'. When I was growing up in Jamaica, the game was all my friends and I were ever interested in. It has always been a massive sport on the island but there has never been any finance to tap the potential. Jamaicans have always considered themselves to be the best footballers in the region so when Trinidad nearly qualified for the 1990 World Cup, I think it stung Jamaican pride.

I know a lot of Jamaican coaches – all of them excellent coaches – and there is a huge amount of talent in Jamaica, so why has it taken until now for Jamaica to make it to the World Cup?

There are many reasons. Jamaicans love Brazilian football and a Brazilian coach was probably what they needed. Rene Simoes added professionalism to the native Jamaican flair but he also changed attitudes. Jamaicans idolised Brazilian footballers for their skills rather than the hard work and dedication they put into the sport. Brazilian flair and skill are admired the world over, but the discipline that goes into making it function within a team is often ignored. The attitude that Brazilians are natural players who operate as individuals held Jamaica back for too long.

It has also always been difficult to keep the best players in the country. Football is a working-class sport and many talented Jamaican footballers were forced to emigrate on soccer scholarships to continue playing. They might have had to stop playing in their early twenties if they had stayed at home because of the need to work and support their families. A lot of the boys did not have boots. They had to travel to matches and no matter how talented they were, many fell by the wayside because they just could not afford to play football.

As well as the English-based Jamaicans, I know many of the older Jamaican players and am delighted they got the opportunity to play in a tournament they had watched avidly on television over the years. They had always dreamt about playing in the World Cup but never thought it possible and they should feel proud that youngsters in Jamaica will now dream of emulating them.

Jamaica has qualified once but it is crucial that they go again and do even better the next time. The World Cup can now give young players in Jamaica something to aim for and it is also important that the best young players are kept on the island. That will take hard work and investment but I am confident the game is now going in the right direction.

The World Cup has snowballed for the African teams and there is no reason why the same should not happen in the Caribbean. I believe that if the football revolution had started earlier, Jamaica would now be on a par with some of the better-known African countries. You have to build on what you have achieved and the more Jamaica can play against top-quality opposition the more they will improve.

People often ask me who I would have supported if results had gone the right way and England faced Jamaica in the last 16 at the World Cup. I am the son of a diplomat so I say I would have supported both teams. Only when the goals started going in would I have had some serious talking to do! Enjoy the book.

Newcastle, 31 August 1998

PART ONE

PREFACE
The Qualifying Match

ROBBIE

16 November 1997

The sound is gently lilting but even through the haze of sleep there is no mistaking that familiar voice: '. . . One hear-ar-at / Let's get together and feel all right . . .' It's 8.30am and the strains of Bob Marley's 'One Love' provide an unusual but curiously pleasant alarm call. I'm on the top bunk in a small bedroom. Opposite, I can see two of my team mates fast asleep in a similar double-decker arrangement. The deep breathing coming from below tells me that I am the only one awake.

Through the window into the garden, I can see that it is already hot outside. The brilliant, clear light hits the mango trees and the noise of car horns rises up from the distance. Footsteps and voices elsewhere in the house confirm that our date with destiny has finally arrived. I rub my eyes, sit up and smile. What a way to start the biggest day of my football career.

Every single person on Jamaica will have come into this day with the same thought on his or her mind. Many will have been to church and prayed for us this morning. The population of Jamaica is showing the advanced symptoms of football fever. From Montego Bay to Mandeville, from the rural parish of West Moreland to Spanish Town, the bumpy roads that lead into Kingston will already be swarming with buses, vans, cars and trucks. This is a day for history making and no one wants to miss it.

From nowhere, we now stand just 90 minutes away from becoming the first English-speaking Caribbean island to qualify for the World Cup finals. We are a team made up of very different people with a modest ability yet we have overcome a lack of experience and short-age of cash to stand on the brink of achieving something very special. It's important that we don't let these considerations distract us today. We must try to treat this momentous match against Mexico just like any other game.

I think back over recent events and reflect how far I have come. Geographically I am 4,000 miles away from my native Potteries – although it feels like I've travelled further as a player. From playing men's football as a 12 year old, to breaking a leg and being rejected by Stoke, then going from Port Vale to Wimbledon – it could be light years. By rights, I should have given up on the idea of playing inter-national football at the age of 32. Yet here I am, just one game away from the pinnacle of any player's career. If you had told me 12 months ago that I would find myself in this position, I would have laughed and told you the sun had gone to your head.

I am a Jamaican citizen now. I have always been eligible for citizenship through my parents but I'd never needed to fill out the paperwork before. When I did, back in June, I was helped by the High Commissioner in London, a good friend of Captain Burrell, president of the Jamaican Football Federation and architect of the national movement I now find myself at the centre of. It made a change, the Commissioner told me, to be able to deal with matters like mine rather than processing paperwork on yardies waiting for deportation. My application went through at unprecedented speed. Two days later I was a Jamaican national.

Yesterday, the prime minister visited the team house. The TV was switched off and the dominoes hastily cleared away, and the players sat up in the sofas that line the day room. Captain Burrell could not hide his excitement when he walked in with the greying P.J. Patterson. The PM addressed us, looking each one of us in the eye. He appeared to be well informed about football and commended us for the vital point we won in El Salvador last week. He spoke of good passing and how we should get the ball wide in order to feed the country's new goalscoring hero, Deon Burton of Derby County. The nation's leader had obviously been thinking long and hard about the tactics we should employ.

'You have done so much for Jamaica,' Patterson told us. 'You have righted a lot of wrong perceptions that outsiders had about our coun-try.' He's right. The football team has generated more positive publicity for a place blighted by poverty and violence than the tourist office could ever dream of. Basically, there were two images of Jamaica: the golden beaches and palm trees of the walled, all-inclusive holiday resorts and people living on the breadline. The murder rate here is one of the highest in the world, yet on match days it drops to virtually nil.

We are trying to make Jamaica famous for something else. Even if it all goes wrong today, the Reggae Boyz have brought unity to a population divided along social and political lines. More than anything, though, we have made Jamaicans feel proud. People now want to wear the colours of the flag and sing the closing line of the national anthem – 'Jamaica land we love' – with feeling.

A rumour had been circulating that Prime Minister Patterson was going to reward the team for its achievements. It was suggested that we might get a gold Rolex watch each. Status is measured by different means in Jamaica and gold, like a title, is a mark of your standing. A state-of-the-art digital watch would never be as desirable as a less expensive gold watch and it's about how much you've got and how you wear it. I've never worn a lot myself but quite a few of the lads have big necklaces and chunky rings. Horace Burrell, known simply as 'The Captain', *always* wears his gold Rolex.

Then there are cars and mobile phones. Behind the walls of our modest compound, the pecking order can be identified through where you park your car. The smartest will be parked nearest the windows of the house. Similarly, those who spend hours chatting into their cellular phones are demonstrating that they have the money to pay the bills. One of my team mates even has a gold chain thick enough for his phone to be suspended from it. There is no need to scratch at the surface to understand Jamaican culture – it is all there to see.

The Captain was dying to tell us what Patterson had up his sleeve and could barely contain himself as he stood behind the prime minister, giving us thumbs-up signals. To own a house in Jamaica is better than gold, cars and phones, so smiles broke out across the room as Patterson announced that we were to be given land. Allotments of government-owned real estate would be made available to each player in the squad and we would be furnished with low-interest mortgages to build houses on them.

Good land is very hard to come by. I'm planning to have a villa built for me and my family and would like to buy one for my parents too, as they are Jamaican born and bred. Seeing their son doing something positive for the island has made them feel that they have given something back after leaving all those years ago.

After we'd seen Patterson, opposition leader Edward Seaga arived. Everyone was still buzzing about the land and naturally we wondered how Patterson's political rival was going to match such a gesture. However, Seaga, a thin white man with dark glasses, delivered a big speech about having to win for the country – and nothing more. He wished us, 'All the best' and left. Some of the Jamaican lads started shouting for Patterson while Seaga was still in earshot. The chant 'Show, show, show' went up as a joke. He had lost face.

Patterson's government has supported the programme since the early days and we are now seeing the political capital that can be made out of football because we have become a vehicle for change in Jamaica. The football team is suddenly a popular cause and politicians want to be associated with our success. If a snap election was to be called today, our Brazilian coach, Professor Rene Simoes, would be swept into Government House on the biggest landslide in history.

At the beginning of this momentous week, we flew back into Jamaica from El Salvador, safe in the knowledge that we only required a point to qualify for the World Cup Finals. Before we set up camp again, I decided to spend some time with one of my close friends in the Jamaican squad, Aaron 'Spider' Lawrence, at his home near the exotic beaches of Negril. Spider and I are often mistaken for twins and we do act that way sometimes. He made me feel especially welcome when I first arrived to play for Jamaica in July. He introduced me to the other players and is the man who now occupies the top bunk on the other side of our cramped bedroom. The reserve goalkeeper, Spider's importance to the squad is far greater than his position on the bench implies.

Spider is confident, eloquent and charismatic, as well as being one of the more entrepreneurial players in the squad. (He is setting up his own taxi firm and has recruited a loyal driver named Stogie.) When I saw what Spider called his family home, however, I was confronted with the reality of where many of my team mates come from. The rest of the lads had warned me that Spider was from an under-developed part of the island, but I wasn't prepared for what I saw. The main dwelling was like a shack with three bedrooms. There was limited lighting, curtains instead of doors and much of the wiring was exposed. I've got to admit that it shocked me. Spider is the breadwinner and has to look after his mother, brother and sister on the modest income he makes from being part of the Jamaican football programme. He is also trying to build a new home, which no doubt will be fantastic when it's finished, and all the more so because 'the Road to France' is paying for every brick.

Spider and the other Jamaica-based players spend Monday to Friday in our team bungalow in Kingston, training, doing physical work and practising set pieces. The players seem to like it, and when I saw how Spider lived I realised why he was happy to share a house with 20 other men. For a start, everything is laid on, and he is well aware that football can buy him things that he could never afford doing any other job.

The only downer for Spider is the fact that he can't really go out while he's in camp. Jamaicans love socialising and Spider is no different. After a game, the players are usually pestered non stop by a public that has got high on hope. We're treated like pop stars on the island, and even the top names in music like DJs Beenie Man or Bounti Killah and reggae stars Jimmy Cliff and Dennis Brown want to be seen with the Reggae Boyz. When he gets the chance, though, Spider still likes to hang out on the corner with friends or pay a visit to his garage. In his own area, locals wish him luck but give him room to relax.

There are many people in Jamaica who live like Spider. Not many of them, however, can say they are on the threshold of going to the World Cup finals to represent their country. And while Spider has not made many appearances on the Road to France campaign, what he brings to the mix cannot be measured in playing statistics alone. Spider radiates warmth and no one deserves this chance more than him.

The happiness his success has brought reminds me of another reason why this team is unique. The players have become stars in their own right but they still live in the same homes and among the same people as they did before being thrust into the spotlight. The only difference now is that they are in a better position to help those less fortunate than themselves. The boys do a lot for charity when they are together as a group and the public appreciate that.

I witnessed how uncelebrity-like they are only days ago. Our bus broke down in the mountains on the way back from Braco Village in Trelawny – where we had been hiding out to get away from all the excitement. Anyone who has crossed the belly of the island will know what a mountainous journey it is and we found ourselves beside an enormous ravine with a stricken bus and basketfuls of equipment.

Can you imagine Glenn Hoddle flagging down passing traffic? That's what Simoes did, packing his players into a convoy of cars, trucks and vans. I wonder what the odds were on me getting a ride with five others in an Englishman's jeep. Bringing up the rear, a flatbed lorry carried our kit, footballs and those unlucky ones at the back of the bus. From nowhere, we then acquired a police escort and drove into Kingston with cheers ringing in our ears. It could only happen in Jamaica.

The routine is the same on every match day. We all have to be up for breakfast together and because Simoes doesn't like anyone to be different, green shirts must be worn. After a hearty start to the day, prepared by the team chef, there are a couple of hours left to kill before we begin the serious preparations for this afternoon's game. Some of the boys take to the draughts board, a game taken very seriously in Jamaica. I'm not exaggerating when I say that friendships have been lost on the outcome of a game. Elsewhere in the large day room, the slap of dominoes on the table top can be heard. Voices are raised and tension is high.

At eleven o'clock, the team Reverend enters the house with some members of his church. The spiritual time has a position of prime importance in our pre-match build-up and we sing, hold hands and pray for guidance in the task ahead. Reverend Al Miller is a hearty man and he speaks with great power and warmth, communicating with every one of us. He instils a sense of inner peace which concentrates our minds on what our devout coach has been saying. Simoes, you see, believes Jamaica is destined to secure qualification for France. It is part of 'God's plan'.

When the Reverend has finished, the coach holds one of his famous team meetings. The little Brazilian is a remarkable character: a motivator, tactician and leader of men. He maps out what he wants us to do on his laptop compter before working on our minds. It is now up to us, he tells us. Do we want to tell our grand-children that we took tiny Jamaica to the World Cup finals? People are smiling round the table but there is a collective churning of stomachs.

The vibe is right. We go back to the rooms and prepare our gear for the match. We are only three miles from the National Stadium but we have to leave early. The roads are rammed and even though our distinctive Reggae Boyz bus has an escort of police outriders, we are unable to make much headway through the traffic. Music blares out of the speakers. Spider is up and shouting, stoking the excitement. Everyone is starting to feel the buzz now and as we look through the dusty windows of the bus, we see the streets lined with men, women and children wearing yellow and shouting 'Good luck'.

People have been arriving at the stadium since early this morn-ing. It was filled to capacity, and the gates were locked hours ago. As we turn right off Arthur Wint Drive, past the bronze statue of Bob Marley, the concrete cauldron comes into view. Where yester-day there were large expanses of scorched earth punctuated by the odd grazing goat, today we are accosted by a sea of simmering nationalism. Roadside vendors, fans desperate for tickets and harassed policemen can be made out amid the blanket of distinc-tive yellow that surrounds the stadium. The deafening din of whistles and horns that greets our arrival intensifies the assault on the senses.

Bob Marley was probably the last person to experience adula-tion like this on Jamaica. It is fitting that the island's patron saint has been honoured with a statue that looks out across the small patch of green where today we will try to emulate his feats: bring-ing Jamaica to the attention of the outside world. Simoes tells to us to stay focused and as we push through the crowds to the stadium entrance, he insists that there are to be no autographs, no photos and no idle chat. This is our workplace. 'The Office' is an appropriate nickname for the cracked, concrete bowl we call home.

Outside the changing room, we can hear the DJs whipping the crowd into a frenzy. Match day in Kingston has become a carnival. Jimmy Cliff takes to the stage to an almighty roar. Beenie Man, current king of the dancefloor, gets a similar ovation soon after. It's a bit claustrophobic in the hot dressing room, so we pad down the tunnel and emerge from the shade of the stand into the bright glare of sunlight that covers most of the pitch. The noise and heat seem to blur my vision and, for a moment, everything sways.

The kick-off comes round sooner than we think possible. I will be on the bench but my colleagues from England, Fitzroy Simpson, Paul Hall and Deon Burton, are in the starting eleven. As we line up in the tunnel we get a good look at our Mexican opponents. They scored a 6–0 win over us back in April so we are out for revenge. Already qualified, they don't look overly concerned and I hear one of them saying, 'Today, you no score goals, we no score goals.' The coach picks this up and pulls us all together before we go out. He does not want any of us to listen to what the guy has said. He tells us that if Mexico get a chance in the last minute, they won't think twice about scoring and putting us out.

The Reverend calls for calm and addresses the stadium using a microphone. His prayer is typically passionate and when he closes with 'Amen', the ground erupts. The stadium is only meant to hold 35,000 but there must be nearer 50,000 inside with people sitting on each other's shoulders. The far side is a bank of yellow which rises as one for the national anthem.

Mexico's nonchalant attitude is evident on the pitch as soon as the referee blows to start the match. Only their captain, Luis Garcia, seems intent on winning, so our defenders have to be vigilant. We try to force the pace but it is hard when the opposition are not snapping into tackles. They seem content to sit back and defend and the first half passes at a subdued, practice-match pace. There is still a palpable tension in the air until a huge roar bursts from the far side and quickly spreads round the ground. El Salvador, who must beat the United States to deny us, are a goal down. Simoes rushes to the touchline and gestures for the team to stay calm. The half ends with the scores tied at 0–0. The coach has to keep a lid on emotions during his half-time team talk because we are now so close.

I come on in the second half to replace the tiring Theodore Whitmore. 'The Professor' has always said that he thinks my big time will come in France at the World Cup. He knows I haven't been totally happy moving from the fringes of the England squad to sitting on the bench for Jamaica. I may be a Premiership player but he is under no pressure to play me, particularly since I have been suffering from a knee injury. I'm here as part of the squad.

With ten minutes to go, another huge chant swells from the crowd: 'France, France, France.' The USA have scored again and, barring a miracle, we are through. I can see Simoes on the sideline, desperately trying to contain a broad smile. We enjoy the final moments before the referee blows to confirm history has been made.

Spectators come streaming from the stands. Some players slump to the floor, wiping tears from their eyes, while others run after Whitmore, who has grabbed a Jamaican flag from the crowd and is sprinting the length of the field. Old favourites pound from the sound system in tribute to our glorious achievement. Simoes somehow calls us all together. Before the match he had told us that when (not if) we qualified, he wanted us to gather in the centre circle to say a prayer. The world's cameras are on us and he wants to send out a message that we remember where we have come from and who we have done this for.

After praying, the players scatter everywhere. Fitzroy and Durrent Brown are at the centre of a ruck of well-wishers, arm in arm with the coach; Whitmore is being chaired from the pitch; Deon is being mobbed by delirious girls. Captain and goalkeeper Warren Barrett is talking breathlessly into a microphone. I tell a reporter that this was not just a football match, it was the entire nation making a point. It is a chance for Jamaica to put its name on the map and generate some interest for an ailing economy.

The prime minister takes the mike and announces that this is 'undoubtedly the greatest day in our sporting history' and that tomorrow will be a national holiday to mark the occasion. The ground erupts again before Jimmy Cliff takes over on the stage and sings 'You Can Get It If You Really Want'. We have united a nation and I realise for the first time just what a powerful force soccer can be.

It takes an age to get back into the dressing room as the world and his wife are trying to join the celebrations. Simoes has been doused with the contents of an ice bucket and his shirt – with JESUS SAVES written on the back – is soaked. Players, officials, technical and backroom staff, fans and complete strangers are jumping up and down, shouting at the tops of their voices. Inside, people are locked in jubilant embraces; outside, the party is just warming up.

We eventually return to the team house on Shortwood Road to see the prime minister, who conveniently lives next door. The city is one giant roadblock. Parties have broken out on every street corner and gunshots can be heard downtown. On this occasion, the sound is one that signifies joy rather than violence. I finally get out of my football gear at 11pm, eight hours after the match kicked off. Taking a shower was out of the question amid the euphoric scenes in the dressing room.

The country has gone crazy so I decide to get away from it all by travelling out of Kingston to meet Garth Crooks. He is almost as emotional as I am, as his parents are Jamaican, and is still finding it hard to fully come to terms with the scenes he has just covered for the BBC. Garth was a big hero of mine in my youth and when I first went to train as a schoolboy with Stoke City, Crooksy and Adrian Heath used to look out for me. He makes me think of home: of people like John Rudge, who taught me so much at Port Vale, and Ray Harford and Joe Kinnear at Wimbledon. I chuckle when I think of what the Crazy Gang will make of 'The Duke' going to the World Cup finals. I will be 33 by then.

I think of my family. My wife and two kids back in London and my mum and dad in Stoke. It was my mother who was the big football fan in the family, travelling to away games on the train with the hooligans. I wouldn't even know she had gone until I saw her face behind the goal when I ran out on to the pitch. I think of my dad, a former miner. He always said that if I was good enough, he would get to hear about it. I think of my two sisters and especially my older brother Neville. He was a PT trainer in the army and eight years ago had a fall which left him paralysed. His attitude to life has been an example throughout and everything I do on the field is dedicated to him. This is for all of them, for Jamaica and for West Indians across the world.

1

The Captain's Dream

DANIEL

Our story starts with a retired army officer who lived in a smart house high in the hills overlooking Kingston. In the summer of 1994, Captain Horace Burrell had a vision as he watched the World Cup on his jumbo television set. In it, he turned tiny Jamaica into a force in world football and led them to the 1998 finals in France. His team would go down in history as representatives of the smallest country ever to qualify for the biggest sporting event on the planet.

Burrell had football on his mind that summer – he had recently been elected president of the Jamaican Football Federation, a grandiose new post that looked like a poisoned chalice to most observers. The JFF administration Burrell inherited from the outgoing president, Heron Dale, was crippled by debt. It was staffed by two clerical workers and a politically appointed general secretary who attempted to run the national team programmes and act as ruling body for the tangled network of local leagues from a tiny office at the ramshackle National Stadium complex in Kingston. The previous administration had made a mess of both tasks and been forced out following a depressingly familiar sequence of bad results and poor management.

It is important to paint a clear picture of Jamaican football in 1994 to put The Captain's vision into context. There was no professional league, local 'club' matches were blighted by violence and facilities were almost non-existent. Many of the players were unemployed or worked in menial, poorly paid jobs. The domestic league, an essentially amateur and often shambolic

13

set-up, was in danger of falling apart at the seams. There had been a glut of abandoned matches, bottles regularly rained on to the field and players were attacked, so sponsors were understandably thin on the ground.

These inherent problems within local football were reflected in the accelerated decline of the national team. That year, Jamaica had failed to qualify for the finals of the annual Shell Cup, a tournament played between the islands of the Caribbean, having been humiliated in the qualifying rounds by the less than mighty Cayman Islands. There were no benefits to be gained from playing for Jamaica in 1994 and professionals from England would not have been given insurance, travel expenses or payment. Some of the island's best players even refused to turn up for internationals, citing differences with the Federation.

Jamaica's international pedigree did not stretch far either. In the past, the national team had never even made it through to the final qualifying group of a World Cup, let alone glimpsed the promised land of a sporting festival watched by billions. The Jamaican team was withdrawn from the qualifying rounds of the 1974 tournament for what the records describe as 'poor behaviour on a tour to Bermuda', although football officials are reluctant to reveal exactly what happened. The reasons Jamaica did not compete in either 1982 or 1986 are clearer: insufficient funds and a poorly prepared team respectively. In 1990, Jamaica was banned from entering for non-payment of FIFA affiliation fees.

Jamaican footballers who had represented their country were, in truth, international players in name only. Few had experienced football outside the Caribbean and pulling on the colours of Jamaica provided a source of pride but little more. Crowds were down and results were dismal, ensuring that the 1994 World Cup from the USA was an event that didn't involve the locals. Like Burrell, they watched it on television, rooting for Brazil or Argentina.

It was just as well the new president liked a challenge. The son of a wealthy landowner from the Clarendon parish to the west of Kingston, Burrell trained as an army officer in Canada and England. Some say he attended Sandhurst although getting him to confirm it is difficult. He took early retirement at the age of 36 and made his fortune from a chain of bakeries, becoming something of a local celebrity in the process. He wore expensive suits, handled large amounts of cash and the lilac Mercedes parked in his front drive was one of the smartest cars in the country. The pistol he carried in a variety of holsters was also testament to the position he occupied within Jamaican society. On an island where a title means respect, 'Captain' was good though '*The* Captain' was better.

A big, imposing 44 year old with a regal moustache and deep voice, The Captain was desperate to get 'turned on again'. He wasn't short of money and had the time to spare – he only needed three hours sleep a night. Burrell had marched through life generally getting what he wanted with a mixture of talk and charm, and believed that the army had taught him discipline and the art of leadership. They were qualities that would be required in abundance.

In the few months after being elected, The Captain spoke of his bold plan but cynics in Jamaica, brought up on a diet of poorly organised, underfunded football, dismissed it as fantasy. The Captain ignored them because he truly believed in the power of his countrymen. He had faith that there was enough talent on the island for it to become a great footballing nation. And now he felt compelled to use his position, the respect he had earned and the skills he had developed to turn his vision into reality. The Captain was on a mission.

Leadership and cash were important qualities, but what sort of football qualifications did The Captain possess? He had been a keen but not particularly successful sportsman and shown energy and enthusiasm in directing the army football team. He had also sat on the committee of a local football association in his spare time. When he left the army, he had a spell as treasurer for the JFF, served as vice-president of the Caribbean Football Union and gradually rose through the layers of local administration to finally take the top job in Jamaican football. The Captain had experience but nothing to suggest that he could start a revolution.

That June, The Captain caught a plane to Florida for a meeting with Austin 'Jack' Warner. The West Indian was president of CONCACAF, the Confederation of North and Central American and Caribbean Association Football. CONCACAF was a football backwater from which only Mexico had made any impact on the outside world. The only other two countries with any money to spend on the sport, Canada and the United States, had taken to football like fish to bicycles, though this small fact had not stopped the USA hosting that summer's tournament. In 1994, Warner's region was making progress without compensurate success on the football field, demonstrated by the extra qualifying spot he had secured for the 1998 World Cup finals. Of 34 eligible football minnows, three would now make it to France. The Captain knew that this additional place would be worth a lot of money to the nation that won it.

The two knew each other from Burrell's time as deputy chairman of CONCACAF's Disciplinary Commission, a job for which he had the perfect mien. The Captain wanted to know how his small island of two and a half million people could ever hope to compete with its bigger group opponents, let alone the likes of Brazil, Germany, Italy and Argentina. That is the question he wanted Warner to answer in Orlando.

The Caribbean had contributed very little to the World Cup finals. Cuba qualified before World War II and Haiti had made it through to the finals in West Germany in '74. Since then, only Trinidad and Tobago had come close, missing out by a point on Italia '90. Warner, nevertheless, felt confident that something could be done, and as The Captain leant forward in his chair, moustache twitching with interest, he sketched out a rough blueprint for transforming Jamaican football. The plan involved hiring a top foreign coach and setting up an efficient federation that could take care of the business of raising the funds necessary for success. It sounded simple, although both men knew the reality would be different.

The first significant decision The Captain made after that meeting was that the technical expertise should be supplied by a Brazilian, because he did not believe that the Jamaican people would accept a coach from any other country. They had long loved Brazilian football and, anyway, European coaches had proved short-lived failures in the past. And Burrell had already come up with additional reasons why the appointment of a coach from the game's spiritual home could be the platform for his grand idea.

First, a Brazilian coach would give the programme a profile, making it easier for the players to gain international exposure and experience. Second, Burrell was also seduced by the notion that there was something in the rhythmic qualities inherent in both nationalities: the Brazilians had samba, the Jamaicans had reggae. The Captain's brainwave was to create a fusion of the spirit of reggae and samba to produce an extraordinary football team and extraordinary product.

Other members of the JFF were less enlightened and called for a local man to be installed as technical director of football and coach of the national team. The Captain reminded them that he was the man in charge.

The initial idea for a well-funded World Cup qualifying bid relied on gathering together business leaders from within the private sector, a think tank that could assist in the generation of income for the fledgling programme. The Captain was well respected, through the success of his eponymous Captain's Bakeries, and he duly approached Howard McIntosh, a finance expert and boss of Jamaica's Workers' Bank. McIntosh – a tall, imposing man with studious small, round glasses – would become the financial brains behind the operation. He liked what The Captain had to say and together they agreed on a name for the project: 'The Highway to France'. With his help, Burrell wanted to assemble a line-up of local businessmen who would become 'godfathers' to Jamaican football. This loose committee of business brains would eventually evolve into the Football Foundation of Jamaica.

The Captain met with the Jamaican prime minister P.J. Patterson, and delivered a detailed address about his plans, outlining how Jamaican football could 'rise up' and a feel-good factor could be generated in a divided, dispirited country. He was, in his own words, 'cogniscent of the fact that football was not only a sport. It could become an integral part of nation-building in Jamaica'.

He explained that the programme would need significant funding and diplomatic assistance in the form of exploiting existing links with Brazil and gently persuading businesses at home to get behind the venture. He reminded the prime minister, in words that would be repeated to media representatives across the world over the next four years, that, 'The Jamaican people are some of the proudest in the world. As people, we want the best and if we don't get it, we make it quite clear that we don't like it.'

Patterson, a reserved, unemotional man on the surface, listened intently as the plan was spelt out. The Captain remembers exactly what he said when he had finished: 'I think it's a marvellous idea. It is unusual but the way you made your presentation gives me confidence in what you are trying to achieve.' The prime minister recognised the economic possibilities that might spring from World Cup qualification and immediately lent his support to the project, despatching a letter to his friend, the President of Brazil.

Burrell had also discussed his ideas with Carl Brown, a man who had coached the Jamaican national team on two separate occasions in the past. Brown had quit in 1993 on the grounds of ill health, at around the same time that Horace Reid, then team manager and a man who would become integral within Burrell's new order, also decided to step away from the national team set-up. It would be fair to say that both recognised Jamaican football was at an all-time low.

Carl Brown was a respected figure in the island's football community. He came from a prominent sporting family which had long links with the Boystown club in Trenchtown. He had represented Jamaica as a player and even enjoyed some success during his tenures as coach, leading Jamaica to Shell Cup triumph in 1991 and a creditable third place in the second CONCACAF Gold Cup two years later. Such a showing should have been the springboard for Jamaican football but, just as the Federation failed to capitalise on Shell Cup success in 1991, the efforts of Brown and his team were again met with apathy.

He too realised that something dramatic would have to be done to reverse the island's footballing fortunes. He told the new president of the JFF that he supported his decision to look outside Jamaica for a coach, but on one condition. Brown appreciated that the Jamaican football public were wary of outsiders and wanted guarantees that the JFF would be prepared to stick by their man through the inevitable, early setbacks. The solution, Brown felt, was to offer the new coach a long contract of four years minimum.

Brown also accepted an invitation to rejoin the JFF, taking up an as yet unspecified coaching role. His agreement to assist the new regime would prove to be crucial in the early months. He knew the players but, more importantly, his experience of leading the national team had made him a realist. He would come back on board with his eyes wide open, the magnitude of the problems facing the nascent programme clearly apparent to him. Having coached the team between 1983 and 1986, he had resigned out of frustration at not being able to get anyone to provide the players with what they needed. There was no funding from the private sector and only a dribble from government coffers. He knew that previous Jamaican coaches had harboured similar dreams of reaching the World Cup finals, but also knew they had never had someone like The Captain to drive the machine.

Horace Reid, another important figure in the story, had also been involved in football for a long time, and he had been a prominent face in local football at community level in the parish of St Catherine's. Although he would later become the bureaucrat who oiled the workings of the JFF machine, Reid had coaching credentials that extended to leading Hazard FC to Jamaica's league title in 1993. He had worked with the national team between 1990 and 1993 but knew little about Captain Burrell when he was approached to join on the hastily retitled 'Road to France' programme. At the time, Reid was a sales representative for a company that made fine rums, but after carefully weighing up the options he found the temptation of The Captain's new challenge too great to resist.

The next stop was the Brazilian embassy and a meeting with Mr Antonio Carlos de Andrade, Brazilian ambassador to Jamaica. He agreed to contact the president-director of the Brazilian Football Academy, Professor Manoel Espezim Neto. Against the advice of a JFF committee, Burrell decided that finding that man should now be the first priority. Making the necessary financial arrangements could wait. By the end of a whirlwind summer, Burrell was in the air, flying to Rio de Janeiro to meet the coaches on a shortlist drawn up by the Brazilian Football Academy. The first step had been taken along the Road to France.

Drumming his fingers on the steering wheel with impatience, Rene Simoes sat in a car outside the main airport in Rio de

Janeiro. A small, dark, 42 year old with a thick Groucho Marx-style moustache and tinted glasses, Simoes had been asked to do a favour for his old university friend Manoel Neto. The academy president had been called away on last-minute business to South Korea.

Neto explained how Captain Burrell was over to interview Brazilian coaches for the job as national coach to Jamaica, describing the novel diplomatic course that had got him this far: the visit to the Jamaican prime minister, a letter to the Brazilian president, contact with the Brazilian Ambassador in Jamaica, the request of assistance from the Brazilian Ministry of Internal Affairs and the approach to the Brazilian Football Academy.

Burrell's list of requirements had served to narrow the field down to a list of five possible coaches. The Brazilian he wanted had to be a former player with a coaching diploma and someone who had coached a Brazilian national team, worked abroad and spoke some English. Simoes had only recently returned home after five years' coaching in the Middle East and when Professor Neto called him to say that he thought he was the most qualified candidate for the post, Simoes had said thank you but no thank you. He had been to the island in 1989 when he was coach to the Brazilian Under 20s side and knew something of the state of Jamaican football. What Simoes did not know, however, was that Neto had already sent a list of names to the Jamaican Federation with his at the top.

Although Neto thought Simoes would be perfect for the Jamaican mission, he was not exactly a household name at the time. Rene himself believed that football was the reason God had put him on this earth. One of 12 children born in Cavalcante, Rio de Janeiro, close to ghetto areas not unlike those found in downtown Kingston, he tells a story of how on the night before he was born his mother had dreamt of a little boy wearing a string round his neck with a whistle attached, and standing with one foot resting on a football. She sounded like a good woman to have in a pools syndicate.

Like many boys from working-class backgrounds, Rene grew up playing football on the streets before working his way through youth and college teams in Brazil's vast football infrastructure. Simoes eventually turned pro and won occasional plaudits as a promising left midfielder. He was headstrong, though, and did not respect authority, falling out with his coach and quitting his club after a blazing row with the president. Despite vowing that he was finished with the game at the age of 22, within six months he had made the decision to become the coach he had never had. He studied PE and enrolled for a further year at college to gain his coaching certificate.

Less than two years later, armed with the title 'Professor of Football' and a passion for psychology, Simoes scored his first success, coaching Rio de Janeiro's Somley College to victory in the University Olympic Day tournament. He moved on to the Vasco da Gama club where he became Under 20s coach. One of his stories has Simoes filling in for his head coach and leading the senior team on a tour of the United States. He remembers the mayor of the town looking straight past him when he got off the bus, not believing he was old enough to head such a prestigious delegation. The year was 1976 and Rene was just 24.

Over the next few years, Simoes' methods continued to bear fruit and after occasional triumphs at college, youth team and regional league level he was lured to Portugal. The Iberian adventure was short-lived, however. Age had not mellowed Simoes much by the mid 1980s and another row, again with the club president, saw him soon packing his bags for home. In 1988 he enjoyed his biggest success when he led the Brazil Under 20s to victory in the South American Youth Championship in Argentina. It was a major coup as it was the first time a Brazilian national team had ever won a trophy on the soil of their great South American rivals.

He had coached the Brazilian Under 17, 20 and 23 sides – working with future World Cup winners like Taffarel and Leonardo in the process – by the turn of the decade, but decided that after 15 years it was time for a change. He packed his bags once more, headed for Qatar in the Middle East and became the desert equivalent of Alex Ferguson.

As he waited for his passenger at the airport, Simoes felt underwhelmed to be back in Brazil at his old club Mesquita. He had won them promotion to the First Division in 1985 but almost ten years on, the club was languishing in the Third Division. So he was certainly open to offers – but not desperate enough to take a job in Jamaica, and even dressed in a T-shirt and trainers to ensure Burrell got the message that he wasn't interested. He made the right impression because, after strolling through the doors of the airport flanked by his business adviser, Burrell got into the car and asked to be taken straight to his hotel. The well-heeled arrival from the Caribbean naturally assumed that the short, scruffy guy with the bushy moustache was a driver the Academy had sent to collect him.

Pride slightly dented, Simoes put his passenger straight and The Captain began to fire questions from the back seat. By the time they arrived at the Copacabana Plaza, his tone had softened from dictatorial to merely presidential. The Captain was a man who knew what he wanted and once inside the hotel, his face betrayed the fact that he was far from impressed. The smile was gone and his eyes darted contemptuously around the lobby. When he spoke, he spoke slowly, telling Simoes that if this hotel reflected what the Brazilian Academy thought about Jamaica, then there could be problems.

The Plaza was one of the most famous hotels in Rio during the sixties and although it was not worthy of five stars in 1994, it was adequate for a man who had invited himself to Brazil. He had not been courted by the Academy to go over and talk business and Simoes had been told that Burrell was to pay his own way. This visit was Mr Burrell's idea and the Academy felt no obligation to foot the bill.

The Captain, though, had other ideas. After turning his nose up at the hotel, he demanded that he be taken to see the President of Brazil. Simoes, feeling slightly awkward in the presence of this expensively suited madman from the Caribbean, informed Burrell that such a meeting would be difficult as the president lived in Brasilia. The Captain stopped for a moment, considered his options and came up with a solution. With the faintest hint of a smile, Burrell said that if the Brazilian authorities would be generous enough to pay for his hotel he would be gracious enough to accept their offer. This 'kind' compromise implied that a refusal could result in a minor diplomatic incident.

Simoes called the Ministry of Foreign Affairs to try to resolve the impasse. 'This man is mad,' he recalls saying to the minister, before getting confirmation that there was no budget for Burrell's expenses. Before the news could be relayed to the small delegation from the Jamaican Football Federation, however, The Captain had snatched the phone impatiently from Simoes' hand. He set about talking to the minister himself and their serious, frank exchange lasted for 15 minutes.

Simoes was still not interested in the job but was by now intrigued by the portentous captain. He asked him what he wanted from his new coach and listened as Burrell again outlined his plan. It seemed far-fetched but Simoes gave his expert advice all the same. He had put together a similar project for the Brazilian Football Confederation and stressed to The Captain how the coach should work. From his limited knowledge of Jamaican football and its complete lack of coaching culture, Simoes explained that it would be important to establish an agenda that was clearly understood by all involved.

In his inimitable form of broken English, a dialect that relied on hybrid words and lots of body movement, Simoes described the coach working along vertical and horizontal lines. The vertical line was the technical director, who would coach the national team, and be in charge of football in the whole country. He would "establish philosphe (sic), plans and follow-ups for the development of players in Jamaica". He would educate local coaches and work with all age groups.

Continuity was the key to success. Each coach would be the assistant to the coach above him – the Under 17s coach would be the assistant to the Under 20s coach and so on. The same would happen every time a squad was called together to travel – five younger players would be invited to join up with the more senior party. Simoes believed in collective effort and organisation and Burrell was quietly impressed: they were themes that fitted in nicely with his vision to market the programme as a nation-building exercise.

The horizontal line, Simoes explained, could be any coach in the world. He believed that every time a coach travelled abroad he had a duty to pass on his knowledge. His experience had shown that national federations sometimes employed coaches who preferred to keep what they had learnt of different football cultures to themselves. In Qatar, Simoes had made a point of trying to teach the natives some of his tricks.

When Simoes had finished, he told The Captain that interviews with the other four coaches on his list had been arranged for later that afternoon. They would start at four and finish at around eight, at which time he would come back to the hotel and chaperone The Captain and his colleague for a night out in Rio. Simoes reflected that Burrell was redoubtable indeed when he received a call from the ministry which confirmed that The Captain's hotel and flight costs would be met.

Simoes returned to the hotel that evening, keen to know if Burrell had selected his coach. The Captain replied that he had, gravely informing Simoes that one of the things his army background had taught him was how to pick out an effective commander. The Brazilian sat down, which was just as well because when Burrell told him his answer, mild surprise at the cheek of the man turned to open-mouthed incredulity. 'I have picked my coach and my coach is you,' boomed Burrell, conveniently ignoring Simoes' clearly stated desire not to be considered.

Simoes laughed, saying that he didn't want to go to Jamaica and Burrell would not have the money to make him an offer worth accepting. The Captain didn't bat an eyelid and informed Simoes that he would work something out with the Brazilian government so that he could be paid a suitable salary. Simoes had never heard of a government paying one of its coaches to go and work abroad but as far as The Captain was concerned, the vacancy was now filled.

As they dined out that night, Simoes tried his best to shake off The Captain's proposal – even taking his two guests to a show in Plataforma where he banked on the dancing girls being able divert The Captain's attention. He was not disappointed and as The Captain's eyes lit up, the business talk subsided. The show ended with music from all the nationalities represented in the audience and when a Bob Marley track was played, The Captain and his colleague David Haughton were invited on to the stage to dance. Their reggae moves brought the house down and Simoes could not help but warm to the dancing behemoth from Kingston.

The next day, Burrell and Haughton flew to Brasilia for further meetings. As he drove away after dropping them off at the airport, Simoes was adamant that he was not going to fall for The Captain's manipulative tactics. But Burrell was now not the only one exerting pressure. Sergio Arruda, director of the Brazilian Association of Cooperation, phoned to encourage Simoes to accept the offer, reminding him of the hit movie *Cool Runnings* which revolved around the Jamaican bobsleigh team that qualified for the Winter Olympics. Arruda felt that if an island without snow could achieve such a feat, then surely Simoes could score similar success on the football field.

And there were others twisting his arm: high-level calls from the Minister of Education, the Chief Ambassador for Caribbean Matters and the Minister of External Relations all urged Simoes to accept. He was told that The Captain had made up his mind: it was 'love at first sight'. Indeed, as Simoes drove downtown to attend a meeting with the Brazilian Association of Travel Agents, Burrell was putting the finishing touches to another piece of shrewd negotiation.

The Captain's meeting in the capital yielded an unprecedented agreement whereby the Brazilian government agreed to pay the first three months of Simoes' salary. They would also establish a project of technical cooperation for the Caribbean which would be backed by the World Bank. To further increase the pressure on Simoes to accept Burrell's offer, he would be placed in charge of the project. As The Captain's target sat through his meeting in Rio, talking about the courses he was to give in American cities where Brazil had played during the recent World Cup, he was oblivious to how his future was being shaped all those miles away. As far as Simoes was concerned, the vacancy was still open.

Burrell told Simoes he had rejected another coach when he flew back into Rio from Sao Paulo but doubts about Burrell's ability to match his salary demands were not alleviated by The Captain's unwillingness to pay the room rate at the five-star Meridien Copacabana. The beachfront hotel was a step up in class from the Plaza but when Simoes saw that Burrell had elected to share a room with Haughton, even more misgivings materialised in his mind. Burrell had revealed nothing about his agreement with the Brazilian government and had thus far bullied and charmed his way into paying for next to nothing. Simoes concluded that either the Jamaican Football Federation was teetering on the brink of bankruptcy or The Captain was a charismatic fraud.

A US $5,000 a month salary secured through the cooperation of the Brazilian government made Simoes revise his opinion slightly, but without being rude, he told The Captain that the figure was nowhere near what he wanted or needed. He figured his best tactic would be to price himself out of Burrell's wage bracket, so he duly rattled off a list of minimum requirements: a regular wage, a lump sum on signing the contract, a house, car, air tickets for him and his family, 60 days' holiday, health insurance and, oh yes, no taxes. Again Burrell smiled and soothed Simoes with assurances that the Brazilian government could make this possible. He left the room and within minutes was back to announce that Brasilia had agreed to bump the salary up to US $10,000 a month.

The talks continued for hours and what started out as an amusing, hypothetical conversation soon became something far more serious. Simoes' patience almost snapped when Burrell suggested that he should dispense with his requests for air fares, a rent-free house and holiday pay, telling him that these concessions would be greatly appreciated by the people of Jamaica. As Simoes slowly managed to up The Captain's opening offer, his base line was dropping at the same rate. He was on the point of walking out many times during the night but five hours later, Burrell had what he wanted. Simoes drove home, exhausted and slightly confused by the events of the past few days. Why had he got riled about something he genuinely did not want? How had he been manoeuvred into a position of giving his word that he would accept the job?

There was still time for the saga to take a couple of late twists. When Simoes got home that night to tell his wife Fatima the news, the phone rang with the offer of a job in Japan. The money was far superior to what Burrell was offering, the facilities would be first class and the local infrastructure would be a world removed from the amateur, cash-starved scenario waiting for him in Jamaica. It was a tough evening for a coach suddenly in great demand. He had told The Captain that he would to take up the Jamaican job in 15 days.

The final stumbling block was the contract, which Simoes insisted should be sent to him before he left for Jamaica. Just days before his date of departure, it had not arrived. Again, Simoes started to get bad vibes about the whole idea and when The Captain phoned to check that everything was still in place, Simoes told him that the deal would be off unless the contract was signed, sealed and delivered before he left Brazil. It was duly faxed but when Simoes read it, he could not believe that the document was the product of that long, arduous night of bartering. His head told him not to sign it. His heart persuaded him otherwise. Simoes was a man who believed God had a plan for him and he found himself incapable of going back on the verbal agreement he had struck with Burrell.

2

Many Rivers to Cross

DANIEL

In October 1994, Captain Burrell introduced Professor Rene Simoes to the press, describing him as 'the new saviour of Jamaican football'. The Brazilian, whose grand title owed itself to a relatively modest coaching certificate, had suddenly been imbued with an aura. 'Professor' gave him a certain mystique and an authority which convinced enough people he would bring a learned, intellectual approach to football on the island. The Captain, flanked by McIntosh, Reid and Simoes, then presented the programme to reporters. To create a professional environment for the players and a national system that would deliver World Cup qualification would cost US $4 million over four years. People laughed and dismissed him as a dreamer.

It did not take long for Professor Rene Simoes to realise the size of the task Captain Burrell had set. When he arrived in Jamaica, Simoes found himself in a developing country that played under developed football. Only a handful of pitches on the island had enough grass to warrant them being referred to as such. Professionalism was anathema. The clubs were loose collections of individuals rather than the well-organised, well-supported institutions found in the recognised football world. The game had no paid administrators – just committee members with little power and less finance to make improvements. 'When I came here,' Simoes said later, 'there was really nothing.'

Teams were born out of communities and frequently changed names. There existed a labyrinth of parish leagues beneath the top national division and winning schools cups was considered more prestigious than taking the club championship. Players moved between clubs almost at will. Their contracts were worth about as much as the registration form an average Sunday league player might fill out every season in Great Britain. Players only turned up when it suited them. In short, the game suffered from an almost total lack of infrastructure.

Simoes likes to tell stories and this is his version of October 1994: 'There are two Brazilian sailor men. When one of the Brazilian sailors arrived in China he said, "I will return immediately. Nobody wears shoes in this community." He sent shoes to China and the second sailor man called him and said, "You are a great man. You have great vision because, until you came, nobody wears shoes." This was my first impression of Jamaica. Nobody played football as they can because the quality was not there. From that position you have to make everything.'

Jamaican football was chaotic and cowered in the shadow of violence. The bitter factionalism that had cost so many lives down the years spilled on to football fields inside Kingston, while elsewhere officials lived in fear of blowing their whistle at an inopportune moment. A bad refereeing decision could be the signal for bottles to rain down from behind the fencing or for a linesman to get his ear 'chopped with a knife'. Football was a sport of the ghettos and it had problems to match.

To those who played it, however, football was a welcome release from the hardships of everyday life. Carl Brown had been a national football hero in his time and knew all about the modest fame that came with playing for Jamaica. He also knew what it was like to walk home from the stadium after a match, the feeling of stardom suddenly dissipated as he joined the throng leaving on foot. Having grown up in the same ghetto as some of the players now joining the programme, he understood that football could never be the *only* thing in a young man's life when food, clothes and money were hard to come by. Indeed, some of the Jamaican footballers about to be groomed for France would not have owned a pair of boots until their late teens.

The players Simoes selected for the programme would have to be handled carefully. If this new man came in and tried to change things too quickly or too drastically, some players might suck their teeth and walk out. Why should they get worked up about a national team that even its fans laughed at? Discipline was conspicuous by its absence in the lives of young ghetto men. Many boys grew up without the guidance of conventional father figures, becoming men with little regard for authority and hair-trigger sensibilities, and being ordered about by another man did not make a Jamaican feel comfortable in his own environment. Respect meant everything and Brown wanted Simoes to understand what and who he was dealing with. He thought he should learn something of the culture that shaped the people and footballers of Jamaica.

Coming from a country where football was a religion, Simoes was accustomed to a structured professional league where players were paid handsomely and could be expected to withstand the demands placed on them. In Jamaica, the top players' idea of a day's work did not involve training after midday and driving a Mercedes back home for an afternoon nap. Local players were often drained when they arrived at the pitch to train in the evening. While things remained as they were a coach could make demands on his players but he also had to understand that there was a cut-off point. For the fishermen, waiters, bartenders and factory workers that Simoes inherited, the onus was on them to be breadwinners first and footballers second. Their priority was to provide for their families and in 1994 playing football full-time in Jamaica did not present a means of doing that.

Yet while football may not have offered financial rewards, it did provide a potential route out of the ghettos for the best players. The Business House League was prestigious, and although it was an essentially white-collar organisation, current and former Jamaican internationals could be found representing large corporations and companies in its midweek fixtures. In a simple return for furthering the firm's chance of victory, players would be given employment and a pay packet at the end of the week.

These were the meagre resources from which Simoes was supposed to fashion a team capable of qualifying for the World Cup finals. Luckily, he was not blind to the situation. He too had encountered the day-to-day reality of trying to survive, having come from a working-class family of 12 children. This particular taste of life had forged a proud, hard-working man of many parts. On the one hand, Simoes was a fiery, hot-blooded disciplinarian with a temper to match. On the other, he was a devout Christian who believed in hard work, loyalty and compassion. Simoes would exhibit all these traits over the next few years.

Wherever in the world he had travelled as a coach, Simoes had worn the badge of Brazil with pride but never sought to force his ideas down other people's throats. As Simoes remembers: 'I lived in Qatar and Portugal so I already knew how to prove myself to players when I came to Jamaic (sic). The secret is relax and start to read the players. Life is like a book. You can open the book and close the book and when I ask you, you will know nothing about the book. You can read but if you don't capture anything about the book you will not learn anything. Life is the same.'

On top of everything else, Jamaica's new technical director and national coach was adaptable. He quickly recognised similarities that existed between his homeland and Jamaica. Both were very spiritual places that nurtured a temperamental streak within their people. The heat dictated the pace of life and while the sun shone and the waves crashed against the shore, everything was cool. A set of values existed in the shanties of Brazil and the board shacks of Kingston's zinc roof communities. A woman could struggle to clothe and feed herself from Monday to Friday yet find the money for a dazzling new hairstyle for the dance on Saturday. A man might buy a huge fridge for his beer and run it on the line he has thrown across the overhead cables. Motivating the terminally relaxed was not going to be easy.

The JFF had appointed a man with charisma to match the credentials all Jamaicans expected of a Brazilian coach. Simoes turned his hand to writing columns in Jamaican newspapers, furthering the cause of the programme in articles imbued with biblical references, anecdotes and florid imagery. He appeared on television and spoke on the radio, becoming one half of an easily identifiable double act with the far larger Captain Burrell. When he talked it was with energy and passion, delivered with a grasp of English that conveyed simple messages in a comical, infectious manner. The way they set about creating a profile for their young football programme and planting a seed of hope was extremely entertaining, but also very shrewd.

The new man's dynamism impressed those who questioned the programme's chances and his eccentric oratory proved a gift for the publicists. But more than anything, it was the Brazilian's willingness to embrace Jamaican culture that began to win over the sceptics. By publicly acclaiming the achievements of Jamaicans in other fields such as music and sport, Simoes pressed the right buttons with those who wondered whether he was another short-term experiment. His intuitive feel for the rhythms of local life meant that he quickly established a rapport with a notoriously fickle Jamaican public. The Captain was delighted: while he wrote letters and fixed appointments there was now someone spearheading the campaign.

The coach also took up Burrell's theme of a revolution created by fusing samba and reggae as he toured the island giving speeches and attending functions. It was a tune that struck right to the heart of popular culture. Like Brazil, music in Jamaica is an everpresent part of life: in workplaces, on the streets and in homes, the sound of reggae can be heard drifting across the airwaves. It was not all easy slow as dancehall, ragga and bashment thumped out of car speakers and neighbourhood sound systems to articulate the everyday frisson of danger. This combination of mellow and malice manifested itself in the people and the way they expressed themselves. Simoes marvelled at how patois could change from sleepy drawl to violent bark in the space of a sentence.

The fibres that intertwined to create the Jamaican identity interested Simoes, so much so that he declared his intention to transplant Jamaica's vibrant culture onto the football field. He even turned the team's consistently poor disciplinary record to his advantage, claiming that the aggression that had previously led to a spate of red cards could now be channelled in the right direction. He was there, he said, to impose a Brazilian football philosophy with strong Jamaican characteristics.

Intuitively, Simoes detected an underlying pride in the yards of the government blocks, the hills of the rural interior and beside the coast, and knew he could massage this through football. Sure, Jamaica was poor but it was also a creative, vibrant nation that embraced its heroes. Through his music, Bob Marley had seduced the world with a laidback sound that conjured up images of sand and palm trees while speaking the language of political freedom. The island's cricketers had brought decades of joy by thrashing their former colonial masters and from the stew that produced Jamaica emerged the fastest sprinters on earth – names like Merlene Ottey and Ben Johnson, who nevertheless represented Canada. These were people who had represented the island on a global stage and sent out a message from a small population determined to punch above its weight. Everywhere Simoes went in those early months, he was told that there was great talent in this, his new home.

Nation-building was all about making people feel good about themselves, but before the country could gain confidence through its football team, the players needed confidence in themselves. Simoes had to be able to offer incentives because simply telling players they were good enough to qualify for the World Cup was not enough. A footballer needed to live like a professional and be paid like a professional in order to compete like one. Yet while the new JFF administration attempted to plug the leaks caused by previous regimes' mismanagement, money remained thin on the ground. The government was on board, albeit with one eye trained firmly on results, but the private sector still needed coaxing into providing some of the things that would make Simoes' players more comfortable.

Attitudes also had to be changed. When Simoes arrived he discovered that Jamaican players looked on football as a simple game where the result didn't always matter. Jamaican fans had been brought up to covet transient pieces of individual magic more than the collective beauty of a well-worked goal. Style was more important than substance, whether it be clothes, DJs, cars, gold or football. Whenever Simoes stopped to watch an impromptu scrimmage on a rough piece of land, marked out at each end by tiny goals made out of metal piping or sticks, he was encouraged by the skill levels required to bring a ball under control while it bounced between stones, flying legs and discarded rubbish.

But while the cheek to push the ball between the shins of an opponent or pull off an audacious turn prompted louder shouts than a tap-in goal that might decide the match, it would be difficult to mould an effective team unit. More attention was needed on the cake, not on the icing, and much later, Simoes would remark that his first impression was that the locals played like 'performing seals'.

Generating funding and support turned out to be a slow, tiring process as the JFF fought to replace the common perception of football as the sport of thugs with something far more positive. Ironically, the origins of the sport's unwanted stigma lay with another Brazilian coach, Jorge Penna, who had taken the Jamaican job in 1962. The first, and possibly worst, thing he did was to choose the majority of his team from ghetto areas, as up until then football had been played and organised by affluent people, the sort who could afford their own boots.

Opening the doors of the national team to what some saw as an 'undesirable element' gradually saw rich people being turned off the game. From then on, football struggled to attract support from the private sector and although lack of funding did not dent the game's popularity, it fatally damaged its prospects. If you went to the Boystown club in Trenchtown you would still see players kicking a ball from dawn till dusk – it was an outlet for youths to let off steam. Penna scored a hit with these people by becoming the first coach to tap into the huge talent pool within the poorer communities but in doing so he simultaneously drove away the sector of society with the capacity to bankroll the game. It is interesting to note that football's biggest benefactors manufactured products relevant to the ghettos: cigarettes and alcohol.

Simoes was therefore trying to build the top storey of a building – the national team – before any foundations had been laid. The national team had to be the priority, yet with no tradition of excellence to fall back on it was hard to know where to start. He needed to focus the minds of his players. He told them that professionalism was a state of mind as much as a weekly pay packet, and the only way to become more professional was to understand what could be achieved through proper preparation. It was tough convincing them. They had watched professional football from Europe and South America on TV and knew that the game bore no resemblance to their soccer. Foreign professionals were not harangued by spectators at half-time. The players returned to the changing room rather than sat on the pitch.

Crowds were controlled, wages were high and the trappings of wealth were conspicuous. None of that applied in Jamaica.

Barely two weeks after he took up the job, Simoes first, hastily put-together team went down 3–0 to the United States in Kingston. A nucleus of older, experienced players existed as the core of Simoes' early squads. From Montego Bay came goalkeeper and captain Warren Barrett. From Seba United, the west coast's biggest club, came defenders Steve Malcolm and Anthony Dennis, midfielders Hector Wright and the exciting 'link' player Thoedore 'Tappa' Whitmore. They were joined from the western, more rural part of the island by the long-serving sweeper, Durrent 'Tatti' Brown and midfielder Gareth Peterkin, both of Wadadah FC.

Kingston was represented by players from inner-city clubs like Tivoli Gardens and Arnett Gardens and Constant Spring; Real Mona and Harbour View contributed players from the outskirts of the capital. Some of Jamaica's best players earned a living in the States, including midfield campaigner Altimont Butler, striker Paul Young and the star of Jamaican football, Walter 'Blacka Pearl' Boyd, who appeared for Colorado Foxes. While Jamaica could not afford to pay its players a wage, their support for the programme would rely purely on patriotism. Boyd, in particular, flew into Jamaica on the morning of a game and was usually on his way back to Denver, where he was coached by Jamaican Lorne Donaldson, later that evening. Many of his fans will tell you that Boyd paid his own way in the early days.

Although Simoes was jumping in and out of his seat during the match, clutching at clumps of his own hair with frustration and kicking every imaginary ball against the USA, he refused to panic at the scoreline. Instead, he stayed calm and spoke to the press about what skill he had seen and what a fine job coach Brown had done during his time in charge. Without being negative, he also pointed out what was wrong and the steps that could be taken to put things right. More support for the programme was a priority; more matches would be a start.

In December, Captain Burrell fulfilled the latter by securing a couple of friendlies against a touring club side from Germany. Borussia Dortmund might not have been well known to the Jamaican public at large but The Captain spoke of them being a 'powerhouse of European football'. Gate revenue from the matches was the drip feed in the arm of the struggling programme and Burrell showed great chutzpah in the way he promoted the games. Jamaica lost the first in Kingston by a single goal but gained revenge three days later in Montego Bay's Jarrett Park to chalk up the first victory of the new era. For the records, local legend Paul 'Tegat' Davis was the scorer.

Simoes also needed to address the problem of access to his players. If Jamaica was to have any chance, he had to have his squad close by at all times. He needed to be able to work intensively on the training field, impose his playing philosophy and instil in many of them the rudimentary tactics required to compete at a higher level. Close proximity to the players would also allow him to improve them psychologically and implant a work ethic. But while some members of his squad were scattered across northern America playing minor league or collegiate football and those at home felt more inclined to turn out for club before country, Simoes was stymied.

However, 1995 was a year of slow but gradual progress. The government donated a house – a white-washed bungalow next to the prime minister's residence – which the squad could use as a base when training camps were called. Captain Burrell wanted the players to get to know each other and to live together when possible to develop, using his military parlance, an *'esprit de corps'*. Simoes used his contacts back home to fund and stage a training camp in Brazil, which would give him a chance to get a better look at the players and introduce them to his new ideas away from the distractions of everyday Jamaican life. Gradually, he wanted to wean them off expressing themselves as individuals in favour of team effort, discipline and commitment. The players started getting paid too. The most lucrative incentive in those early days was around £40 a week.

Simoes kept up the flow of media appearances, constantly reminding Jamaica that support and dedication were needed and that the problems football faced could be related to the daily struggles of everyday life. He also made sure that he was seen to be as equally 'hands on' with the younger teams and local coaches. He toured the island to give coaching workshops and although the sudden intrusion of this foreigner was not always appreciated by men who had run local teams for years, Simoes smiled and continued to drive home his message. When they felt their toes were being stepped on, Simoes spoke in riddles, tying his critics up in words.

Many local coaches, for instance, believed that school football on the island was the best in the world. Simoes had to overcome this myopic view and one of his favourite fictional tales was about an uncle who owned a farm. This uncle thought that his farm was the best in the world so he built a high wall round it and did not go outside for 20 years. Then, one night, a hurricane blew the walls down. When the uncle looked outside, he saw that the farm next door was more modern. 'Sometimes you find that what you have is fantastic and the best in the world,' said Simoes, 'and sometimes you find that what you have needs to be developed.'

Things were improving by the second half of 1995. Captain Burrell tied up the most high-profile sponsorship to date when American Airlines pledged to transport the team and their luggage. It was a vital agreement as Simoes had insisted from the start that the main difference between the 'first world and third world' footballers was the number of stamps they had in their passports. While he was careful not to be overly critical of what Jamaica had achieved in the past, he stressed the need to travel in order to gain exposure to new cultures and different types of football. When he first met the team, however, some of the players did not even *own* a passport.

Travel required money and for the first part of the year Simoes had to make do with matches against nearby St Lucia and Trinidad and Tobago. Results were looking up, though, and when the Zambian national team flew in for two games in August, Walter Boyd underlined the team's progress with goals in successive victories. Four straight wins against Costa Rica and Honduras at home, and away to Trinidad and Tobago and the Cayman Islands, saw confidence rising. In November, a year after the launch of the programme, The Captain found enough money in the kitty to send Simoes and his team on tour to Zambia. It was the first stop on a trek that would take them to every continent over the next four years.

The Zambian tour was significant for other reasons. On arrival at the airport, the Jamaican party were met by an enthusiastic crowd of local fans and among the placards was written the message 'Welcome to Jamaica's Reggae Boyz'. The nickname was picked up by a journalist, who wired his story across the globe, and it immediately stuck. The Captain was delighted. The team had been given a sense of identity and purpose and he vowed that wherever the Reggae Boyz travelled, they would be responsible for exporting Jamaican culture. The new name suggested a young, cool and entertaining team, and on belatedly realising the potential of his 'brand', The Captain licensed the name in 11 different countries. The Jamaicans won friends and an identity in Africa – but lost both matches.

The team reached another landmark when Burrell enticed the highly rated Norwegian national side to visit Jamaica for a match at the end of November. Egil Olsen fielded a weakened line-up but it was still Jamaica's toughest test to date, and a goal on his debut from 18-year-old Kevin 'Pele' Wilson of Arnett Gardens was good enough to earn a 1–1 draw.

Four days later, however, the mood of mild euphoria was tempered when the JFF announced the indefinite suspension of the country's football season because of increasing violence at matches. The Jamaican Referees' Association said referees refused to work because of attacks on players, referees and linesmen after a riot at a match between two college sides. The Manning Cup in Jamaica was not a competition that bore comparison with Ivy League college events in the States or school football in England. It stirred local rivalries which occasionally degenerated into running battles. Many officials with firearms licences had started carrying guns during matches and it was a timely reminder that while progress was being made on the international front, problems still existed closer to home.

A fudged agreement with the police to step up security saw the domestic season restarted in December but nothing seemed capable of derailing the national team bandwagon. Three more wins – away to Antigua and St Kitts and then only a second ever victory over fancied Mexico before 30,000 fans in Kingston – saw Jamaica rise 40 places in the world rankings to 56th. Fourteen wins from 19 matches over the year meant that the newly titled Reggae Boyz had won FIFA's 'Mover of the Year' award. The Under 23s team also topped the Caribbean Zone in the Olympic qualifying tournament. It was just the start The Captain had hoped for. A message had been sent to the world, boasted Burrell. Jamaica should be taken seriously.

Growing confidence in the new administration was reflected in sponsorship deals with Bargain Rent-a-Car and Courts, the latter furnishing the expanding office space occupied by the JFF and the former supplying transport on the island. The deals were worth something in the region of JA $8 million (approx. £145,000) and enabled funds to be ploughed into the team and into clearing the debts inherited by The Captain's team on taking office. The government also came good, investing JA $10 million to upgrade the island's pitches, and smaller donations were secured elsewhere as the Football Foundation of Jamaica cranked into gear. The crowds started drifting back to the National Stadium.

Both abroad and, more importantly, at home, the team was now taking shape and making news. Alongside the commuting Walter Boyd, Simoes had now blooded a cadre of new players who appealed to people in the game's traditional heartlands. Gregory Messam, the left-sided defender from Harbour View, became a big hit with the girls, who had now started attending matches in numbers. He had the gold, he had the hair, he had the tattoos. The same could be said for defender Donald Stewart, the baby-faced Ricardo Gardener and the giant Onandi Lowe. These players were from the same backgrounds as many of the fans and had the attitude to match. Pictures from the early days invariably show them pulling rap star poses for the camera. Unlike previous coaches, Simoes positively encouraged his young bucks to express themselves – the prominent gold jewellery and extravagant hairstyles gave them star quality and enhanced the product.

In January 1996, the well-heeled Captain Burrell flew to Milan to collect the FIFA award from Pele, and the senior squad, after drawing 1–1 at home to Cuba in a friendly, flew off for another training camp in Brazil. There, Simoes met a young fitness trainer named Alfredo Montesso, whom he persuaded to join him on the Road to France programme. For all the tributes he had paid publicly to his Jamaican backroom staff, Simoes felt that making the next step would rely on increasing the fund of specialist knowledge within the programme. Montesso, who up until 1992 had been a professional footballer with a Second Division club in

Sao Paulo, spoke no English at the time. He would not be the last Brazilian to join up.

Club bosses – often minor businessmen or community leaders – were still a problem, and Simoes' patience began to wear thin when they refused to understand that the existing system could not support a national team capable of qualifying for France. He told them repeatedly that World Cup success would be beneficial to the clubs and that it could pave the way for professionalism but there was no way success could be achieved while the players were fulfilling club obligations. He needed them full-time, living in the team bungalow and available for travel, to be improved as footballers.

The clubs were not comfortable with this arrangement at first, insisting that their traditional Jamaican style of football was perfectly adequate for an effective World Cup bid. Simoes called a meeting of all presidents of the clubs in Jamaica and asked them how many clubs there were on the island. He listened to a different answer from each president before announcing that they were all wrong. A club, he said, must have a field, a stadium and administrative offices. There were no clubs on Jamaica. Simoes then reminded them that he was the technical director and if they did not like it, he would return to Brazil.

In March, Simoes handed a debut to a young player with a big personality. Ian 'Pepe' Goodison had grown up in Tivoli Gardens, one of the toughest areas in downtown Kingston, and he was an unknown 17 year old when he first came into contact with Simoes. The coach had been advised to go down to Second Division club Olympic Gardens to check out a player but had got the names mixed up. Simoes was advised again and when he finally sat down to watch the burly Goodison in action, he immediately recognised a boy blessed with football skills and leadership qualities. Twenty-eight days before Jamaica's first match on the long road to qualification, Goodison marked his arrival with a debut goal in a 2–0 home win over Guatemala.

Although the Road to France can be traced back beyond 1994, the first qualifying match took place away to Surinam in Paramaribo on 31 March 1996. By that two-legged, second-round tie, Simoes had laid the bricks: Warren Barrett in goal, protected by the three pillars – Ian 'Pepe' Goodison, the more experienced Durrent 'Tatti' Brown and Linval 'Rudi' Dixon of Hazard FC. Thoedore Whitmore scored the only goal in the 56th minute to get the campaign off to a flying start but only 2,500 watched a match that now represents a significant milestone.

Three weeks later, Paul Young repeated the dose in Kingston. Two goals from Walter Boyd and another from Whitmore were then enough to see off Barbados in both legs to ensure qualification for the semi-final group of four teams. Boyd's late winner in the first match is rumoured to be the finest of Jamaica's entire World Cup campaign though precious few saw it as Jamaican television's coverage cut out before the final whistle. Funding of the programme relied heavily on gate receipts and the stadium was only half full for the home tie.

The JFF worked overtime to fix up friendlies before the crucial semi-final round began in September. In July, an All-African XI delighted an enthusiastic crowd in the National Stadium, now known by the fans as 'The Office'. Whitmore and Christopher Dawes got their names on the scoresheet in an impressive 3–0 win. All was far from rosy behind the scenes, however, and the new administration had been forced to take the programme 'one day at a time'. Early FFJ meetings had been well attended but despite the upswing in results, the cash flow had slowed to a trickle. By August 1996, the programme had almost reached a standstill. The anticipated backing from corporate Jamaica had not materialised, crowds were down and players were disgruntled at the low levels of payment.

Walter Boyd was losing money by returning home to play for his country and if, as Simoes wanted, he was to give up his contract in the States to join the programme full-time, an adequate financial package would have to be put in place. It would mean the JFF having to find JA $250,000 (approximately US $6,000) a month. Boyd was a guaranteed crowd puller but more importantly, he scored goals.

Before playing Costa Rica at home, just 11 days before their first World Cup match in the next round, seven players threatened to walk out. Simoes, who thought about quitting himself, retaliated by stating that if any of them left they would be expelled for good.

The Brazilian had recently taken matters into his own hands, going to a friend who ran a small supermarket to ask for help. He wanted US $1,000 a month to keep the programme alive. When he got the money, Simoes realised that this might be the kernel of an idea – a way for companies to make smaller but no less effective donations. He recommended that the progamme launch a scheme called 'Adopt a Player', in which businesses would sponsor an individual player, paying him a wage and meeting his expenses in return for endorsement opportunities – the sort of scheme operated by poorer clubs in Britain to raise sponsorship for players kits. It proved to be another turning point and, as Simoes pointed out, 'The money is not in the pocket but in the head of the administrator.'

The drought in finances was particularly frustrating given the improvements that had been made in so many areas. Psychologically, the players were now starting to believe in themselves. They had never before been convinced that they could build the future of their families through football but the mental diet Simoes had put them on was now producing more confident individuals. He believed that if you want to lose weight, you should eat low-calorie food. If you want to increase weight, you should eat high-calorie food. If, however, you want to feel positive about yourself, you must be fed a mental diet of positive food. All Simoes players were told, 'You are able to do things. You have the potential. You can do it.'

Peter Cargill, the experienced midfielder who had made his international debut back in 1984, had returned to the island after being impressed with the new set-up and was available after injury. He had spent seven years playing in Israel and was one of the only players in the squad who knew what it was to live and work as a professional footballer. 'Jair', as he was known to his team mates, also commanded huge respect among his peers. He was calm, assured and could be relied on to carry out the coach's orders. He was an all-important old head among the youth Simoes had gathered around him. Playing in the heart of midfield, Cargill dictated the rhythm of the team. In fact, Simoes said he was 'like my wife on the football pitch'.

In the penultimate group of four, Jamaica found themselves up against Mexico, St Vincent and Honduras. On 15 September

Simoes patched up morale sufficiently to send his team out to face Honduras before 21,000 fans in Kingston. Despite the atmosphere created by the whistles and the rhythms run by the selector on the stadium sound system, many of those who assembled at 'The Office' doubted their team's chance of advancing beyond this stage. But as Jamaica's opponents, qualifiers for the finals of 1982, trudged in 2–0 down at half-time, a new feeling of optimism swept round the ground. For good measure, Boyd made it 3–0 eight minutes after the break with his second goal of the match. Eight days later, Jamaica made it two wins out of two as Paul Young scored both goals to secure an away win over St Vincent.

The big test was now at hand – Mexico away in the mighty Azteca Stadium – and Jamaica played two friendlies in five days before setting off to face the strongest team in the region. The Azteca was a far cry from 'The Office' and 110,000 passionate Mexicans engulfed the handful of intrepid fans who had travelled from Jamaica. The two teams walked out to a deafening ticker-tape reception, but as soon as the game began, Mexico were all over Jamaica. Only a mixture of profligate finishing and heroic defending kept the scores level until a minute before half-time, when Luis Alves Zague tore through the Jamaican defence to put Mexico in front.

Ten minutes after the break, Mexico made it 2–0 through Carlos Hermosillo. Baying for Jamaican blood, the crowd looked like being satisfied as Durrent Brown hobbled off, injured in a desperate attempt to stop the second fatal strike on goal. Simoes switched things round, bringing on Wolde Harris to partner Boyd up front and pushing the huge Lowe back into the sweeper position. It worked. The Mexican crowd grew restless and Lowe started to dictate the tempo from deep in the Jamaican half. In the 70th minute, Jamaican hearts missed a beat as Boyd beat his man before sending a scorching shot past Jorge Campos at his near post. Jamaica could not find the equaliser but had recorded their best ever result on Mexican soil.

The schedule showed no signs of slacking and ten days later, Jamaica were in San Pedro Sula for the potentially hazardous away tie with Honduras. The players had already experienced the hostility of Central American crowds when they were pelted with large coins during a 'friendly' in Costa Rica and the treatment in Honduras sank lower still. The team hotel was surrounded by local fans the night before the game and the incessant banging of drums and blaring of car horns ensured that sleep was an impossibility. The Captain stormed downstairs to confront the mob and when Simoes joined him, a minor fracas developed in the street.

After walking out to a barrage of urine-filled bottles and used toilet paper, the match itself was one long rearguard action. Hopes sank when Walter Boyd received his second yellow card for kicking the ball away. The players protested that they could not hear the whistle above the folk and samba blaring from the tinny stadium PA system and the crowd's constant decibel level. Jamaica defended like lions and held on to record an invaluable goalless draw.

A home win against St Vincent and a favourable result against Mexico in Kingston would see Jamaica make history. Never before had they made it to the final qualifying stage. Five goals against St Vincent put the team in good heart for the visit of Bora Milutinovic and his Mexican team for the final match of the semi-final round. Elsewhere, Honduras knew that they would have to run up a cricket score against the hapless Venetians and hope that Mexico could do them a favour. The National Stadium was full to capacity, scuffles breaking out on the pavements outside as anxious fans rushed through the gates. Some climbed over walls or shinned up floodlights for a better look. All of Jamaica was out for this crucial match.

Mexico started well and in the 16th minute, Goodison had to scramble the ball off his own line. Tension mounted as a big screen flashed up scores from Honduras where, worryingly, St Vincent were already trailing 6–1 by half-time. Fifteen minutes after the break, Honduras had stretched their advantage to eight goals, leading by the unlikely score of 11–3. Nerves were in tatters as Boyd, back from suspension, and Onandi Lowe attempted to pick the lock of the Mexican defence. The Central Americans responded with renewed efforts on Barrett's goal but with 15 minutes to go they seemed content to take their foot off the gas and stroll to a draw that was purely academic for them.

Simoes scampered to the touchline. He wanted to replace the limping 'Pepe' Goodison but there was just time for a corner to be swung in from the left foot of Gregory Messam. Straining every sinew, Goodison rose unmarked to meet it with a powerful header and put Jamaica in front. The stadium had never witnessed such joy. A bouncing riot of green, gold and black rose as one on all sides. Umbrellas, shading their owners from the fierce sun, were twirled in delight and the wail of air horns filled the blue skies. Goodison wheeled away before breaking into his own personalised goal celebration, a funky strut with his chest puffed out. At the final whistle the players were engulfed by their jubilant fans. The sweating Simoes, wearing his familiar 'JESUS SAVES' T-shirt, was chaired from the pitch.

Jamaica had arrived.

3

One Door Closes, Another One Opens

ROBBIE

The game against Mexico in the semi-final round was still some months off when the idea of playing for Jamaica first came into my head. My parents had always made us aware of our Jamaican roots and we went over four or five times during my childhood. I had been to the island on holiday to see my grandmother and cousins since, but I must admit, becoming a Jamaican international was not something that had been a big ambition.

The prospect had crossed my mind because every so often circulars would be sent round professional clubs in England, enquiring whether players had Scottish, Irish or Welsh grandparents. I wondered why more players had not explored their Caribbean roots and every so often I received a call from some complete stranger saying that he represented the Jamaican FA. The idea started to take shape, however, a good year before I made my debut – prompted by a phone call from an associate of Winston Clarke, the black sports promoter.

Winston was exploring opportunities in the West Indies at the time and seemed keen to generate momentum for the Caribbean Football Union. I got the impression that he felt there was money to be made in finding players in Europe who might qualify for international caps back in the West Indies and vice versa in terms of finding contracts in Europe for Caribbean players.

His company wanted to recruit players in England who would be eligible, under FIFA rules, for the Jamaican national team. It sounded like an interesting idea but I still had hopes for England at the time. However, there was no point burning any bridges so I told him that if he could show me something official we would take it further. I wasn't prepared to commit myself to anything on the basis of a phone call so I was not best pleased when a story appeared in the *Sun* soon after, duly listing a number of players, myself included, who would be eligible for Jamaica under FIFA rules. Clarke was definitely behind it.

I made some enquiries and found out a little bit about the Jamaican team: they had a new coach and had beaten Barbados, but that was about it. I spoke to Clarke himself over the course of the next couple of weeks but then the whole idea suddenly seemed to fizzle out. For six months, I concentrated on my football with Wimbledon, scored goals and pressed ahead with trying to break into the England squad. I heard nothing more about Jamaica.

Then, around Christmas, I received a call from Mr Horace Reid, the general manager of the Jamaican national team. He explained that the Jamaican Football Federation was putting together a serious bid to qualify for the World Cup and asked whether I would consider playing for Jamaica. In theory, I said, I would. Though I didn't know much about Jamaican football, I strongly suspected that it was pretty rudimentary.

Prior to this first contact with the Jamaican Football Federation, I had been watching *Jamaican ER* on television – and I must admit that the series sowed a few seeds of doubt in my mind. On the evidence of the show, the last place I would want to be treated in the event of an injury was a poorly equipped, understaffed hospital in Kingston, one of the world's most dangerous cities. If I broke my leg in Jamaica, would there be anaesthetic or would I get a bamboo shoot strapped to the side of my leg and told to be on my way? I bought some time, asking Reid to find out whether things like air fares, medical insurance and expenses would be taken care of. Looking back, my fears about treatment of injuries were totally groundless and the medical side is one of the most professional aspects of the national team set-up in Jamaica.

While Mr Reid was looking into matters, I learnt that a number of English-based players were being watched by the JFF. Bob Hazel, formerly of QPR, was doing a bit of scouting work for them and I was one of the players on his shortlist. Bob duly contacted me and said that the JFF's interest was serious. Other players on the list included Danny Maddix and Rufus Brevett of QPR, Dean Sturridge and Daryl Powell of Derby County, my Dons team mate Marcus Gayle and the

Portsmouth lads, Fitzroy Simpson, Paul Hall and Deon Burton.

Bob asked again whether I'd consider playing for Jamaica and again I said that I was not going to do anything rash that might jeopardise my chances with Glenn Hoddle. I had made the standby squad for the match against Mexico (of all people) in late 1996, so it was too early to be able to give him a firm decision. I was playing well and believed that I still had a chance with England.

I thought about it more after a meeting in January 1997 with a contingent from the JFF – Rene Simoes, Captain Horace Burrell and Mr Reid. Their very presence in Britain suggested that their intentions were serious. They watched me play for Wimbledon against QPR in the fifth round of the FA Cup and then invited me to join them that evening at the Selsdon Park Hotel near Croydon.

I found Rene Simoes quite guarded. There was no question of him coming cap in hand to request assistance from England. It was more like he had something that I wanted – the opportunity to play international football and maybe even a World Cup. He gave the impression that was up to him whether I was going to get a piece of it. It was certainly not my choice.

Simoes didn't seem sure that I had what he needed. 'The way my teams play is totally alien to the way Wimbledon play,' he explained. Obviously he was aware of the criticism that has so often been fired at the Crazy Gang. Although everyone labels us 'route one', at the club we know that there is a lot more to Wimbledon's success than hard work and high balls. We can play a bit too. The little Brazilian with the big moustache and strange pronunciation went to great lengths to tell me that his teams played a typical South American passing game, slower in tempo and with the ball on the ground rather than in the air. I listened to what he had to say, mentally biting my lip.

His philosophy, he said, was not to give the ball away. At Wimbledon we go long and are prepared to lose the ball in the opponent's half because we always fancy ourselves to win it back. Simoes liked to build the play up slowly, Brazilian style, and told me that there was no place in his side for a box-to-box player like me.

I would have to change my style to fit in with what Jamaica needed – that much was obvious. I reminded Simoes that I was an experienced professional who had played in different teams with different styles. You have to be able to adapt your style to the team you are playing for, and that's why I play the way I do for Wimbledon. It didn't take a genius to work out that it would be nigh on impossible to keep boxing it on a boiling afternoon in Kingston. It made sense to play a slower game and I understood what Simoes was saying. I still felt that he had reservations, however.

I would have to comply with certain conditions, he explained. I wouldn't be staying in luxury hotels or getting any extra benefits. Instead, I'd be living in the team house, training with all the other players and on the same bonus system as everyone else. Before introducing anyone new to a team he had already taken a long way, he wanted me to know how hard he had worked on forging team spirit. Nothing would be allowed to upset the applecart, not even a 'big name' from the English Premiership, which suited me fine because if I decided to take the plunge I wanted to do my work on the pitch and feel on a level with everyone else.

Simoes was obviously very conscious of creating and maintaining the right chemistry between people but the way he described the vibe inside the Jamaican camp reminded me of the dressing-room atmosphere we have at Wimbledon – that old 'us against the world' mentality. I knew exactly what he was talking about but Simoes clearly felt compelled to spell it out to me – he didn't want me to have any false expectations about what things would be like should I decide to play for Jamaica (if he wanted me, that is).

He also warned me that I would have trouble winning the players over and that he would let them be the judge of whether I was suitable or not. I would have to go into a strange environment and prove myself, both as a player and as a Jamaican. This lion's den – as he seemed to want me to think of it – wouldn't be alien to me. Emotions are the same the world over. Whenever a player joins a new club, he has to find his level within the dressing-room hierarchy. Like starting a new school or job, the first few days are a bit daunting but then you start to relax as you feel more settled and accepted. I had survived the most notorious initiation tests in English football at Wimbledon so I felt reasonably confident that I could handle what Simoes was describing.

Yet while Wimbledon were going well and an England chance was still being talked about, I felt that I had enough on my plate and was happy to let things run their natural course. I spoke to Jamaican officials on a couple of occasions after that meeting and Simoes kept me informed on how things were going with his team.

During that 1996–97 season, Joe Kinnear had spoken to Glenn Hoddle about my chances. The new national coach had been complimentary about me and Wimbledon's up and coming defender Chris Perry. Joe told us to be patient – Hoddle would have a look at us when he got the chance. I made the standby squad again for the World Cup qualifying game against Italy in February 1997 and still felt that there was an outside chance I might force my way into Hoddle's plans.

Whether that would mean getting the nod for the B team – something I think Hoddle was looking to resurrect even back then – or for the full squad, I didn't know at that point. If the opportunity with England B had presented itself, however, I would have taken it and tried to prove my worth. I've never denied that I would have played for England. It was only natural that England should be my first choice; it is the country where I was born and grew up.

Having reached the top division at the relatively late age of 26, I have always felt that I have been playing 'catch up'. The first hurdle was to establish myself as a top-flight player and the next was to get an England call-up, which I did in 1992. After that, though, I got no further than being talked about as someone who was perpetually on the fringes. While that attitude persisted, I felt that I would have to work fast if I was ever to establish myself as an England player. I set a deadline for the end of the season. If I hadn't had a chance by then, I knew it would be difficult or even impossible, to force my way in during the 12 months before the team went to France.

My fears were realised when, after finishing the best season of my career as one of the highest-scoring midfielders in the country, I was not picked for the squad that Glenn Hoddle took to Le Tournoi in France that summer. My dreams of playing for England had all but died.

Six months had passed between that first meeting with Simoes and Burrell in London. The picture was now a lot clearer in my mind but I had just finished a long season and needed a holiday with my family. I had booked a three-week trip to Jamaica months back because I wanted to take my kids to see their grandparents and show them a bit of their heritage.

I tried to speak to Simoes again at the beginning of the pre-season period, a month or so before Jamaica would be competing in the Caribbean Shell Cup, but could not get through. God works in mysterious ways, though, as I was to find out during my three weeks on the island.

We stayed in Ocho Rios and one evening during the holiday, I was having dinner with my wife Sandra when I spotted a familiar face on the other side of the restaurant. You see a lot of people you recognise in football and I thought this guy with the moustache and glasses might be a supporter or someone I had met along the way. Half an hour later there was a tap on my shoulder. As soon as I heard the voice, I knew it was Professor Simoes.

My immediate thought was that he'd tracked me down. It seemed too much of a coincidence that we should now find ourselves having dinner in the same hotel. As Simoes went to pull up a chair and join us, I said to my wife that I thought it was all a bit spooky. Simoes explained that he had been in the area to run a coaching course and had come over to the hotel to see his daughter, who was the entertainments manager. He assured me that our meeting was pure chance and looking back, Simoes had no reason to lie.

We talked some football but Simoes obviously realised that we were in Jamaica to get away after a long season and went to great lengths to be very polite and courteous to my wife. Our conversation ended with Simoes inviting me to Kingston to continue our talks, find out what football meant in the country and meet a few people in influential positions.

I said I'd have to discuss it with my wife because, to be fair, she'd also had her quota of football by then. I wouldn't go if she didn't want me to. By the same token, if I did not take this opportunity I would only have to fly back out after we had returned from holiday. In the end, Sandra and I decided to give ourselves two nights in Kingston.

Simoes arranged for us to be picked up a couple of days later. When I got to the front of the hotel, there to collect us was the biggest limousine I'd ever seen, complete with drinks cabinet and television. It was so long the front bumper looked like it was already in Kingston. Other hotel guests stopped and stared as we boarded this huge monstrosity. They must have thought we were local dignitaries.

It took about an hour and half to get to Kingston and when we arrived we discovered that the JFF had booked us into The Wyndham, the city's top hotel. We were met by Mr Reid, who told us that the Federation would pick up the tab for whatever we wanted. After catching the lift to the tenth floor, Reid presented us with a key for a lift which took us up another couple of floors. When we got out at the penthouse, our room – if you can call it that – was located opposite the Presidential Suite. It was absolutely enormous – bedroom, conference facilities, living room, kitchen area. We could not have been treated better if we were Bill and Hilary Clinton.

We had two nights living it up before Captain Burrell joined us. We went out to lunch with some government officials and it felt like I was being paraded in front of his business contacts. Burrell struck me as an honest, down-to-earth sort of man although I had been told prior to going out to lunch with him in Kingston that he was not afraid of showing his wealth. From what I could make out, he was happy to have me with him. I was a Premiership player and he seemed to enjoy the kudos that brought him. I met with Mr Reid and we discussed details before The Captain, as I would soon know him, did what he does best. He held a press conference.

The Captain told the press that we could do great things for each other if I decided to come out and play for the Reggae Boyz. I knew him well enough now to know he was pretty shrewd and I suspected he wanted me to commit early so that other eligible Premiership players might be persuaded to do the same. We went to watch a game in Montego Bay and the message came across the Jarrett Park tannoy system that I was in the crowd. If he was trying to charm me, he was doing a good job.

There were about five or six thousand people there to watch Seba United and it was quite unusual to watch football on a ground they use for cricket. I was told the ground was one of the best in the country – I wouldn't like to see the worst. But it was good to be shown sides of Jamaica that you don't see as a tourist and there was certainly a 'heady' atmosphere at the match. The spectators did get pretty involved in the game but there were no songs or chants like in British football – it was more like people shouting their friends on from the stands. I was interested to see the state of Jamaican domestic football and it was obvious the country desperately needed a professional league if the game was to progress. In the two games I saw, Burrell pointed out five players who were in the international squad. I was relieved to see that they were head and shoulders above the rest.

Simoes explained that many clubs don't have their own pitch in Jamaica. Security also seems to be a problem judging by the size and weaponry of the police presence. He was not impressed by club football in Jamaica and said that the national programme was trying to set up a professional league for the year 2000. Taking all these factors into consideration, I left with the impression that the standard was not that bad but not that good. I'd say it was on a par with the English Vauxhall Conference or Third Division.

After the game in Montego Bay, we got down to business. Burrell, Simoes and I spent a couple of hours talking in a hotel room and they asked me again whether I wanted to play for Jamaica. Obviously I had to speak to my wife but in principle I said the answer was yes. To be honest, the hospitality did not sway me that much (although I did enjoy it!) The fact was, once I'd got a feel for the whole situation, I knew I wanted to be a part of it. I felt that playing for Jamaica would be like playing for Wimbledon. Marcus Gayle, my Wimbledon team mate, flew in from his honeymoon on Barbados and we talked through the technical and administrative details with Mr Reid, shook hands with The Captain and Simoes and agreed, club permitting, to return back out for the forthcoming Shell Cup.

The JFF were aware of the good relationship I had with my employers at Wimbledon so agreed not to broadcast anything until I had a meeting with Sam Hammam and Joe Kinnear. I wanted to make sure they had no major problems with my decision. Deep down, I felt that Joe would be all right about the situation. He knew that I had international ambitions and he had helped to push me for England, even speaking out in the press on a few occasions to say that he thought I deserved a chance over people who had already been picked. If I had the opportunity to play international football, Joe knew I'd be looking to take it.

Sam, on the other hand, was less enthusiastic, probably because he didn't know about any of this before I told him at the meeting. I hadn't said anything previously because I hadn't known what was going to happen. Sam was reservedly pleased for me but understandably concerned that I would be missing for Wimbledon matches which, depending on how the season went, could see the club in a relegation battle. He was looking out for the interests of the club and I did not expect him to be any other way. Although I didn't exactly have to win Sam over, I expressed that I had a right to play and pointed out that international football would improve me as a player and enhance the reputation of the club. After all, if I got to play in the World Cup, I would go as a Wimbledon footballer.

4

Learning the Hard Way

DANIEL

While Robbie spent the year between the summer of 1996 and the Shell Cup of July 1997 considering his options, careful assessment of the team's strengths and weaknesses clarified the overall picture for Simoes. What happened in the six months between that win over Mexico and the point when Simoes formally added the names of English-based players to his squad roster is crucial. This period formed the backbone of the World Cup squad but also exposed their limitations. Simoes had just over a year to turn them into a team that could not only compete in this final stage but grab one of the top three spots.

As Robbie's account reveals, the JFF opened talks with English-based players at least four months before the first match of the final round in March '97. Simoes liked to consult the senior members of his squad and did so regularly at strategic points along the Road to France. He spoke frankly with Peter Cargill, Warren Barrett and Durrent Brown when the team topped the semi-final group and wanted to know whether they believed they now needed outside assistance to go further. The coach knew that members of this experienced inner council could be trusted to take a level-headed look at the situation and he also knew that if *they* were persuaded of the merits of outside help, he could counter any public criticism by saying, 'This is what the players want.'

Back in the late eighties, Jamaica had experimented with introducing players born in England but it had not worked. The imports had been put up in posh hotels while the local players had to pay their own way. Simoes had no intention of making the same mistakes and when he set off to England in the company of The Captain and Horace Reid in January 1997, he knew that anyone who took his fancy and accepted the offer would come to Jamaica on his terms. Preferential treatment for well-paid stars from the Premiership would rip holes in a team that had showed great fighting spirit in getting this far. Simoes told his senior players as much and consequently could set off on his first foreign recruitment drive with their blessing.

Exploring the possibility of injecting the programme with a shot of overseas professionalism would be upping the ante and the JFF knew that it would have to be able to meet new challenges if the experiment was to work. Simoes had kept an eye on developments across the water, noting the form of players on a hit list drawn up by Clarke and co. in England. The coach was aware that professionals would improve the squad technically while Captain Burrell could see the promise of marketing his 'product' to a wider audience. Plucking players from across the diaspora fitted with the island's 'Out of many, one nation' credo. It is not hard to imagine The Captain standing in front of the mirror, practising his new sales pitch: 'The match next Sunday afternoon will feature players from some of the top clubs in England – Jamaicans from across the seas.' This was nation-building gone global.

Brazilian Simoes showed more delicacy in handling this situation than his Jamaican colleague. He insists that he actively resisted the temptation to rush in overseas talent in the early days, preferring instead to achieve the first stage of what he calls 'a cultural revolution' through the efforts of an exclusively Jamaican-born squad of players. This was important for two reasons. First, it convinced those same players of their own worth, proving to them that they could reach the standards that Simoes had promised. Second, it got the country behind him.

By January 1997, however, Simoes had been in the job for 15 months and had had enough time to assess the strengths and weaknesses of his squad. Additional experience and know-how were now necessary if The Captain's dream was to come to fruition and to do that, he had to change opinion in Jamaica and demonstrate that without new players the Road to France would be routed down a dead end. Patience would be required to educate an expectant public about what Jamaica would find in the next round. Simoes knew that his team would probably struggle and that public opposition to the introduction of overseas players would diminish as a result. Timing was, therefore, of the essence.

Simoes planned the World Cup schedule carefully, taking advantage of CONCACAF's willingness to let national coaches and associations draw up the fixture list. He pencilled in the USA as his first game. For Jamaica, the first consideration had to be money, and a home match to start the campaign would pump some much-needed revenue into JFF coffers. Simoes also fancied Steve Sampson's side to be one of three to qualify so an early chance to pit his team against a group 'heavyweight' would leave him and the public with a better idea of where Jamaica stood in relation to her bigger, richer rivals. At least Glenn Hoddle and Cesare Maldini didn't need to worry about the cash from the first game being enough for them to play in the second.

If they could weather the early storms, Simoes fancied his chances at home in the latter stages. Four of the last six games were scheduled for Kingston. The coach liked to play mind games with his better-equipped opponents and after putting together an excellent sequence of home results since losing to the USA in November 1994, he knew that none of his CONCACAF rivals would relish the prospect of an energy-sapping, midday kick-off in the searing heat of Kingston. Bora Milutinovic, in particular, would not relish bringing his team to the boiling cauldron of the National Stadium after their last defeat, especially if they still needed points to qualify. Both coaches predicted that Mexico would be through by that stage so they agreed on making Jamaica v. Mexico the last game of the group. Simoes figured that Jamaica would be better off facing a complacent Mexico rather than another team battling it out for the final spot. It proved a clever strategy although it did not shape up that way at first.

Simoes was quite open about his plans to disrupt opponents as much as was legally permitted and was not upset when football writers from the US filed reports about the shabby treatment of their team: cartons of drink on the American bus were left untouched for fear they had been spiked, the bus was 'conve-

Though he did not enjoy the best of luck during the tournament, Warren 'Boopie' Barrett (right) always led by example.

The giant Onandi Lowe clashes with Croatia's Davor Suker in Lens during Jamaica's historic first match at the World Cup finals.

The Portsmouth pioneers (left to right): Paul Hall,
Deon Burton and Fitzroy Simpson.

Steve 'Shorty' Malcolm: a quiet man with a famous temper.

The man with the vision, Captain Horace Burrell.

Professor Rene Simoes was adamant that he didn't want to coach Jamaica but when Captain Burrell met the Brazilian it was love 'at first sight'.

© ALLSPORT

© DEVON CHIN

At the end of a hard week's training at Braco, the Boys enjoy a game of head tennis in the pool.

The impressively pouting Ian 'Pepe' Goodison and fans.

Jamaican fans came in
many shapes and sizes at
the World Cup. The Ouch
Girls (above) became firm
favourites.

A bouncing sea of yellow, green and black: Jamaica's fans congregate
at 'The Office' for the biggest party since Independence in 1962, November 1997.

© EMPICS

The team that made history by becoming the first English-speaking Caribbean
island to qualify for the World Cup finals: (back row from left to right) Warren
Barrett, Peter Cargill, Dean Sewell, Ricardo Gardener, Theodore Whitmore, Ian
Goodison, Fitzroy Simpson, Alfredo Montessa (trainer); (front row from left to
right) Linval Dixon, Deon Burton, Durrent Brown, Paul Hall.

© ALLSPORT

World Cup fever just before all hell
broke loose at Reggae Boyz Market at
Devon House, May 1998. (Top)

The King and the President: Pele and
Captain Burrell take centre stage before
Jamaica play Santos of Brazil in
Kingston. (Above right)

The last man to experience adulation like
this. A statue of Bob Marley overlooks
the National Stadium in Kingston. (Left)

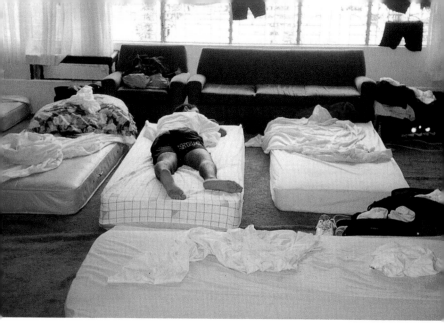

The team house in Kingston more than made up for its lack of
luxury with atmosphere. Here, a squad member indulges in a
favourite Jamaican pastime.

Pre-match prayer session in the team house. Rene Simoes and his 'brother in
Christ' Carl Brown (left) get the vibe right before the crunch match against Mexico,
November 1997.

niently' blocked in after training sessions and the US team was allocated a miniscule changing room. American journalists painted a grim picture of Jamaica. Simoes shrugged. 'The point is, it's a psychological war – how much you can interefere with the balance of the opposing team. At 3.30, when games are usually played, the temperature is 90 degrees, so there is not much difference [to America]. But when you put the game at 12 o'clock, you change everything for the United States camp. You are saying, "Hey, prepare yourself. Jamaica awaits you." It is a message that the game is not only on the field. Respect us: we are here in the final six not by accident. We are here because we have worked very hard. Don't consider us Third World because this is football.'

Excellent stuff indeed.

The Captain joined in, announcing that the United States should expect the unexpected. The Jamaican crowd and the local DJs would combine to create an atmosphere unlike any other the USA players had experienced. If the USA were not in the best frame of mind by the time they walked out into the blistering midday heat, then Simoes and The Captain could feel pleased that they had done their job well. It's called turning problems to your own advantage.

Over 35,000 squeezed into the National Stadium to see Jamaica dominate large tracts of play against the US but for all the encouragement of this bumper crowd, the Reggae Boyz could not get the goal that would have got the campaign off to a flyer. In the 30th minute Walter Boyd, now in the programme full-time, saw a shot from ten yards clawed away by United States keeper Kasey Keller and Whitmore was put through but delayed long enough for Mike Burns to make a last-ditch, goal-line clearance. Jamaica played pretty well and might have nicked it.

The United States were the more experienced team but offered little as they struggled to come to terms with strong gusts blowing down off the Blue Mountains and the uneven bounce on a rock-hard pitch. Eric Wynalda could have put them in front on the hour but Barrett made a flying save. Similarly, only the dependable Durrent 'Tatti' Brown stood between Roy Lassiter and a clear run on the Jamaican goal. The Americans were pleased to get out with a point. Coach Sampson had done something others would prove incapable of. He had survived a visit to 'The Office'.

The national team party flew straight out to Bolivia after the USA game to begin the build-up to another defining match on the Road to France. Mexico had followed an opening 3–0 win over Canada with a limp 0–0 draw in Costa Rica and as favourites to qualify from the group in first place, were now expected to hand the minnows from the Caribbean a sound thrashing. They need-n't have worried because the team they faced on 13 April was a pale shadow of the side that had previously beaten them in Kingston.

By the time Jamaica ran out to a spine-chilling reception at the Azteca, they were broken men. There are numerous reasons why this happened, but scheduling a match against Bolivia, 12,000 feet above sea level and just two days after the physical exertion of a World Cup qualifying game, was certainly one of them. Playing and travelling had left the team exhausted and after recent experiences in Mexico, Honduras and Costa Rica, they felt more than a little wary of their surroundings. Playing so soon after arrival was also potentially dangerous because one should normally take two weeks to acclimatise. Jamaica had less than 12 hours, four of which were spent on the bus which took them from the airport to the mining town of Orura in the moun-tains.

When the party arrived at the hotel, some members of the team couldn't even climb more than two flights of stairs without having to sit down for a breather. Next day, goalkeeper Warren Barrett was also surprised to watch his first goal kick of the train-ing session keep climbing over the halfway line before finally touching down beyond the opposition goal.

The match against Bolivia quickly descended into farce and from the stands it looked as if the Jamaicans were not taking things seriously. Collapsing like deckchairs all over the pitch, the physio was called on at almost every break in play. What perhaps those who slow hand-clapped their derision did not know was that many of the Reggae Boyz were experiencing difficulties breathing in the rarified atmosphere and were having to be given oxygen. Bolivia were 6–0 up by half-time.

The hosts eased off in the second half, sensing that they were not facing any real opposition. They contented themselves play-ing keep ball and ridiculed the Jamaicans by just passing it round them. Ian Goodison and Onandi Lowe did not take well to being dissed so publicly and were shown red cards for X-rated tackles. Afterwards, Bolivian coach Antonio Lopez was furious, claiming that Jamaica had offered only 15 minutes of resistance.

All the hard work of establishing some semblance of foot-balling credibility had almost been undone in the space of 90 minutes. Press reports that the Jamaican players had rolled round on the floor giggling or booted the ball as far out of play as they could, did nothing to enhance the team's status as serious contenders. Across the world, people read reports that described the Reggae Boyz as a gimmick team. Simoes had his work cut out to lift spirits and immediately went back on the offensive, claim-ing that the reports were scurrilous lies written by a Bolivian journalist. His side were not a team of jokers, he argued. The Jamaican problems were for real, he continued, and defenders Dean Sewell and Steve Malcolm had both needed specialist medical attention in the dressing room. He also pointed out that Jamaica were without Gregory Messam, Peter Cargill, Durrent Brown, Andy Williams, Theodore Whitmore and the injured Walter Boyd, all of whom had played against the USA. He did agree, however, that it had been dangerous to play after such limited preparation. It was a catastrophic start to the tour.

The team moved on to Mexico, to the training base in Toluca they had used in 1996. Simoes had allowed 21 days for his team to get acclimatised for the crunch game in Mexcio City because after giving the home team a scare in the previous round, he believed Jamaica could now go one better and take a point at the Azteca. But the boys had to be given time to prepare properly, especially in the light of what had happened in Bolivia.

The coach had wanted to play a couple of friendlies against local club sides before moving on to the capital but for some reason no plans were made. Eventually a warm-up match against Mexican club side Toros Neza was hastily arranged by embar-rassed Federation officials. It was agreed that the game would be played near the local brewery although Simoes had stipulated that it must be behind closed doors. Under no circumstances were any journalists or cameramen to be allowed in.

The team arrived on a bus that The Captain had persuaded Nestlé to lend them to find more than 200 fans and a large contingent of Mexican reporters in the ground. No stranger to tricks and certainly nobody's fool, Simoes told the assembled crowd that he would not play the game until the ground had been emptied and the gates locked. When he found out that in among the local hacks were reporters from some of the larger dailies in the capital, the smell of rat grew stronger. It is not clear whether the Federation were making any money out of the match but despite his gut feeling that this game could go very wrong, Simoes eventually backed down and agreed to play. It was a decision that could have cost him his life.

Toros Neza had drafted in three Argentinians, a Venezualan and a Chilean for a game which immediately demonstrated that it would be anything but a mild-mannered work-out. From the first whistle, a violent undercurrent flowed in the tackles and Simoes was immediately concerned by the referee's unwillingness to take control. Jamaica took the lead after 45 seconds when Onandi Lowe converted a chance from a corner. They then hit the post before being denied a certain penalty. Simoes spent the first ten minutes on the touchline, shouting at the referee.

As the X-rated challenges flew in thick and fast, tempers frayed still further. The Jamaican players were being elbowed at corner kicks and Simoes urged all involved to take a deep breath and calm down. Unfortunately, one of Toros Neza's Argentinians, a notorious hatchet man, was trying to systematically maim the entire Jamaican team. Simoes was furious by now, encroaching on to the pitch on two or three occasions to urge the referee to take a firmer grip – genuinely afraid that somebody was going to get seriously hurt. His young team did not have the discipline to turn the other cheek and when Steve Malcolm was cut in half with a brutal tackle, emotions reached boiling point.

Malcolm, known as 'Shorty' because of his stocky, five foot four build, was the wrong man to mess with. He had a notoriously short fuse. The coach had even been advised not to pick him when he had first called together a squad because Malcolm was a former 'rude boy'. Anyone in the Jamaican squad will tell you that he is a man more than capable of looking after himself. While playing a match for Seba United against Wadadah at Jarrett Park in 1996, he jumped into the crowd and threatened a spectator with a bottle. The local authority in charge of the stadium, the island's second biggest, promptly banned Shorty from playing at Jarrett Park for two months. Seba responded by moving their games *en bloc* to a much smaller venue in the hills of St James.

Malcolm's past caught up with him in the 19th minute when he retaliated with an equally vicious tackle. The Toros Neza players were immediately on him, punching him to the ground. The other Jamaican players went to Shorty's rescue and individual fights broke out all over the pitch. Simoes tried to part the warring factions but was smashed full in the face with a blindside punch. It was landed by the Toros Neza doctor.

From their places in the stand, other members of the Jamaican party vaulted over the hoardings to join the fray. Local fans wanted a bit of the action too, throwing bottles at the visitors. Within a minute, the 29 Jamaicans were up against 200 and more. Simoes crawled back to the touchline and gasped to Montessa that they had to stop this 'madness', before being struck with another punch to the throat, this time from one of the Toros Neza players.

The Jamaican players returned fire with bottles and as they retreated, totally outnumbered, some threw rocks and hacked pieces of wood from the fencing. It was desperate stuff. When they could go back no further, Simoes screamed at the Mexicans that someone would die if they took a step closer. One of the Jamaican players had already almost killed a fan in an attack with a wooden stake and Ian Goodison had knocked another unconscious. Onandi Lowe had broken a finger in the process of handing out a severe beating to the person stupid enough to have taken him on in the first place. The sight of Lowe in full flow and the other Jamaican players returning to the scene armed with makeshift spears and lumps of masonry significantly reduced the locals' hunger for a fight. Eventually, the Jamaican delegation bunched together and backed out of the ground towards the team coach.

Simoes boarded the bus with a hideously swollen face, Gregory Messam had damaged his knee doing karate kicks and almost every other member of the squad sported a scar as a souvenir of the match from hell. The Mexican press were about to have a field day and early reports that reached Mexico City laid the blame squarely on the shoulders of the Reggae Boyz. Meanwhile, the pictures had been broadcast round the world. No mention had been made of the racial abuse or physical provocation.

Simoes suspected that the brawl had been planned as a way of upsetting Jamaican preparations. Before the match had even taken place, the team had suddenly been denied use of their training pitch and were forced to practise on a small ground at the hotel. The team bus had also been withdrawn. Simoes later learnt that the Mexican First Division side were renowned for this sort of thing and decided not to arrange any further 'friendlies' before the 13 April showdown for fear of being stitched up again. Indeed, the team spent much of the next two weeks locked inside their hotel.

If the atmosphere within the Azteca was hostile for their last visit, all sentiments were multiplied in the wake of the Toros Neza affair. The team were totally demoralised after a miserable few weeks and were 3–0 down by half-time. In the midst of this carnage, Onandi Lowe disobeyed instructions from the bench to drop back to play sweeper following another injury to Durrent Brown. Lowe was immediately replaced by the hobbling Walter Boyd and banished to the dressing room. Barrett, who was having a bit of a nightmare, picked up his second booking and would be out of the next game, away to Canada. Messam was clearly unfit and Whitmore, who had sustained an injury to his instep during the fight in Toluca, was a pale shadow of his normal self. Hermosillo completed his hat-trick a minute after the restart before Joaquin Del Olmo and Luis Hernandez rounded off a second 6–0 annihilation in the space of three weeks.

Jamaica returned home with their heads bowed. Opinion had changed and the old doubts began to circulate. In *The Gleaner*, Jamaica's main daily paper, sociologist Peter Espeut's commentary cast doubts on the 'national psyche' in the wake of the Mexico humiliation. A Jamaican footballer, he said, played as an individual who was more interested in 'creating a skill or a "Pele", taking on the whole opposition by himself; "bruckin" the whole side and scoring a goal'. He highlighted the disciplinary problems that had escalated within the last month, 'Some prima donnas won't turn up for training, they take holidays without permission, or will only play if they get their way,' he added. 'We also have to teach teamwork and discipline.' It seemed that all the strides made by Simoes had been forgotten in the space of three weeks.

There was also criticism of the JFF. The plans for the tour had been a disaster from start to finish. Simoes might have been privately pleased that his players were now ready to fight for each other but the Federation's decision to schedule a match at altitude so soon after arriving in Bolivia and then walk into a potentially fatal match in Toluca were both signs that they still had a lot to learn.

Simoes was also seething about Lowe's act of mutiny and in the week following the party's return from Mexico, the Harbour View man was slapped with a four-year international ban. Clearly, Simoes was determined to make an example of anyone who stepped out of line. Newspaper reports in Jamaica said that Lowe had walked off the pitch of his own accord although the striker would later protest his innocence. Boyd, who had fallen out with Simoes briefly in 1994, was also put on guard. His goals had dried up and the coach detected signs that his main striker was slipping back into old habits: he was increasingly sullen, moody and difficult to work with.

But little more than a week after the decimation by Mexico, the Reggae Boyz were on the road again. This time the destination was Burnaby in British Columbia for a match with Canada. The Canadians shared the responsibility of propping up the group and only a marginally worse goal difference kept Simoes' team off the bottom. Jamaica would have five days to prepare for a match they simply could not afford to lose. Barrett was suspended and Peter Cargill, who had missed the Mexico game after two previous yellow cards, was out with a foot injury. Spirits were *not* high.

Canadian coach Bob Lenarduzzi had slated his side after three previous goalless performances and luckily for Simoes, they were in the same torpid mood against Jamaica. Boyd occasionally dazzled but goals were going to be hard to come by when Jamaica's best player on the day was at the other end of the field. Spider Lawrence, or 'Wildboy' as he was known in Jamaica, was having the game of his life and capped an heroic all-round display with a flying stop from Canadian Alex Bunbury in the 80th minute. The run of indiscipline continued when Gregory Messam was sent off for a late tackle on Tomasz Radzinski four minutes later. Messam would later accuse a female Canadian official of racist comments in the build-up to the match and was given a three-match ban by FIFA after being found guilty of kicking a ball at her during the CONCACAF Gold Cup in 1998.

A goalless draw gave Jamaica a hard-earned second point but the bubble was deflating fast at home. Simoes flew back to a fresh row with prominent members of the local football community. He had reacted angrily to criticism of his team tactics and selection for the Canada match and made some less than flattering remarks about Jimmy Chin, president of Galaxy United – the National Premier League side from Clarendon. Among other things, Simoes had dismissed Chin, a local businessman, as 'that guy from Galaxy'. Chin was so offended that he consulted his lawyers and threatened to take the matter to the Supreme Court unless he got an apology from both Simoes and the JFF. Clyde Juredini, general manager of Harbour View, put the knife in and was joined by Waterhouse coach Geoffrey Maxwell. It was something out of nothing yet the reaction from within the Jamaican football community was telling. Simoes had been patient with them, using the squad system judiciously in order to let the teams have their players whenever possible, but the coaches had now shown their true colours.

In July, FIFA handed down its sentence for the unsavoury scenes in Toluca. Jamaica bore the brunt, slapped with a $34,000 fine compared with the $17,000 and $7,000 imposed on the Mexican Football Association and Toros Neza respectively. Reports from the hearing suggested that the disciplinary committee focused on the stones and wooden posts rather than the initial punches thrown by Argentinian German Arangio. Nothing much was made of Simoes' attempts to come between the warring factions or the fact that the crowd was allowed to invade the pitch and join the fracas. It was a financial blow the JFF could ill afford.

A miserable two months was completed with a 3–1 defeat to Costa Rica in San José. The shaky-looking Barrett spilled a cross which allowed Derby County's Paulo Wanchope to walk the ball into an empty net. The listless Boyd was brought off at half-time and replaced by Paul Young, while midfielder Altimont Butler was also starting to show his age. Concerns about Barrett's loss of form continued when he nearly gifted the Costa Ricans a second. Cargill worked tirelessly to lift Jamaican spirits and the veteran midfielder's persistence paid off on the hour when Andy Williams beat his man on the edge of the box to equalise from 18 yards. It should have been the platform for Jamaica to go on and get a result but instead the team again lost its discipline. Wanchope, a third-generation Jamaican himself, got a second, and the towel came in as substitute Allan Oviedo crowned a comfortable Costa Rican victory with a third goal in the last minute.

The carping grew louder still and Simoes almost lost his temper with the critics at home after suggestions that he had been ignoring the younger teams in favour of concentrating solely on the faltering national eleven. He bit his lip and reminded them that this was meant to be a learning process not only for the team but for himself, his coaching staff and the Jamaican Football Federation. The man who had been acclaimed a national hero less than seven months earlier found his credentials now being called into doubt.

It seemed very harsh. Simoes had worked tirelessly to fashion a side that the public could relate to. He wanted his players to be genuine heroes and had insisted that ten per cent of the players' earnings from World Cup qualifiers should go to charity. In May, Ricardo Gardener and Steve Green handed over two cheques of JA $30,000 each (approximately US $1,000) to Food for the Poor and the SOS Children's Village from their cut of the gate money against the United States. The team's constant round of fund-raising functions and hospital visits, had served to cement a bond between the players and the public.

The 'Adopt a Player' scheme had also started to bear fruit and the JFF were detecting the first signs of genuine interest from the private sector. To mark the new-found solvency of the programme, the JFF printed a souvenir programme for the CONCACAF World Cup qualifying round which serves as a historical document on the campaign's aims, ideals and sponsors.

It revealed that the Sports Development Foundation, a government body that collected a heavy tax on the national lottery, funded Simoes' salary and overseas training camps. Its motto was 'Developing A Nation Through Sports' and Simoes wore their T-shirt for Jamaica matches.

In the programme, Warren Barrett can be seen leaping for a catch against the backdrop of a bottle of Red Stripe, his sponsor. Cargill is pictured clutching a small football in a photocopier showroom, alongside Simoes and the general manager of Toshiba. Shell announced that they had adopted national striker Paul Young as part of its 'continuing belief in the talent and aspirations of the Jamaican people'. Jamaican Money Market Brokers Ltd offered financial advice to the new football stars. Grace Kennedy boasted that it provided nutrition for the national football team; food cooked by a chef donated by the Jamaican Defence Force. Walter Boyd was sponsored by Corporate Group Ltd; Ian Goodison by auto appliance dealers Caribrake, Durrent Brown by Empire Supermarket and Gregory Messam by Burger King. Kingston Music backed Donald Stewart and young Winston Griffiths was sponsored by Juici Beef Patties. The fleet-footed Theodore Whitmore drew his wage from a cement company. It was a tremendously innovative approach and the JFF were rightly applauded for their efforts. The players were now operating on a professional level but if they lost their next match, the experience would almost certainly prove short-lived.

But ultimately, and importantly, the fans had become increasingly disillusioned. The poor form of the team and hikes in ticket prices for big games meant that only a tiny crowd watched Jamaica play El Salvador in a match they had to win. The critics said that Jamaica were down and out but a second successive strike from the promising Andy Williams just about kept hopes alive. It was a goal that was celebrated with nothing of the passion that greeted the last scored at The Office in the World Cup, but it gave Jamaica its first win in the group, to put her level on points with third-placed America. The inability of away teams to claim victory in Kingston was about the only crumb of comfort for Simoes as he contemplated his next move.

Two weeks later he announced what that move would be. Nine overseas-based footballers were to be evaluated at a one-week training camp. Simoes was careful in his choice of wording and went to great lengths to underline the fact that these players were being tried out by Jamaica and not the other way round.

The JFF's statement read: 'For these players to represent Jamaica, there are a number of things that are mandatory for them to do. They have to show interest that they want to serve Jamaica and not only take something from Jamaica. They have to show some commitment for this purpose and they have to follow all instructions. They will have to sleep with the other players, travel in the same bus, eat the same food. There will be no concessions for anyone as this will make a different team within the team.'

The Captain then informed the Jamaican press that only the two Wimbledon players, Robbie Earle and Marcus Gayle, would be paid for as they were guests of the JFF. 'They have to be treated differently than the others because they are in the English Premier League,' said Burrell, 'and are professionals.'

On the plane from England were Luton's Dwight Marshall, and Fitzroy Simpson and Paul Hall from Portsmouth. They had also persuaded Deon Burton to come along for the ride and reminded him to pack his boots.

Whether The Captain already knew it or not, they were all professionals too.

5

Final Steps Along the Road to France

ROBBIE

I met the other Jamaican players for the first time in July 1997. I had gone out for the Shell Cup and arrived on a typically blazing hot day. The team house, a modest, white-washed bungalow set in lovely grounds next door to the Prime Minister's official residence, came as a big culture shock. People were lying on mattresses spread out across the floor of the front room and kit was hanging up on the windows.

After talking to the players, a lot of whom knew exactly who I was and where I was at, I was led to a room where the older, more experienced players sleep. After struggling down a narrow corridor lugging two big Nike bags, I discovered that it would be nigh-on impossible to get me and them inside. There was a double bunk-bed on one side, a gap of two feet, and then a double bunk-bed on the other side. My room mates were Peter Cargill, an older-looking guy with a friendly face, Aaron Lawrence, who I seemed to click with immediately, and the giant Donnovan Ricketts who was the third-choice keeper.

We had three or four hours to kill before the first training session. Some of the lads played cards, some played dominoes, and others sprawled across the mattresses to watch TV. I elected to keep myself to myself so I buried my nose in a book. I was very aware that a lot of eyes were going to be on me and I wanted to avoid being conspicuous. I thought it best to play it very cool as we were going to be in the house for two days before flying off to Antigua for the annual tournament between the Caribbean islands.

Paul Hall and Fitzroy Simpson had been out in Jamaica with their new team mates for a while before I arrived. I had played against Fitz a number of times when he was at Swindon and Man City and met Paul on a couple of occasions, but I didn't know either of them – or Deon Burton – particularly well. The three of them knew each other from Portsmouth so they had natural allies within the camp. I was pretty much on my own and wanted to win them over as much as I did the Jamaican-based players.

I was quite surprised by the amount of influence Hall and Simpson already seemed to have within the squad. To all intents and purposes, they were as Jamaican as any of their team mates and it was clear they genuinely wanted to play for Jamaica. They had gone to great lengths to prove it - writing letters, paying their own air fare over for a trial and running the risk of falling out with their club at home – and had both won caps by the time I arrived. All three seemed to have integrated into the group remarkably well and were not afraid of voicing their opinions. Deon seemed a bit less confident but it did not take long to discover that Fitz more than made up for him. I found out later that he had already exchanged words with one of the Jamaican lads on the training ground.

At about seven that evening we got ready for training. Peter Cargill, who was to become a close friend and confidant over the next 12 months, told me that some of the players would be more guarded than others. Steven 'Shorty' Malcolm was one of the blokes Peter warned me not to cross. He was not a giant, as his name might suggest, but one of those people who if he says he is going to get you, he'll get you. Even if it takes him ten years!

Although the atmosphere was never hostile, I did sense a few people thinking, 'We know you're a bigger fish but we still think we could get by without you'. They were not necessarily players in my position; they were what I would call the more Jamaican Jamaicans. Ian Goodison, captain Warren Barrett and striker Paul Young were all a bit standoffish.

Paul Young, who had been in the Jamaican system for about ten years, had not been picked for the last two squads. He was a reserve striker and to him I must have looked like a threat because he probably felt that I could play that bit further forward if necessary. If I came in and was accepted I would move up a notch and he would get pushed down one in the process, so I could understand his reservations about getting too friendly.

My second big culture shock was getting on the team bus to go training. The stereo was turned right up and reggae blasted out all the way to the ground. It was impossible to hear yourself think but people waved and cheered as the distinctive, government-donated Reggae Boyz bus sped past in a cloud of dust and throbbing bass.

I knew that the coach would be looking for me to win over the players at training and Cargill told me how to go about it. When we had a game of head tennis, I should deliberately pair up with one of the lads who had a problem. If I could get a bit of banter going it would help to break the ice.

Simoes put on a really hard session, even by Wimbledon's rigorous standards, and afterwards Paul Hall admitted that it was one of the toughest he'd had since being with the team. We were out there for about three hours and it was near enough pitch black by the time we'd finished.

The coach is one of those guys who can sometimes get a bit carried away and although I believe he was trying to make a point to the new boy from the Premiership, this was also going to be the last main training session before the team left for Antigua. We did a lot of running and some ball drills I'd never seen before, and then we finished with a highly competitive practice game.

I got through that first training session in Kingston doing just enough to impress, even getting a couple of laughs out of some of the lads. Getting a nutmeg was a bonus because the Jamaicans love their tricks. Ian Goodison likes to go for 'megs' more than most but he reacted well when I did him with one, so I felt a lot more comfortable in my new surroundings.

Initiations are part of a footballer's life and turning up for my first training session at Wimbledon was possibly one of the most daunting I'll ever have. John Fashanu was still the main man in the summer of 1991 and I remember his greeting: 'Welcome, baby. You have just joined the family. I'm the main man here and if there is anything you want, you come and see me.'

Lawrie Sanchez and Alan Cork were also at the club then. Sanch was a senior member of the squad and like some of the Jamaicans, he seemed a bit wary at first. To be fair, though, that was just his manner and he helped me quite a lot in the early days, warning me to keep myself to myself and not be too loud too early as there were some sharp people in the dressing room. The most important thing to remember, however, was not to cross Fash.

Right from the start, it was rammed into every player that this was a team game and individuals who got the limelight should stress that Wimbledon's success was a collective effort. I was the record signing at the time and felt that I had a lot to prove. During cross-country runs, I was aware of a few of the lads whose position I now threatened pulling up on my shoulder. They would usually try to stretch away with a mile to go, or hit me with some hard tackles on the training pitch.

I got slaughtered for the first couple of weeks and the infamous Wimbledon stripping came after about three days. It was actually quite a relief because at least it was over and done with then. The odd pair of trousers still got cut up after that but once Fash took me under his wing everything calmed down. On a tour in Stirlingshire, soon after, he said that I'd made the right impression and had worked hard. If I kept my head down and scored a few goals, he told me, everything would be all right. He also said that he'd be watching my back from then on.

To become a Wimbledon player you need a strong survival instinct so I was fairly confident about coping with the first few days as part of the Jamaican squad. Obviously, I was a bit apprehensive about what to expect but the one thing that seemed to bring this group of disparate individuals together was the football. Whatever lifestyles we had, wherever we came from, once we were on the football pitch everything else was forgotten.

After a couple of days in Jamaica, we set off for Antigua, where my real initiation would take place. Until I had played with the team, represented Jamaica and worn the shirt, I knew that I would not be totally accepted. The trip also gave me the opportunity to spend more time with the Jamaican-based players and I soon felt that I was starting to bat off one or two people and beginning to enjoy myself.

Once in Antigua, we played the hosts, St Kitts and Trinidad, who we eventually went out to at the semi-final stage. The first game on tour was a tight 1–1 draw and I got on as a substitute for the last 20 minutes. It was an ideal way to get some fitness back and get used to the other players. My new team mates were technically a lot better than I had expected and I was surprised to see that ability-wise they were more impressive than some people I'd played against in the

Premiership. Their inexperience only really revealed itself in tactical situations.

As Simoes had told me back in January, Jamaica played a Brazilian style that relied on passing and rhythm. Sometimes teams can pass the ball without purpose but the coach liked us to keep the ball and work it to certain areas. He used a theory called 'the three doors'. As you are playing up the pitch, there is a door on the right, the middle and the left, and by passing across the pitch you are effectively knocking on these three doors. If you move the ball quickly enough, he says, the opposition won't be able to defend all the doors at once. When one is left unguarded, that is the time to step up the pace and pour through. Peter Cargill, the central midfield player and fulcrum of the team, was the key to the system. It reminded me of a basketball move in that the ball would be worked to a certain area before the point called the play.

The coach pulled me to one side after the game and explained that the reason he hadn't thrown me on from the start was because he didn't want people back in Jamaica to blame me if we got beaten. Likewise, if we had won he didn't want the new boy getting all the credit. He was obviously very aware of the bigger picture.

There was real ability in the side and, crucially, Simoes had given the players tremendous belief in themselves. His method of motivating people wasn't exactly brainwashing but it was certainly somewhere close. He would talk to you on an individual basis and only afterwards did you realise that these discussions would invariably be testing you out.

The coach is also a very philosophical man. One night, as a few of us walked on the beach, he talked about the stars in the sky. He pointed out the brightest star and said, 'Right now, that star is Theodore Whitmore.' Then, pointing to a different star, he said, 'That little one there, by the time of the World Cup, will be bright and it will represent someone else.' He insisted that everybody's star would play a part.

We had a couple of good chats while I was out in Antigua, Simoes being keen to find out how well I had fitted in. He had asked the players for their opinions and now wanted to know whether I was picking up the same vibes. I felt it had gone OK so far and I hoped the other players could now see that I wasn't the sort of person to go shouting the odds. I think they realised that I was committed, having taken time out of my own holidays to be there. Simoes agreed, but warned me not to get above my station. I wouldn't have a problem as long as I stayed humble, he told me.

Things did go well with the players on that first trip, even to the extent where the leg-pulling started. Some of the boys liked to wind me up, saying I talked 'too English', with a plum in my mouth. They would put on posh English accents and say things like, 'Would you like a cup of tea this morning, darling?' They also liked to test me out with the patois. A couple of times the boys would say something and check to see whether I'd caught it. Little did they know that I understood a lot because my parents have always spoken in patois at home. I can even talk a bit as well. But even though I knew exactly what they were saying, I thought I'd let them get away with it at first. Deon Burton, on the other hand, was like a chameleon in that he put on the broadest Jamaican accent you've ever heard.

I tended to speak in my normal voice and my Jamaican team mates spoke English to me. At times, usually on the football pitch, I'd talk patois with them but generally I thought that I went across as an English person and shouldn't have to compromise. Whatever language I spoke, they now knew that I was one of them.

In footballing terms, however, the jury was still out because I had only played two hours in four games.

After ten days in Antigua I flew straight back to England in time for pre-season training. On reflection, I was very glad I had gone out. I knew that I had to endure the settling-in period but now that it was over I could go back out for the World Cup qualifiers knowing what to expect. I would also be a lot fitter by then and, hopefully, more of an asset to the team.

I thought over the last fortnight as I sat back on the long transatlantic flight home. Even at that early stage, Simoes liked to ask my opinion, firing slightly unexpected questions about how I thought the session had gone or how the team was playing. At the time, however, I was a bit wary of being too critical as I had just come into the set-up. The coach also liked to run through things with Cargill, though he was careful not to do it in front of the other players.

I did tell Simoes that I didn't think we defended set pieces well and that better teams would punish us for that. He agreed and admitted that he sometimes had a problem communicating the importance of organisation to some of the Jamaican-based players. They did not readily accept information on the pitch, he told me, and they worked on different thought processes than other footballers. He had trained with some great players in his time yet he was incredibly patient with the Jamaican lads. 'Just 12 just months ago,' he said, 'this Jamaican team did not even know how to hold a defensive line.' He had achieved so much already and he was not about to give up now.

It is very important that you form a good impression of the manager and I have had great respect for nearly all of the men I've played under. I like football people who talk about how you will fit into their system rather than about money or dressing-room politics. Psychology was definitely one of Simoes' biggest strengths and when he said that he thought we could qualify if the English-born players bedded in well, I believed him.

DANIEL

Robbie arrived back in Jamaica a couple of months later, the night after the Reggae Boyz had beaten the Calypso Boys of Trinidad and Tobago 6–1 at the National Stadium. It had not been been a pretty match by all accounts. Two Trinidadian players had been sent off and Ian 'Pepe' Goodison got his marching orders for retaliating against a foul on Gregory Messam. Coach Simoes had also got in on the act, being banished to the stands after reportedly saying something out of turn to the referee. Paul Hall had continued his impressive start with two goals. Jamaica was badly in need of someone capable of finding the net because Walter Boyd had been thrown off the programme for certain inappropriate remarks he made about Simoes and Reid.

ROBBIE

I felt positive when I arrived back in Jamaica in September, a week before the World Cup qualifier against Canada. If we could win that game and then beat Costa Rica a week later, also in Kingston, we would be nicely set up for the final three matches. They involved travelling to Washington to play the USA at the beginning of October, before rounding off the campaign with a potentially hazardous away match in El Salvador followed by the final match against Mexico at home seven days later. There was an encouraging wave of confidence running through the squad after the demolition of Trinidad.

Coach Brown had not been at the Trinidad game and rumours were rife that there had been a dispute with Simoes. Simoes had a Brazilian fitness trainer and a Portuguese masseur and at times it almost seemed like Brown was the token Jamaican on the backroom staff. He had been involved with the national programme from the start and I imagine he felt his role had been undermined since the arrival of Simoes, as he wasn't allowed much input on the training pitch. Apparently, only some last-minute mediating by Captain Burrell had healed the rift.

Simoes seemed pleased to have us all together again and joked with me about having to leave my club instincts at home. It would take him a week, he said, to turn me back into a Brazilian. Only after he'd had a chance to work with me would the movement come naturally and make me look less English!

Naturally, there was a lot of talk about Walter Boyd, who had recently made comments about the coach wanting to 'play God in his life'. Boyd had made the remarks while he was in England on trial with West Brom and they had not gone down at all well. Boyd was a big star in Jamaica but he had fallen out with the coach on a regular basis. On his return from England, he was expected to play against Trinidad and Tobago but Simoes demanded that he apologise first. It all seemed like a storm in a teacup but the upshot was that Boyd was not recalled to the squad in the build-up to Canada.

It was during the week before the match that I started to feel more at home in the team house. There was always a rush for the shower after training so I generally took the next best option and plumped for washing al fresco under the garden hose. Set back from the road behind imposing iron gates, the white-washed maisonette with grills on the windows made up for its lack of luxury with the atmosphere inside. Arguments broke out over games of dominoes or about who was next on the phone but ultimately we were a strong group. The rest of the lads weren't aware of the parallels that existed with Wimbledon: we were both small outfits, looking for an identity.

The younger Jamaican players really looked up to Peter Cargill and my friendship with him developed. The 6–0 defeat in Mexico had been a big turning point for all the players in the programme, he explained. He also talked about the problem with Onandi Lowe, a turning point for the coach because he knew then that he needed to bring in professionals from England. When the other players knew we were coming, fresh impetus was added to a process that was probably on the wane. Everyone in the squad changed their attitude at that point.

As a result, there was a lot of pressure on the English-based players because if we lost the game against Canada we were going to be really up against it. The honeymoon period was now over and this was the first big test. The others had been over in Jamaica for two weeks. Hally had been accepted and become an integral part of the group whereas the Jamaican players seemed to reserve their judgement a bit more on Deon. He was quite a bit younger than the rest of us and maybe the fact that he had come over to Jamaica on the back of Fitz and Paul also meant that he had to try that bit harder to prove himself both as a person and a footballer.

We bonded for two important reasons: we had been brought in to give the squad a lift and had to try to pull the group towards us, and although we had Jamaican citizenship we were still in a strange country and were not quite sure how things worked yet.

The intensity of my World Cup debut took me totally by surprise. Following the Reverend's visit to the house, we drove to the ground on the team bus and it was then that I started to get a feeling for just how important qualification had become to the nation. It seemed like the whole country had descended on Kingston to see what these new boys from England could do.

Deon Burton scored his first goal for the country to put us 1–0 up. The noise that greeted it was something else; the whole stadium seemed to explode and the hairs stood up on the back of my neck. As I looked round the ground, everyone was hugging each other and jumping up and down with joy. I just wanted to get on there and get involved and when I finally did get the chance, it was Jamaica's new goalscoring hero that I replaced.

I was without doubt the most nervous I had ever been. I'm normally a calm person and never used to get uptight about doing exams at school or appearing on TV. But when the coach called me off the bench and said I'd be going on, a weird feeling came over me. Once I got to the touchline, I felt almost overwhelmed by the noise.

The heat must have had a lot to do with it because as I looked across the pitch to the far side of the stadium, the grass was shimmering and hot air was visibly rising off the concrete. I had seen Paul Peschisolido in the tunnel before the game and he had turned to me and said, 'Christ knows how you can play in this heat.' Simoes had wanted us to play at midday but FIFA had told him that it was too dangerous. Peschisolido came off after about 50 minutes and looked absolutely drained.

This moment was one I'd been waiting for for almost 17 years. I'd played nearly 600 League games, 300 at Premiership level, but when it came to World Cup qualifiers I was a complete novice compared to some of those guys out on the pitch. Durrent Brown and Warren Barrett alone had nearly 200 caps between them. But having spent time with the lads, I knew how much this meant to them, so I ran on to the pitch at the National Stadium for the first time knowing that I could not let anyone down. My first touch was OK; I controlled it, got past the guy and laid it off. I was in the game.

We held on for the win against Canada and then stayed in Kingston for the following week, training every day at either the National Stadium or the Water Commission field on the outskirts. It was an upbeat camp because we had got the result we needed and everyone on the island was very excited. The only down point was Andy Williams breaking his shoulder in training.

Peter Cargill showed me round Kingston a couple of times when we had an afternoon off. We went to the barbers and toured parts of the city that very few tourists see. It was the first time I had been downtown since I was a little kid. I vividly remembered all the hustle and bustle and my dad holding my hand. It was an eye-opening experience to go back and although people everywhere were congratulating us, Peter reminded me of my dad by telling me to stick close to him. He was obviously a lot better known than I was and, though I never felt threatened, it was still a daunting place.

On September 14 we played Costa Rica in the second of the two qualifying matches in Kingston. Before the game, Simoes made the English lads parade in front of the Costa Rican players in the tunnel – presumably all part of the psychological games he liked to play. It worked. You could see the Costa Ricans whispering to each other, slightly anxious when they realised that English professionals were now part of a Jamaican set-up they once dismissed as amateurish.

It was a tight, scrappy game and the coach was about to change things round when Deon Burton scored just after half-time. Simoes had walked down to my end of the bench during the game and asked me whether I could play right wing back. I told him that I could although it wasn't really my position. It would have been easy to say yes just to get on the pitch but when I did go on, I slotted into midfield, under orders to keep things tight and make sure the boys stayed calm. It seemed to work.

Later that evening, Fitz, Hally, Deon and I travelled back to London on a British Airways flight. We were all buzzing: we had given the camp a lift and Jamaica were now equal on points with Mexico at the top of the group. Any negative vibes about English-born players taking the place of Jamaicans had been replaced by talk of what a good influence we had been on the programme. Deon scored two vital goals, Fitz had given the midfield some bite and discipline and Hally was a big hit with the other lads. I'd done my bit and given the team experience when they needed it. Without those six points it was doubtful whether the programme could have continued.

We were now in a position where we only needed another three points to qualify. The cabin crew presented us with bottles of champagne on the flight home. They nicknamed us 'The Fab Four' – which just about summed up how we felt.

The games came thick and fast and at the beginning of October I left London bound for Washington. There were five days before we took on the United States at the RFK Stadium in a match we fancied getting something out of. I had picked up a knee injury and knew I wouldn't be playing, however.

Captain Burrell kept me busy, liking the idea of having a player who could act as the public face of the campaign. Ricardo Gardener and Ian Goodison had become big favourites and were exciting young players but neither was particularly good in front of the camera. Burrell wanted a media-friendly spokesman who could sell the programme abroad. Simoes had told him that Brazilian football had been aided by foreign investment and I became a small part of Burrell's plan to try something similar with Jamaica.

During that week, The Captain announced the new kit deal he had tied up with Kappa and I was asked to take the press conference. Burrell and Reid sorted out the commercial side of the operation between them and I was brought in to talk football and add a bit of gloss to the package. Sometimes I wondered if The Captain had been more attracted by my media contacts than my football ability.

Simoes continued to impress me with his attention to detail. He left absolutely nothing to chance, even making sure that all the thermostats in the players' hotel rooms were set to the right temperature because he wanted the boys to get used to the colder climate before they went out to play. He was also a big fan of technology and rather than using a blackboard to demonstrate team patterns and moves, he had a laptop computer. It must have been a curious sight to the uninitiated: 22 large men craning their necks to get a look at the graphic print-out of what they were meant to be doing on the pitch. It was a refreshing approach which held the players' attention.

He also proved himself to be a tactile, caring coach, always ready to put a reassuring arm round a player or act like a father figure. He was a disciplinarian with a tough streak but he also knew that a sympathetic arm round the shoulders could have a massive therapeutic effect.

The game against the USA was truly memorable. Two-thirds of the stadium was filled with noisy Jamaican fans, turning the atmosphere into something like Kingston on match day. People had travelled from far and wide; the huge Caribbean population of New York had mobilised for the night and thousands more had flown in from Miami. Jamaica might be a small country but there are millions of Jamaicans scattered across the world. This wasn't just about our island any more, though. We now had the backing of the entire West Indian community. There could be no thought of defeat in front of a crowd like that.

At half-time the score was 0–0 and Simoes asked me what I thought. I genuinely believed the boys were playing better than I'd ever seen them play and that we just needed to have faith in ourselves. It was almost as though the coach needed an independent opinion. He knew that I would give him an honest answer rather than the one he wanted to hear.

It's always refreshing to have a manager who is happy for players to have their say. In any football situation, you can see things in the blink of an eye that the manager might have missed. Joe Kinnear has always encouraged me to have an opinion at Wimbledon and we have grown to really respect each other over the years. I'm one of those people who likes to be able to talk about things with the manager. At other clubs you might need an appointment to see the boss but that has never been the case with Joe.

He might ask me how I would line up the side if we were to play, say, Liverpool. Though I would never talk about personnel, we'd discuss systems and formations. He worries that we might get too blinkered at Wimbledon so he asks a few of the players just to check that he isn't missing anything obvious. Joe doesn't believe his way is the only way but he still likes to remind people who's boss now and again. Lots of managers succumb to the pressures but Joe's got that inner belief that what he's doing is right. I got the same feeling about Simoes.

Four minutes after the break, however, the United States went in front through a dubious penalty; the ball hit Ian Goodison's hand but it was clearly outside the area. It was time for the boys to hit back. Hally intercepted a pass and Deon buried it from eight yards. The whole place went up and it looked like Deon's head was going to explode as he sprinted towards the bench. The game finished at 1–1 though we were unlucky not to go on and win it.

Simoes was delighted that we had given such a good account of ourselves. The United States camp had been critical of the pitch at the National Stadium after their goalless draw in Kingston and Simoes took great joy in showing the world how the Jamaicans could play on a good surface. It was a big psychological boost for the team and Simoes started to talk about destiny. 'God helped us for Deon's goal', he announced. Whether he had or not, the statistics spoke for them-selves: Jamaica were now top of the group.

By November we had been overtaken again by Mexico and the USA. Our week of destiny beckoned – El Salvador away followed by the final match at home to Mexico. A win in the first match would guar-antee us a place in France and a draw would probably be good enough.

If Washington was one big celebration, El Salvador was like one long nightmare. The sign on arrival said, 'Welcome to El Salvador', but our welcoming party did not quite fit the bill. After a long wait in customs, we found our coach surrounded by 50 or more El Salvadorian fanatics waving banners, blowing horns and shouting obscenities. We knew this was going to be far from peaceful.

It didn't take long for the mind games to start. We arrived for our first training session to find a helicopter parked on the pitch. We were told that it was being used by government officials and could not be moved for at least 45 minutes. Simoes gathered us round and told everyone to stay calm and concentrate on what we were there for. Our hosts would do everything possible to distract us, he said, and the local press were just waiting for us to show signs of stress. The chopper was finally moved, to ironic cheers, and we enjoyed a hard, competitive session.

We continued with the same routine for the next couple of days but strange things kept happening. One day there would be no bottled water for the players, the next the cones we used for training would have mysteriously disappeared. Through all this, I was impressed by my team mates' ability to stay relaxed. They were determined that nothing was going to distract them from the task and seeing them adapt to unfamiliar surroundings like these convinced me that many of them could handle a move abroad.

The morning of the match was spent in an unnerving silence. We had been kept awake for much of the night by the racket going on outside: 500 El Salvador fans had congregated at the hotel. Everyone's thoughts were on the match and how close we now were to qualification. The coach called a team meeting and with his usual unique insight, came up with an excellent analogy with two credit card-style room keys, saying that they represented the two teams. On first inspection, he said, the two keys looked identical, but inside, the magnetic strips meant that they were very different. He stressed that both keys were capable of opening the door to France. This, though, was our time.

The match was played in front of 42,000 of the most hostile, partisan fans I have ever come across. Arriving at the ground at about 1.30, we had to muscle our way through the crowd into the changing rooms. The locals were out for our blood and when we went out to have a stroll on the pitch, we were met by four men dressed as witchdoctors. This was obviously meant to psyche us out but the boys handled themselves well, even having the cheek to wave to the banks of blue and white on all sides.

All sorts of things were thrown at us during the game. At one point, Hally went to take a corner and at least eight bags of urine rained down on him. We held out until the break but then two minutes into the second half, El Salvador took the lead. Some slack marking at a corner had allowed de Mello to glance in a near-post header. El Salvador needed a win but they seemed strangely reluctant to go forward and the boys showed their resolve by equalising soon after. Fitz floated a free kick across the box and there was that man again, Deon Burton, to head the ball back beyond the keeper and into the net. 'Ronaldo', as they had started calling him in Jamaica, was certainly living up to his name.

The ground went very quiet for the next half-hour, save for the odd lamentable monkey chant. Then, in the 78th minute, Paul Hall set off on a solo run down the wing. He flew past a couple of challenges and slipped the ball past the keeper into the far corner of the net. It was an incredible goal. Suddenly we were 2–1 up and the tickets to France looked like they were in the bag.

Simoes was shouting to keep the ball and slow the match right down while everyone on the bench was urging the referee to blow his whistle. Sadly, the team's inexperience showed in the last moments of the game. Less than two minutes from time, a specu-lative cross shot somehow evaded Warren Barrett and El Salvador scored an undeserved equaliser. Instead of celebrating the victory required to qualify, dejection hung in the air when we got back to the dressing room. Nevertheless, a vital away point in an inhos-pitable Central American country was a sign of how far the team had come.

It would only be another week before the job was completed.

6

Reggae Boyz On Tour

DANIEL

After a week of hard partying to celebrate qualification to the World Cup Finals, bleary-eyed Jamaicans nursed national-sized hangovers but could think clearly enough to know that the country had turned a corner. The Captain and Simoes had done something that the politicians never could: conjured up a 'feel-good factor' that swept across the island. 'France' became a magical word; the promised land at the end of the road. But it was more than just a word that brought smiles to people's faces. 'France' was a concept that brought ceasefires in warring neighbourhoods. The Captain had been so right when he had called it 'nation building'.

The players were held up in newspapers as an example of what could be achieved through discipline, organisation and team effort. They were attributes that became a clarion call and academics debated whether the JFF's model held the key to dealing with the island's social and economic problems. On the morning after the Mexico game, an editorial in one of Jamaica's daily papers captured the mood: 'Soccer, the national team and its quest to reach France, is giving us the opportunity to redefine ourselves as a people and as a country. The game and our success thus far have provided us with a new window to see what is possible when several Jamaicans act in concert.'

The Jamaican flag had never been so important – or so prominent. It dominated one end of the National Stadium, painted on to a huge panel that looked like it should have supported an electronic scoreboard. They fluttered from windows or were stuck to car bumpers. Yellow, a colour previously considered feminine in such a macho culture, burst into full bloom on the streets. Older Jamaicans reminisced about 1962, when this small outcrop in the northern Caribbean achieved its independence. They shook their heads in disbelief, never imagining that such elation would sweep through the land again. Simoes would indeed have been elected prime minister if he had decided to run. Perhaps the prime minister sensed this because he called an election for the week before Christmas.

Perhaps Prime Minister Patterson wanted a cocktail of jubilation at qualification and Christmas spirit to intoxicate the electorate. He had made a promising start by supporting the programme with government money and could rightly boast that he was one of the first to appreciate the potential of a successful football team. And of course, awarding the population a day off after the Mexico game was a gesture that guaranteed a few extra votes at the polls. However, Simoes was not stupid and he publicly stated that he did not want his team used for a game of political football. At a luncheon hosted by American Airlines, he admitted that he had gone to Patterson's house and expressed his doubts about doing so. The Reggae Boyz had been lined up for a number of government organised public functions and some felt that they were being used to win Patterson votes.

The coach explained, in his own inimitable fashion, that the Reggae Boyz were not about politics, but about dreams: 'The Reggae Boyz will go the next time to civic events, because you must go there and show happiness to Jamaicans. I encourage everyone to dream. Without dream nothing is possible. But dream and work. Don't sit and wait, nothing will happen. I read days ago when I toured America that when they go to the baseball games [the crowd] like to catch the ball. But if you go [to the stadium] and sit in your chair the chance is one in a billion that the ball will come in your hand. But if you move –' He paused, smiling. 'Maybe you will catch the ball.'

The communities in Kingston are clearly defined by their graffiti. You can tell which sector you are in by the PNP or JLP slogans that are daubed on every stretch of bare wall. Downtown, the political landscape is measured not in towns or boroughs but in blocks. But when Jamaica played, barriers came down. Ingrained differences were put aside for the Reggae Boyz. Nowhere else in the social or political life of the country could you see opposite factions fraternising as openly as they did in the grandstand at the National Stadium. If the gangs downtown called a truce for football, then they were following their political paymasters. All three parties included footage of cheering football fans in their campaign videos, but two weeks after calling the country to the polls, Patterson won another term in the most peaceful election in living memory.

Perhaps The Captain *should* have run, but he savoured instead the universal appreciation of a country that just could not stop smiling. He had promised to take Jamaica to the World Cup finals and kept that promise. He felt invincible at the tail end of 1997, brushing off a police investigation into claims that he had gone out to El Salvador with suitcases of cash, checked into a hotel room under a false name and tried to bribe the El Salvadorian team before the penultimate qualifying match. When the scandal was shown to be baseless he extracted a public apology from the country's Soccer Federation.

Then, when the beleagured British Sports Minister, Tony Banks, proved unable to set up a lucrative friendly against England at Wembley, as previously discussed, Burrell wasted no time in pouring on the scorn. The Captain had lent his support to England's bid for the 2006 World Cup in a typical piece of bargaining at a meeting of FIFA representatives in Trinidad. Jamaica's vote was in return for a match that was sure to 'big up' the Reggae Boyz' profile because, in addition to the prestige of playing at the famous old stadium, Burrell knew that he could count on huge support from the UK's West Indian population. A capacity crowd would have done wonders for the JFF's bank balance. Burrell's parting shot was a comment that it would have been a wonderful gesture to receive an invitation from 'England, the home of football, the country that colonised these islands . . .'

Jamaicans had barely had time to come down from the clouds, however, when the moustachioed pied pipers decided on their next tune. Simoes wanted to play 25 matches in the six months leading up to June. The boys had a long way to go before becoming world-class players and travel would broaden their horizons. He argued that Caribbean islands traditionally played no more than six or seven games a year and by cramming four years' experience into half that time, he might just be able to get his team ready to compete effectively in France. The Reggae Boyz were to go on tour.

The administration would need to find an extra gear to fly a 30-strong delegation around the world and back. It would also take serious funding. The Captain revealed that qualification had cost JA $100 million and the same would now be required to match Simoes's requirements. His Federation would take money from wherever they could find it.

Before this tour, however, Burrell, Simoes and Horace Reid were to set off overseas for a fresh recruitment drive. The public did not welcome the prospect of its local heroes being replaced in the team by more strangers from England but it was accepted that The Captain knew what he was doing. To make great waves at the World Cup, the programme had to go after the best possible players, Burrell argued.

It was in December that talks were held with Darryl Powell and Dean Sturridge of Derby County, Danny Maddix of QPR and Chelsea's Frank Sinclair. Simoes had monitored Marcus Gayle's contractual dispute with Wimbledon and was satisfied that the player, who had attended a training get-together in Jamaica, was on the point of getting FIFA clearance. Robbie, Fitzroy, Paul and Deon had attracted column inches in Britain and since qualification Federation HQ had been inundated with fresh enquiries from players who had been checking up with Grandma about which island she was born on.

After England, the party travelled on to France to take in the World Cup draw in Marseilles. Deon Burton represented Jamaica in the curtain-raising exhibition match – coming on to replace Ronaldo in the Rest of the World team – and was on stage to see his team get pulled out of the hat with Argentina, Croatia and Japan in Group H. Simoes looked happy with the outcome and told the people back in Jamaica to keep dreaming. From Marseilles the party travelled north to select a base for June, before returning to Jamaica via Italy and Germany.

Simoes began the new year by taking his team to Brazil for intensive training and assessment. The three-week camp would include a series of testing friendlies against top Brazilian club sides and Simoes emphasised that discipline would be of utmost importance. He had extended good will to all men over the festive period and invited Walter Boyd and Onandi Lowe back into the fold. The squad had been warned, though, that anyone stepping out of line between now and June would be thrown out without question. And, he bluntly informed them, they would have to show at least 30 per cent improvement if they were to reach the standards required in France.

The team received a hero's welcome in Brazil. Simoes had always stated that Jamaica's success was down to mixing local flair with Brazilian football philosophy, and fans of the world's 'second team' lapped it up, taking the Reggae Boyz to their hearts. The tourists proved they could play a bit too, winning their first two games against First Division club sides.

A 4–0 defeat against Corinthians in São Paulo redressed the balance before Jamaica headed for the showpiece match of the tour. Flamengo, the biggest club in Brazil and a team that boasted internationals such as Romario, Ze Roberto and Junior Baiano, would be the most probing examination to date. Jamaica were without all the English-based players so the coach pitched in his youngsters for a match that served as a wake-up call for all those who had got carried away. Flamengo strolled to a 3–0 victory and further defeats to Coritiba and Caixas completed an eye-opening three weeks for the Reggae Boyz.

On his return to Jamaica, Simoes refused to be downcast, pointing out how much his players had learnt in such a short space of time. The defeats also allowed the coach to say 'told you so' to his critics. 'I remember in December, many experts in Jamaica said we could go to the World Cup with only Jamaicans and that we don't need English-based players,' said the coach. 'I hope they now understand how different it is in high-level football.'

Extensive testing of the players' diet, nutrition and physiological conditions showed how far Jamaica still lagged behind in the competition. Six of the men Simoes was preparing for World Cup duty had worms.

While debate raged in Jamaica on the recruitment of English-born players for the team, Simoes introduced more Brazilian faces to the backroom staff. He returned to the island with Professor Walter Ghama and Professor Oswaldo Filho, who were to be employed as consultants. The coach defused the inevitable questions by reminding critics of his agenda. 'When I bring expertise from Brazil everybody start to get upset,' Simoes told reporters. 'I never say that there is no talent in Jamaica but people have to understand what expertise means. Expertise means somebody who knows everything about his professional life.'

Despite the setbacks in South America the awards continued to pile up for the team. The governor general presented Burrell with the prestigious Gleanor Honour Award at a gala ceremony in January. One of the speeches described the team as a 'microcosm of what the nation must become: audacious in setting goals, resilient in the face of setbacks, confident in adversity, respectful of expertise, intolerant of indiscipline and gracious in victory.' An emotional Simoes agreed, adding that the players had showed the positive sides of a country that had once been labelled a 'paradise of drugs'.

Wednesday 28 January demonstrated how the sporting landscape of Jamaica had shifted. In the morning there was national embarrassment as the Test Match between England and the West Indies was called off after 35 minutes due to the atrocious state of the Sabina Park pitch. The evening saw all the razzamatazz of a game under lights at the National Stadium. Although the stadium was not full to capacity for the goalless draw against Sweden, radio phone-ins buzzed with talk of how football was now more relevant than its mismanaged, colonial counterpart.

The Federation wanted to capitalise on this groundswell of public goodwill and took a proactive approach to fundraising. The team had been invited to play in the Gold Cup in the United States and a huge rally staged in the AT&T amphitheatre in Miami was billed as 'South Florida's salute to the Reggae Boyz'. It was the only JFF-sanctioned event during the tournament fortnight. Of the $10 it cost to get in to see special guest stars, reggae and soca bands, a percentage went towards covering the expenses of 'the team's preparations for France'. Captain Burrell pressed flesh on a grand scale and reflected that fundraising had never been such fun.

A day later, the Reggae Boyz hype span into a new orbit. In

Miami's Orange Bowl stadium, Jamaica held world champions Brazil, the guest team, to a 0–0 draw. It was the greatest result in Jamaican football history. Fitzroy, Paul and Deon were back and Frank Sinclair made his debut in defence.

Simoes marvelled at the spirit of his men in an inspired defensive display against some of the most potent forwards in football. He had braced himself for defeat but urged the players not to be intimidated. Using his knowledge of the Brazilian psyche, he laid psychological traps for the illustrious opposition. The first Jamaican to commit a foul would be surrounded by Brazilian players and that, he told his team, would be their signal to show that reputations counted for nothing. Romario had not banked on having an angry-looking Ian Goodison in his face and the Brazilians eventually fell for the ploy. Junior Baiano's dismissal for elbowing Theodore Whitmore on the edge of the box confirmed that Jamaica had won the mind games.

The coach acknowledged that holding Brazil was a milestone but played down its significance by reminding reporters that Brazil had fielded a weakened side. It was a side that nevertheless featured Romario, Taffarel and Denilson and a side that felt compelled in the aftermath to whinge about the referee. But the public was in no mood for sobriety, even if Simoes was determined to pull on the reins. It was a match watched by millions of Jamaicans across the world and the result sparked fresh parties.

The symbolic significance of matching Brazil, a country that had a mythical importance for generations of Jamaican footballers, cannot be understated. It made people genuinely believe that nothing was beyond them. 'If Brazil could not beat Jamaica then who could?' was an outlook shared by most Jamaicans. The momentum was kept up with successive wins against Guatemala and El Salvador, and Jamaica were through to the semi-final where, inevitably, another clash with Mexico awaited them in Los Angeles.

Sides that had looked at each other across a chasm of six goals less than a year before were finally separated by a golden goal 15 minutes into extra time by Luis Hernandez. It was Jamaica's third game in five days. The Reggae Boyz finished the tournament in fourth position after going down to a 77th minute Romario goal in the play-off against Brazil. It had been a hugely successful tour and when Simoes arrived back at the Norman Manley International Airport in Kingston, he told the press that the biggest plus had been the amount of invaluable experience his side had gained.

The players were to stay in camp full-time until the summer and on their return from the States, began to prepare for a home friendly against Nigeria almost immediately. Discipline and dedication were required more than ever before. Although the JFF will not release figures, each player was being paid somewhere between US $700 and US $1000 a month, so Simoes could legitimately make demands on their time, however difficult they found it. Family commitments had to come second for those who lived in Jamaica; club commitments for those who played in England. After the Gold Cup, a further five days away from Portsmouth and Derby for the 'original three' did nothing for relations with their domestic paymasters. Frank Sinclair and Marcus Gayle returned to England while Walter Boyd was recalled after missing the Gold Cup through injury.

In the early hours of Thursday 19 February, the course of this story could have taken a deadly turn. Just days before the match against Nigeria, the four Montego Bay-based members of the squad were involved in a car crash in Falmouth when Warren Barrett's Nissan Sunny was hit by another vehicle which had broken a stop sign. Durrent Brown was knocked unconscious and spent the night in hospital while Barrett, Theodore Whitmore and Steve Malcolm were all treated for minor injuries.

Back in September, Horace Reid had inadvertently admitted that there were still problems with discipline, and Goodison, Gardener, Stewart, Altimont Butler and Aaron Lawrence had all been fined for reporting late to camp. Reid had been responding to criticism that the coach tended to punish some members of the squad more severely than others, following on from Walter Boyd losing his JA $250,000 monthly salary after being thrown off the programme in August. Simoes was becoming more of a disciplinarian by the day and though he must have recognised that time keeping did not figure highly on a Jamaican man's list of priorities, he could not allow laid-back attitudes to hamper progress. So naturally he felt a mixture of relief and rage when he learnt of his players' car crash.

Nigeria's 'Super Eagles' nevertheless represented a good catch for The Captain and he expected a bumper gate for the visit of Africa's premier football nation. Ticket prices reflected Jamaica's new status as World Cup qualifiers. News crews and reporters were now sending accreditation requests from all over the world but for a second game running, the public baulked at the admission fee. Crowd figures were not announced but witnesses say that the stadium was nowhere near capacity to see a makeshift team earn a creditable 2–2 draw. Nothing could be done to deflate the mood so The Captain kept his disappointment largely under wraps. The coach did not, however, declaring that he might include as many as ten players from England in his World Cup squad. It was an implicit threat to the Jamaican-based players in the programme.

They needed to shape up, particularly because at the beginning of March, the JFF unveiled a fixture list that promised some gruelling long-haul flights, weeks in strange hotels and stop-offs in outposts like Iran and South Korea.

Horace Reid could feel proud that his administration had met Simoes' demands yet hinted that JFF finances were again in a parlous state. Cable and Wireless had stumped up JA $15 million and Desnoe and Geddes and Kentucky Fried Chicken had both pumped in JA $2.5 million into the programme. JA $600,000 was donated by Crazy Jim.

Businesses were falling over each other to jump aboard the Reggae Boyz bandwagon but it simply wasn't enough. In February, Simoes, Captain Burrell and Carl Brown visited a company in Spanish Town in order to be presented with 40 beds for the team house. Genuinely grateful, they posed for pictures with a mountain of mattresses, but it was not the type of assistance the JFF really needed. The cost of foreign camps, hotels and training the national team had to be duplicated for the age-group sides that Simoes was now bringing through. Potential sponsors were reminded that the programme needed cash. Dissenting voices, however, had begun to ask where all the money was going.

The two-match tour of Britain looked destined to deliver cash by the barrowload. It was also my first chance to meet this new football phenomenon face-to-face and seeing the Reggae Boyz in the flesh only confirmed that they were a long way from home. The pitch at Loftus Road could have been in the Arctic Circle for all the thick, quilted tracksuits and padded jackets that were on display on that warm Saturday morning in March. Despite the watery sunshine that filtered down on to west London, many of the players had their faces buried deep in the collars of their Kappa bench coats or wore woolly hats pulled down over their ears. Only Robbie, Marcus Gayle and a bemused-looking Darryl Powell arrived for the press call and pitch inspection without gloves on.

Some of the younger players – Messam, Goodison, Whitmore, Gardener and Lowe – huddled together in one of the dug-outs looking like big birds in a small cage. Gardener was the most eye-catching, with his youthful looks and red-dyed braids. They met requests for interviews with blank looks or pretended that they hadn't heard. I had been told by Robbie that some of the Jamaican-based players, especially the younger ones, were not keen on talking to the press, and that was certainly the impression they gave. Establishing eye contact was difficult and they exuded an attitude that warned off those tempted to encroach into their personal space.

In front of the other dug-out, the experienced Peter Cargill propped himself against an advertising hoarding and blew into his hands. Robbie introduced me and a pained smile briefly lit a face that looked like it wore the worries of the world. 'This is a nice stadium,' offered the midfielder sagely. 'It's like Dortmund – compact. A bit too cold though.' Spider Lawrence approached and slung an arm round Robbie, who was then called away to do his umpteenth interview of the morning.

Elsewhere on the pitch, the barrel-chested Captain Burrell cut an imposing figure in a dark cashmere coat over a well-cut double-breasted suit. He had the voice and deportment of a statesman yet reminded me somehow of Don King. Maybe it was that isolated patch of grey hair above his hairline. Horace Reid, who never strayed far from The Captain's side, was similarly immaculate but did not have the same ready smile and prepossessing manner.

Rene Simoes was surprisingly young-looking, wearing the uniform of coaches the world over: a thick anorak, tracksuit trousers and a pair of black trainers, the make of which I'd never seen before. He was every bit as hirsute as the reports had made out.

Watching him rattle off soundbites to press, TV and radio, it quickly became apparent that he was an interviewer's dream. While he listens to questions put to him, his eyebrows rise up over his glasses and he cocks one ear forward in an exaggerated manner. When he speaks his hair wobbles while his face contorts into strange shapes. His answers are always entertaining. 'We are the Cinderellas of this World Cup,' he told a delighted female reporter, more accustomed to the monosyllabic fare dished out by managers in England. 'Now it is up to us to stop midnight for as long as possible.' If he had known the English for pumpkin and fairy godmother, I suspected that the woman holding the mike could have been delayed for hours.

That Simoes has an easy manner with his players was instantly evident. Every time one of them ambled past, the coach tried (and failed) to drag them into the interview. When they smiled, pulled themselves free and wandered off, Simoes gazed after them with paternal fondness. In the absence of Fitzroy, Paul, Deon and Frank, who were all away on club duty, much of the responsibility of projecting the Reggae Boyz to the British media fell to Robbie and Marcus Gayle. Darryl Powell, who had only joined up with the squad the night before, looked like a boy on his first day at a new school.

The 45-minute meet-and-greet session was brought to a close and the players trudged back down the tunnel and on to the bus. Asking what arrangements had been made for a pre-match training session, Simoes was met with a mixture of shrugged shoulders and downward glances. So The Captain elected to flex his muscles, booming to no-one in particular, 'I thought we are supposed to be partners in this match with Queens Park Rangers.' After spending the morning talking about 'capturing France with reggae and football', The Captain's men had apparently overlooked the small matter of capturing a pitch to practise on. The public relations team hired by the JFF, a firm run by two young, British-born West Indians, tried to placate Burrell as quietly and quickly as possible. Now was not the time for an incident.

A match against First Division QPR was perhaps not what Simoes had envisaged when he presented his list of demands to the JFF. For Burrell and the club's long-serving midfielder Simon Barker, however, the game was a Godsend. Barker might have expected a generous turn-out for his testimonial match but nothing like the crowd that descended on Shepherds Bush that glorious spring Sunday. The Notting Hill Carnival, which takes place just a couple of miles up the road, was five months away, yet the large Caribbean population in the area got warmed up nice and early for the visit of the 'all-conquering' Jamaican team.

The atmosphere will live long in the memory of those who sampled it. The side streets around Rangers' compact ground echoed with the sound of whistles, horns and drums. Cars with huge stereos swept in from all corners of the capital and women were conspicuous by their numbers. Rather than pockets of young men walking briskly in packs, whole families took time to soak up the unseasonal warmth. People were dressed to impress: Tommy Hilfiger puffers, freshly styled hair and an abundance of designer labels made the occasion a fashion parade as much as a football match. Street vendors threw open van doors and set up makeshift stalls selling Reggae Boyz T-shirts, posters and slightly dubious-looking replica shirts. Local off-licences did a roaring trade in Red Stripe. It was a day of West Indian pride and as one elderly Rasta commented: 'It's not every day that Jamaica make it to the World Cup.' Even the police were smiling.

On the side of the main stand, Ellerslie Road was crammed. Fitzroy couldn't have wished for more as he weaved through the crowds in his convertible BMW. With Paul Hall on one side and Deon Burton in the back, they were guaranteed a superstars' welcome. For players more used to slipping in and out of grounds unnoticed, this was a dream come true. Hall and Donald Stewart's unofficial World Cup song track throbbed from the car speakers and all three revelled in the adulation being heaped upon them. They had got used to being treated like stars in Jamaica but to win the respect of their own people in Britain was a fantastic feeling.

Inside the ground, it was clear that this was not your average testimonial but a West Indian occasion. A specially imported sound system blasted out the sounds of reggae and dancehall and each time a crowd favourite ripped round the ground, whistles were blown in ear-splitting approval. A steel band played in the top balcony behind one goal and next to me in the paddock, a couple of guys unzipped massive bongo drums and slapped out a rhythm. Even the players seemed to be getting in on the act during their warm-up, stretching to the beat and looking funkier than anything previously seen at Loftus Road.

Peter Cargill donned green boots, Whitmore wore red and keeper Warren Barrett looked resplendent in a pair of white Pumas. *And* there was substance to back up the style. Gardener showed the promise Simoes had talked about, looking as fragile as a new-born foal but tough enough to withstand some typically British tackling. He possessed the subtle touch of a player with more experience than his 19 years. Up front, Onandi Lowe made defenders nervous with his huge physique and Andy Williams demonstrated what neat feet he had. For the first half, a line-up of exclusively Jamaican-born players moved the ball with precision and speed and, though the final pass was lacking, their 'skills' brought roars from the crowd. A close range effort by Whitmore and a second-half header from Robbie, his first goal for Jamaica, were enough for a deserved and thoroughly enjoyable 2–1 victory.

ROBBIE

It didn't take long for the emotions of that wonderful afternoon to turn slightly sour. Captain Burrell called a meeting in our London hotel because the atmosphere within the camp was now rife with discontent. The JFF seemed to be struggling to pay the outstanding monies owed to us from qualification and though they said we would all be paid up by the time we arrived in France, doubts still lingered. The main bone of contention, though, was to leave a bad taste in the mouths of the players for weeks and months to follow.

Within the squad, Fitzroy, Paul Hall, Peter Cargill, Warren Barrett and myself had been elected to lay the foundations for a players' pool (where all monies from promotional activities are shared out equally amongst the team). It is normal practice for teams to operate a pool system once they have made it to a cup final or to the final stages of a major tournament and everything was falling into the place for the

Reggae Boyz to capitalise on their new-found earning potential. Our view was that the pool would provide an opportunity for some of the players to earn a sizeable chunk of money, helping them to start up a business or put the finishing touches to that dream home, maybe even on the piece of land we had been given by the government.

One of the first things mentioned in the contract drawn up with the PR firm we had enlisted to run the pool was that the coach agreed to the proposal. Captain Burrell, however, went absolutely ballistic when he found out because Simoes was a paid employee of the JFF, and Burrell, as we soon discovered, had big problems with money going anywhere other the JFF coffers. We knew, therefore, that when he called a meeting for 7pm we were going to be in for a tough time. Having said that, I thought it would only last for an hour so I told the friends I was meeting to pick me up at half past nine.

We went in determined to stick together, knowing that we might have to give in on certain things but that there were other areas where we had to stay strong. Burrell bowled into the meeting and immediately took centre stage, bellowing, 'I'm the president of the Jamaican Football Federation, you are players. I've paid your wages for the last three years and you are not going to take money out of my pocket and kill the Federation I have worked so hard to build up.' Fair play: The Captain had made a fast start.

We put forward our case as to why we felt the need for the pool, in line with all the other soccer nations at the World Cup, explaining that we had the capacity to raise sponsorship and finance for the group without impingeing on any of the JFF's existing financial arrangements. We believed we could strike deals in Europe that the JFF would never have considered.

The Captain sat and listened for all of two minutes before bringing our argument to an abrupt end. As long as he was president of the Federation there would not be a players' pool under any circumstances, we were told. The Federation was in a unique position because it paid its players a weekly wage and he believed that any outside finances that could be generated should be directed straight into the fund. Then, and only then, would they decide on what sort of cut went to the players.

While I understood the thrust of his argument, I still felt there was room to operate the players' pool alongside the JFF's existing deals. It was not to be. Captain Burrell left us in no doubt as to who was chairing the meeting and went on to spell out the consequences for anyone who went behind his back. 'Two things will happen if this players' pool goes ahead,' he said. 'The first is that I'll resign and sack the coach. I'll tell the world that the Jamaican World Cup dream has been blown apart by the greed of the players and we'll go to France with the Under 23 team.

'The second thing,' he continued, 'is that any player who gets involved in any commercial deal that I don't approve of will be dropped from the squad immediately.' He was referring to the other topic to be 'discussed' in the meeting: the record that Paul Hall had made with Donald 'Foley' Stewart. Burrell had already signed a deal with Sony on an official Reggae Boyz record featuring Ziggy Marley, Maxi Priest and Diane King but when it became apparent that the players were behind Hall's record, Sony suggested that they pull out of the original deal in order to throw their weight behind our track. TransWorld International, who were going to make the video to supplement sales of the record, also threatened to pull out of the official song. The deal was believed to be worth millions to the JFF.

The players were to give up on their own record, Burrell ordered, so that the original Sony deal could be reinstated. Nobody was allowed to get involved with any other recording venture. At around midnight, we phoned one of the partners in the firm that was going to be setting up the players' pool to see if he could establish some sort of middle ground. What we were trying to propose was that we reinstate the original Sony deal but that some of the revenue would go to the players. Burrell didn't seem too unhappy with that but it was becoming clear that there was a crucial reason why he needed this Sony deal to go through.

At two o'clock in the morning, we finally rang the people who had arranged the launch of Hally's record for the following day and told them the whole thing was off. We had wanted Sony to buy Hall and Foley's record and put it out after the release of the original, official 'Rise Up' song, but the coach later told us that the reason Burrell was so keen to kill the players' record was that the Jamaican government had got involved in the original Sony deal.

We were all agreed that The Captain was starting to flex his muscles a little bit too much. A couple of days before, he had tried to talk down Warren Barrett during a team meeting. Warren was speaking on behalf of the players when The Captain suddenly sprang to his feet and interrupted. Burrell said something along the lines of, 'I'm the president of the JFF and no one tells me the way to do things,' to which Warren had replied, 'I'm the captain of the team and you have no right to tell *me* what to do.' Simoes had to step in to calm the situation down. Warren was furious and you could tell there was still tension between the pair at the players' pool meeting.

The Captain was not finished there, though. He went on to say that he was disappointed with the English-based Jamaicans, almost implying that we had been stoking up the other players. He told us how hard he had worked to get us into the programme and how we had now let him down. It was the first time I remember Burrell making the distinction between the English-based players and those born and bred in Jamaica.

In terms of being on the field, Burrell had always said we were a group who worked hard for each other. It was ironic that he was now suggesting that we were a disruptive influence considering that he had used his recruits from England for propaganda purposes in the past. Fitz was furious.

Despite trying to calm him down, I was angry at both the The Captain's insinuations and his point-blank refusal to listen to our case. From my perspective, the potential £15 to £20,000 each we could earn from the pool would not have made a significant difference to my life. To some of the Jamaican-based players, however, it would have brought some fundamental changes. I would have been more than happy to throw my share of the pool back into the central pot or offer it to one of the homeless charities in Jamaica. But Burrell was not interested.

At the end of that epic meeting, we had reached a compromise that suited The Captain better than it suited us. All outside revenue would go through the JFF and a percentage would be paid to the players. The original JFF-approved record deal would stand and the outstanding debts to the PR company would have to be met out of the players' pockets. Six hours after it began, the meeting was drawn to a close. We were now in the early hours of Monday morning.

We were up against dictatorship in the shape of the garrulous captain. When we had asked where the basis for discussion was he told us that there was no basis for discussion. I saw a different side to our glorious leader that night. He had never been afraid of talking 'big money' if that's what it took to get the job done, yet rumblings of discontent were now being heard from those who questioned whether all the revenue that was being generated through tours, friendlies and fundraising functions had been properly accounted for. I was sure Burrell had political ambitions but to get anywhere he would first have to learn the lessons of diplomacy.

DANIEL

The players showed no obvious signs of discontent when I met up with the team in Cardiff a couple of days later. Still in the woolly hats, but now sporting the Joe Bloggs logo thanks to a sponsorship deal delivered by the new PR gurus, they seemed more concerned with what there was to do to pass the time before their friendly against Wales. Apart from breakfast, a light stretch, lunch and more training, there was little more to look forward to than the coach's daily team meeting. Posted in a soulless motorway hotel, most elected to stay in bed while the rain drizzled from pigeon-grey skies.

A training session at the ground helped to relieve the boredom. Gloves, thermal vests and hats were again in evidence as the players clattered out of the tunnel on to Cardiff City's soggy pitch. Alfredo Montessa spent 20 minutes warming the players up before Simoes paired them off for a series of light exercises. New boy Darryl Powell was selected by the coach for a game of foot tennis and found out, like many before him, that Simoes still had a magical touch. The object of the game was to receive and return without letting the ball touch the ground and despite the condensation dripping from his nose, Simoes barely lost a point.

The session finished in customary fashion: a 15-a-side match between the professor's team and coach Brown's team. It was a fast, physical encounter played along the width of the pitch. The rules meant that no more than two touches could be taken before passing and no-one was allowed to play in their normal position. Denise Nicholls, the team's travelling physiotherapist, told me that a complex transfer system allowed movement between the two teams on the one condition that Simoes always got who he wanted. Robbie and most of the English-based players found themselves lining up on the Brazilian's team. As raised voices from the field disputed Simoes' less than impartial refereeing decisions, local and international film crews lined the pitch – reporters from as far afield as Holland, Germany and Japan braving a cold, wet night to grab a word or two with the men behind the miracle.

Later on, back at the hotel, the bar slowly filled up. Pockets of Jamaican fans, Welsh football officials in nasty burgundy blazers and an assortment of agents and boot company reps were all in town for the game. Fitzroy Simpson wandered down in a pair of plastic shower sandals and chatted to some friends. Deon, 'Bibi' Gardener and Donald Stewart sauntered through in baseball caps before plonking themselves in front of the TV to watch the cricket highlights.

Sticking close to his club mate, Darryl Powell looked tall and more composed than before. I called him over to find out how he was settling in. 'It's been superb, very enjoyable,' he said earnestly. 'The first day I felt a little bit apprehensive because you don't know what to expect. You sort of introduce yourself to a few of the players and then take it from there really.' Having been at Portsmouth with Deon and Paul Hall before joining Derby, Powell had pestered them to get Simoes to have a look at him. 'He wasn't too sure at first and they went away but then all of a sudden, out of nowhere, the call-up came.'

Both Darryl's parents are Jamaican and like all of the English-based players in the squad, representing his country has been the source of much family pride. 'My father brought me down to the hotel on the Thursday before the QPR game and that was the first time I had met any of the Jamaican-based players. He was saying that he wished I had been part of the team during qualification, not for the land but just to have been there. I suppose some things are just meant to happen.'

A brief smile flickered across Powell's 'interview face' when he spied Deon pulling faces at him, and it remained there when the conversation turned to Sunday's match against QPR. Hall, Simpson and Burton had been wearing beatific grins ever since and Powell too was still high on the occasion. 'Lovely, lovely, beautiful,' he offered of his debut as a second-half substitute. 'I felt so proud, all of my family felt so proud – just to represent your culture is such a brilliant feeling. The fans behaved so well;

they came out just to enjoy the day and it was a totally different atmosphere than most people are used to in England. I think you have got to be in that culture to really understand it.

'Before the QPR game [Simoes] told me just to relax and enjoy it. All he kept saying was, "Powell, no tension, relax everything, play, don't worry about anything and just play." I don't know if I'll even be going to the World Cup as of yet but if I am then I'd like to go to the camp in Jamaica and get a real feel of it with all the players. It's all about bonding. If you're going to be successful you have got to have strong team spirit and a love for each other.'

Like Robbie, Darryl admitted that he would have answered the call from England if it had come a year ago. Now, though, he is nothing but Jamaican. Did the Jamaican players sense that or was there any tension because of the recent influx of more players from the English Premiership? 'Do you see any tension?' snapped Powell. It was obviously a delicate subject. 'I think that's a case of the press trying to break things down and ruin things. There's a big unity about this side. From the time that you come in here and they know that you're representing Jamaica and you're Jamaican, that's all that matters. It doesn't matter whether you're English born or not – if you are Jamaican and you can play football then they're happy.' As if to prove the point, he revealed that he was considering going the whole hog and trying out a pair of gold boots for his full international debut.

Next day, another one of the new boys, Marcus Gayle, sat on a sofa in the hotel lounge, running a hand over his freshly cut hair. It is tradition that players go for a trim on the morning of a match. 'I've got to keep myself looking sharp for my mum at home, so she'll be proud of her son,' he joked, 'and so my wife will think I'm handsome.'

Marcus finally made his Jamaican debut at the Gold Cup in the USA after waiting seven months to join up with the team. Wimbledon, he revealed, had never thought of him as a potential international and when he began to make fast progress, inserted a clause in his contract that prevented him accepting a call-up from anyone other than England. He had been out in Jamaica when Fitz, Paul and Deon were there for the trial. Back in June, however, Marcus had put his club first. 'It was a tricky time. I didn't really know the Jamaicans that well and even though they were offering me everything, Wimbledon had been my whole life for the last three years. Then suddenly everything was flying in [the club's] face. It was a bit dodgy for me at that time. Sam Hamman and the rest of his boys have given me a bit of a hard time. They look at it like it's a holiday, a little excursion. I told them, "Look, you don't have a holiday playing against Brazil twice a week." '

Like Powell, Marcus had Peter Cargill looking out for him at first but he now felt confident enough to move around. 'You get to know the guys, which is good. Myself and Frank [Sinclair] went out to the Gold Cup together and if we had roomed together we wouldn't have really got to know the guys. We are all unified, we are all good friends. There's no segregation among the players and there's a good crack. "Shorty" Malcolm, "Pepe" Goodison and Dean Sewell are all jokers. Ricardo and "Pepe" are like Pinky and Perky – they come in a twosome all the time.' Right on cue, 'Bibi' meandered past, walking with an exaggerated limp, closely followed by his impressively pouting sidekick 'Pepe'. We both smiled.

Marcus is a great character and it is hard not to warm to him. He has a kind face and does not take himself too seriously. It was quite touching to discover how overwhelmed he had been by the reaction to the famous goal he scored to knock Manchester United out of the previous season's FA Cup. 'I didn't know how big that feeling was until the next day,' he said, smirking. 'I went out to go and buy the papers and everyone was just, like, stopping me. There were little kids whispering and pointing when I went past, even though I was wearing shades and a cap. It does give a bit of a buzz but most of the time I'm in shock about it all. Before that it was just an ordinary life. I'm still new to all this. My wife can't believe it at times and even my mum can't. She believes it a bit more now because she takes all the praise at work.'

Marcus too was extremely proud to play at QPR in front of his native west London community. He thought the team was missing the Reverend. 'The Reverend was out in the States with us – he was amazing, man. He keeps us all focused spiritually.

You get pregnant with it in a way. It's a big thing in my life so I related to what he was saying quite a lot. It's what I practise every week.'

Meanwhile, Marcus had to go. Lunch was ready and then the players had to retire to their rooms for a sleep. Spider walked past, smiling, and issued a husky greeting. He looked as though he had just got up. Fitz appeared at the top of stairs leading up from the basement gymnasium, followed by a film crew. The four-man team were in the process of making a fly-on-the-wall documentary about the Reggae Boyz and seemed to have secured remarkable access, flitting in and out of the players' rooms and constantly pulling Simoes aside to whisper something in his ear. The Captain, who they were keen to talk to, was still in London.

Jamaican fans, decked in bright colours and dripping in gold, filtered into the foyer. A youth in a tracksuit with one trouser leg rolled up to the knee asked me to take some pictures of him. 'They're for my girlfriend,' he said. We went out through some glass doors on to a concrete balcony into rain that felt like a fine, wet blanket. As he pulled a variety of poses with his bare calf hooked over a railing and a mobile phone clamped to his head, he told me that he had come from Leeds.

'On one of the coaches?' I asked.

'No,' he replied, smiling. 'We came in a Lexus.'

The Captain finally arrived at the hotel just an hour before the team were due to leave for the game. A well-known bald British agent rose to greet him, having waited in a drab spot next to the lifts for some six hours. Burrell brushed him aside and immediately went to greet his public, swelling with pride when he discovered that over 50 coaches had made the journey from Brixton alone. 'So,' said The Captain, beaming, 'London is empty.' He repeated the phrase as he disappeared down the corridor, a deep baritone chuckle echoing as the film crew scurried in his wake.

Outside Ninian Park, Jamaican fans congregated to create scenes similar to those in west London. Rastas hawking more bootleg merchandise filled the car park and the familiar shriek of whistles livened up a hideous evening. The kick-off was delayed for ten minutes because of the huge crush of Jamaica fans outside. When they gained access, some looked unfamilar with the old-style terracing at the open end behind one goal. Unfortunately for all those who made the long journey, the Reggae Boyz's play did not prove as popular as their rhythmic warm-up. A very average Welsh side created the best chances and the highlight of an otherwise drab match was Simoes getting into a heated touchline row with an official. The amount of pushing and finger-pointing and Onandi Lowe's red card for elbowing an opponent in the face probably explained why the Brazilian refused to face the press afterwards. Instead, Wales boss Bobby Gould emitted the odour of sour grapes by disputing Jamaica's superior position in the FIFA World Rankings.

The party travelled back to the capital, due to fly back to Jamaica the following day, but there was just time to catch them at Millwall's New Den stadium in south-east London. They were there to shoot a Japanese-funded video and for a press conference to announce a new sponsorship deal. After larking about for the cameras, members of the team and JFF staff filed into a small function room and sat behind a long table. Flanked by The Captain and Simoes, Joe Bloggs chief Shami Ahmed announced that his company had signed up to become the official outfitters of the Reggae Boyz. The team would receive £100,000 for their World Cup bid, £100,000 if they progressed from the group stage and £1,000,000 if they won the World Cup. Captain Burrell made a grand acceptance speech and Simoes talked of dreams, while models in green, yellow and black bikinis stood around looking somewhat incongruous next to the overcoats, scarves and hats being worn by the players. On the other side of the room, Marcus raised his eyebrows wryly.

PART TWO

7

A Different Sense of Belonging

ROBBIE

The matches at Loftus Road and Ninian Park filled me with pride and though I never thought I would be part of such joyous, black football occasions in Britain, in many ways they confirmed beliefs that I have always held. For too long, it has been assumed that black people are not interested in football, and the game at QPR was a day for all the West Indian communities to show how much they love the game. I was so emotional that day: when black people come together to watch football, they produce a friendly atmosphere where the emphasis is firmly on fun, and I was pleased to be a part of that.

Obviously, I hope the achievements of players such as myself, Fitz, Paul Hall, Deon, Marcus, Frank and Darryl will open doors for black players in the future. I have had letters from players across the UK enquiring about the chance of playing for Jamaica, even at under 16 and under 18 level, which means there are young players, perhaps the stars of the future, who are prepared to come out at an early stage and declare their allegiance to Jamaica. That must be down to the emergence of the Jamaican team over the last two years, so it's good to think that one day our efforts will be seen as the start of something much bigger. After all, the population of Jamaica might only be two and a half million but there are ten million Jamaicans around the world – and as they say 'Once you're a Jamaican, you're always a Jamaican.'

A few fellow professionals in England were a bit surprised when I first made the decision to play for Jamaica, seeing it as a small country with no footballing tradition. It would be a culture shock after the relative luxury of life in the Premiership, they said. John Barnes understood why I made the choice because he appreciated the lure of an opportunity to play on the greatest stage of all. Maybe people didn't realise how close Jamaica were to qualification at the time, because once we had made it through to France, everybody was pleased for me and the country.

I get the feeling that a number of players who have represented England, but who would also have been eligible to play for a Caribbean country, would have taken a similar chance seriously if their circumstances had been different. There is an unspoken community between the second-generation West Indians playing football in the United Kingdom and although some of the lads who have played for England could not come out and say, 'I wish I played for Jamaica,' my gut reaction is that some of them would have given it a go.

I have always believed that the English-based players in the Jamaican squad are representing not only the population of the island but all those exiled Jamaicans in Britain and across the world. Second-generation Jamaicans playing in the World Cup finals are a fitting tribute to those people who sailed to Britain on the ss *Windrush* 50 years ago, and this has been brought home to me by the numbers of well-wishing letters I have received on my return from trips away with the Reggae Boyz. Many exiled Jamaicans are realising their dreams through the team, and that means a lot to us.

It is difficult to describe how I feel when I play for Jamaica. Within English clubs, black players can sometimes feel no better than an employee, but with Jamaica, you have a stake in the company. It is a different sense of belonging. I have a strange sense of calm when I am in Jamaica. It's perhaps hard for a white person to understand how strange it is for a black guy, who has lived his life in England, to feel that he doesn't have to look over his shoulder, despite the fact that it is far more dangerous for a relatively wealthy person to stroll about in certain parts of Jamaica than it is in Britain.

Wimbledon is a cosmopolitan club renowned for having a healthy number of black players. Race is not an issue and never has been. Thankfully, I've only had very, very isolated instances of racial abuse on the pitch during my time as a professional, perhaps because bigoted opponents thought twice about making an abusive comment while Fash was around.

I am aware, however, that the problem has not completely disappeared, and there are places in England, and across the world, where you still get inappropriate comments from the crowd. Traditonally, Everton's supporters have been among the worst although it should be said that there has been a vast improvement at Goodison Park in recent years. Clubs in Yorkshire and the north-east have had similar problems with sections of their crowds. It usually follows that the worst racial abuse is found in areas where there is not much of an ethnic population, such as Newcastle, although the success Les Ferdinand enjoyed at St James's Park broke down a lot of racist feeling there. The fact that he did community work also helped.

Things are undoubtedly improving but it is still important to black players in Britain that campaigns like 'Kick Racism Out of Football' and 'Kick it Out' do not become token gestures. They tend to get wheeled out at the start of every new season, which makes you suspect that it's a case of the game wanting to be seen to act in a politically correct manner rather than any overriding desire to do something about the problem. Campaigns like these should be ongoing and fulfil some actual service.

If someone in the stand racially abuses either the players or other people in the ground then clearly something has to be done about it. It's no use identifying a problem and then sitting back, and that very little has been done about it is probably why black players have always been a little wary of allowing their names to be linked with such initiatives. Before they commit themselves to campaigns that deal with racial issues, players have to know that the offenders will be actively weeded out.

That was one of my concerns when the opportunity arose to join the government's Football Task Force. Before getting involved, I wanted to make sure that I wasn't just the token black player they needed to gain a bit of credibility and that they were serious about addressing the problem of racial abuse and discrimination within the game. One of the things that pleased me was that the Task Force's remit wasn't just about racial abuse from the terraces, because that is only a small element of the problem. Racism in football and within the industry runs a lot deeper than that. Allegations have suggested that it has reached as far as the FA and the boardrooms, scouting systems and club administrations. If more ethnic minorities were represented in areas of power and decision-making within the industry, it would help to solve problems all the way down and create a culture within the management of the game that reflects the multi-racial nature of football both on the pitch and in the stands.

A good start would obviously be to have more black managers. I believe there is a glass ceiling within the game when it comes to certain black players going on to take the step up into management. We are now seeing more black players move into coaching but traditionally there has been a school of thought, articulated by Ron Noades a few years ago, whilst discussing the roots of racism, that has persisted long past its natural shelf life.

The sad fact is that the Brentford owner was just being honest when he made those crass comments about black players, and if nothing else, it served to bring out into the open what other people were thinking. Among other things, he said that black players are not generally students of the game and are not good on tactics. Maybe the fact that black players are thought to be athletic, rather than intuitive like a midfield general would be, is one of the reasons why more black players are dissuaded from going into management. While it is not up to the FA to fast-track black players into such positions, I think it would be a start if more were invited to coaching weekends or meetings. At least it would give players a feel for the job and perhaps prove that it might not be as daunting as they first suspected.

Although we have some great black reporters and pundits in TV, black representation within Lancaster Gate bears no relation to the number of black professionals playing in England. If the likes of John Barnes, Paul Ince, Les Ferdinand or Ian Wright succeeded at management level, it would open the door for many other players, but for that to happen the game needs more black or ethnic minority people in decision-making areas so that they can be on the look-out for like-minded people.

How to deal with offenders is also a problem. The higher echelons of the FA hierarchy are almost totally white so those who pass sentence are not really qualified to judge how insulting it is for, say, a black player to be called a 'black bastard' by another player. To call someone a 'black bastard' is as unacceptable on the field as it is off it, and the FA should act accordingly. In the case of the Schmeichel v. Wright feud where, thanks to the use of video evidence, there was absolutely no denying what Schmeichel had said, the FA should have stepped in. It was a missed opportunity to set a precedent. If the authorities had acted decisively in a case involving two players at the highest level of the game, then the effect would have filtered down. If the bloke in the stand knows that he will be ejected or banned from the ground, he will think twice about shouting racial abuse.

If I punched a player off the ball and it was caught on camera then I could expect to be hauled before an FA Disciplinary Hearing. By the same token, if someone launches a racial attack on me or another black player, then the FA should be seen to take decisive action, either through a fine or suspension. The FA can't just pay lip service to campaigns to rid football of racism: it needs to send a positive message to players and fans alike.

Given the number of black players in England, it is worrying that there is not more representation within the corridors of power, and inevitably there will be wider repercussions while that situation is allowed to continue. I know that certain black players have represented England without feeling 100 per cent sure that everything they are doing is appreciated. There have been people within the national set-up who have harboured racial prejudices.

Former England international Cyrille Regis received hate mail when he played for England, around the time when the NF were particularly active within the hardcore of England's following. Ian Wright was treated in a similar way when he first played for his country, especially when he wasn't scoring regularly.

Playing for Jamaica, where black people are obviously in the huge majority, you don't come into contact with those feelings or tendencies. From management right up to the top of the Jamaican Football Federation, everyone is behind us. I feel totally at ease and comfortable with the fact that everyone is coming from the same place.

That's not to say I haven't encountered the problem of racial abuse during my time as a Jamaican international. Indeed, it was very disappointing to witness some of the worst of its kind in El Salvador during our penultimate qualifying match for the World Cup. Witchdoctors trying to indicate that we were monkeys by dancing round us and Jamaican dolls being stabbed while the crowd cheered are not just meant to intimidate: they are derogatory to our race.

As players, we were amazed that this was allowed to happen, and the JFF officials were livid. Typically, the coach turned it to our advantage, however, by telling us that we were not only fighting for ourselves but for the reputation of black people all over the world. He told us that the El Salvadorians did not know how to treat people from other parts of the world. We were going to have to teach them a lesson and he wanted us to channel our aggression to win the game.

I was particularly disappointed because FIFA officials were in attendance yet failed to act. The monkey noises I heard coming from the crowd during that match took me back to the late seventies and early eighties when racism was much worse in England than it is now. I watched a lot of Man City during that time but I also used to go and see a bit of my local club, Stoke. Garth Crooks, my one-time hero and now a good friend, got a lot of stick from the opposition fans in one particular game. Bananas were thrown at him and he had to endure those same monkey impressions. But it upset me more when the home fans turned on him for a missed chance or a poor pass. I clearly remember my acute embarrassment standing among a group of people who would shout racial abuse at one of their own.

Apart from Garth Crooks, the three black players at West Brom – Cyrille Regis, Brendan Batson and Laurie Cunningham – were the glamour boys at the time. Remi Moses was another favourite, perhaps because he played in midfield or maybe because he sometimes looked like he was fighting his colour. Not that he could be seen verbally attacking opponents on a regular basis – where you saw it was in his challenges. He imposed himself with his play and I always like to think that I have followed that example.

One of the things I know is that your football can discolour your face. If you're playing well, you are more likely to be accepted because people almost forget that you're black. Things tend to go the other way if you move to a club and start poorly. The people will make the colour of your skin an issue. It's fascinating that people used to lament that there weren't any black managers in England when Ruud Gullit was boss at Chelsea. Gullit – due to what he had achieved as a player and because of who he was – was never considered black.

John Barnes is a fine example for young black players coming into the game, having overcome prejudices at Liverpool with his performances on the field. Barnes handles things in exactly the right way and like him, I'm not particularly keen to play the race card. I don't see myself as the token black player who has to stand up for black rights. I much prefer to let people know who I am and what I'm about by what I do.

Racial abuse is something that I handle in my own way, but I was aware that some of the other players in the Jamaican squad might not be able to cope so well. Having been brought up in a black society and only coming into contact with black people, they are not used to dealing with racism like we are in Britain.

After growing up in a predominantly white communuty, being the norm in Jamaica has been an interesting experience. When I started out at Port Vale, I remember black players were ridiculed for using moisturisers. Black skin dries a lot more quickly than white skin so after showering most black players apply baby oil or moisturiser. Black players also tend to use wax in their hair, previously regarded as a bit of a gimmick. Now, if you go into a dressing room, you will find every player with gel in one hand and moisturiser in the other. The whole thing has been turned on its head and many aspects of black culture are now embraced in the dressing room. The music we play on the team stereo in the Wimbledon changing room is predominantly black. Footballers' dress sense is often quite street orientated, a style which looks to popular black culture for the lead.

I can understand why a lot of Jamaican people who have come over and made a life in England end up wanting to go back. I think my parents will move back to Jamaica eventually and I certainly intend to spend a lot more time there, especially after I've built my house. It is a place that has always been special to me and my experiences with the national team have only enhanced those feelings.

8

Braco and Beyond

DANIEL

As the tyres of the plane screeched on to the runway in Montego Bay, I looked out of the window into a dark Caribbean night and felt a very different sense of belonging – a sense of not belonging.

The idea had been to come out to Jamaica to find out more about some of the characters at the heart of this story. The previous week, however, had seen all attempts to secure access to the team through the JFF lost in the call-holding system at the Federation offices. Long periods listening to reggae on a transatlantic phone tariff confirmed that 'bigging up' the profile of the national programme did not stretch to telling visiting journalists where the team would be on certain dates. I had almost given up hope of going when a flight came up at the last minute.

There was the normal apprehension of travelling alone and although an interesting eight hours on the national airline – fashion show, chairobics, unlimited Red Stripe and rum – had loosened me up, I was not yet at Jamaica speed. If I had been, the pilot's announcement that the flight would be terminating at Montego Bay Airport – they were digging the runway up in Kingston – would have been met with a 'no problem' instead of punching tension into my guts. In the total absence of an itinerary, the plan for the week relied on presenting myself in person to the JFF in Kingston and politely requesting assistance in arranging some interviews.

The most important meeting was to be with Captain Burrell, the barrel-chested, moustachioed giant who had greeted the brethren in Cardiff with an effusive 'One Love my children' before urging them to tell the film cameras that going to the

World Cup finals was bigger than gaining independence in 1962. The 'Road to France' was gaining an evangelical, dare I say it, political impetus as The Captain introduced his pride of the Caribbean to exiled fans across the world. Support for the Reggae Boyz had bordered on the fanatical in the States and the band-wagon just kept rolling in Britain.

Following his movements, observing him at close quarters and talking to people in and around the camp had provided a rough outline of the ample figure navigating Jamaica's course. He visibly grew in the company of more than three people and punctuated his sentences with dramatic pauses for impact. He had perfected an inflection that was part Pathé newsreel, part smiling menace.

But what was also fascinating about The Captain was how evasive he could be. The film crew had chuckled knowingly when I had asked them how hard it was to pin him down and the fact that he checked his watch at ten-minute intervals over the course of a day convinced me that he was either very busy or deliberately trying to avoid certain people. After the grandstanding and genial handshakes of that Saturday morning press call at QPR, The Captain that breezed through the sliding doors in Cardiff was an altogether more anxious-looking character.

On his last day in Britain I appealed to his vanity by asking him to grant me an interview on his part in the development of Jamaican football. I could not hope to write the story of the Road to France, I told him, without a testimony from the plot's main visionary. He said a meeting would be almost impossible but urged, 'Come to Jamaica, my child,' anyway.

Tracking him down on home turf would be harder still and to get his attention for just five minutes would almost certainly require staking him out. If he was not calling the shots from his office on the top floor of JFF headquarters he might just as easily be at his own private office or chucking dough around and bellowing at his loyal staff at The Captain's Bakery in Maypen.

When I did speak to someone at the JFF, they verified that it was a difficult time for The Captain. Good Friday was fast approaching and they did not expect him to make the journey from Kingston to Braco Village, the official training ground on the north coast. 'It would disturb the flow of the Easter holiday,' the woman said. 'This is a really bad time for him, what with all the work he had been doing in football. He must get his business back on stream.' Pause. 'I even heard that he's been sleeping at the bakery.' It was just as well he only needed three hours' sleep a night, what with buns to bake and the World Cup only a couple of months away.

In addition to the big man, there was of course the likeable and enthusiastic Simoes, the charming Peter Cargill and Aaron Lawrence to get to know better. Spider was best understood in the company of his team mates; he came alive and provided a facial circus for those around him. Whether swaggering through a hotel foyer doing a human beatbox, play fighting with pals who would pat him away affectionately or at the centre of a huddle of people waiting wide-eyed for the punchline, he was a definite one-off. He could have been as cool and taciturn as his colleagues but chose to operate no colour bar with his charm.

There would be no English-based players at Braco and I had been advised to go bearing gifts. The first thought was to buy a consignment of Hilfiger aftershave; an article in the *London Evening Standard* on what the Reggae Boyz thought about personal grooming – an acid test of burgeoning stardom in itself – had thrown up the odd revelation about some of the younger Jamaicans in the side. Sadly, even at duty free prices, enough to avoid an Edward Seaga-type incident would have wiped out the hotel budget.

Surprisingly, inspiration came in WH Smiths and three biographies (always a favourite with footballers) were eventually tucked in the bag: a copy of Ian Wright's *Mr Wright* was for the older Peter Cargill, the real plum choice – *Shankly* – was to appeal to the intellect and motivational genius of Simoes and *Dalglish* was to be used in one of two ways – either as the darling of Anfield for Liverpool fan Gregory Messam or as the grim-faced mumbler at Newcastle for the colder Horace Reid.

As I stepped off that plane into the muggy warmth, I remembered one piece of advice that I had been given: 'Call Stogie when you get there.'

On a map of the world Jamaica is only a tiny pin-prick, so I had figured that the four inches or so between Montego Bay and the outcrop in Trelawny that housed Braco Village would not take long in a taxi. Next day, I was picked up by the driver who had somehow secreted me away from the other stricken passengers waiting to be transported to hotels for the night. 'Stogie' had not been an option.

It would be fair to say that the journey was an eye-opener but only if you discount the fact that mine were closed for most of it. Once out of Montego Bay, the driver careered along bumpy roads in his Honda, always maintaining a safe distance of four inches from the car in front. The tinted windows did nothing to keep out the heat and the black plastic seats turned into instruments designed for human torture. The knot in my stomach doubled in size.

The north coast was tourist country although once out of Montego Bay, the buildings gradually shrank until they were no more than small blocks with corrugated zinc roofs. Many people were sitting outside or walking by the roadside carrying bundles of something or other. The landscape looked like it had been squeezed from the sides; the trees seemed impossibly tall and the terrain dipped and rose like a blanket shaken at one end. It was hard to focus in the fierce light and the verdant climbs up to the mountains inland were almost bleached white by the sun.

The driver looked at me disapprovingly and asked me what I was doing. I explained that I had originally intended to go to Kingston first, have a look at some of the local football clubs and maybe meet Alan 'Skill' Cole – the mythical star of Jamaican football in the 1970s. After that I would have hired a car and driven cross-country to Braco. 'And you alone?' the driver barked, sucking his teeth with the sort of disdain you would normally reserve for scolding a child. 'You get shot man, I tell you that for sure. Ain't you heard?' he asked, 'Jamaica is a dangerous place.'

As if to prove the point, he then weaved around a cavernous pothole, took the racing line into a blind corner and got back behind the next car just in time to avoid us both being sprayed across the grill of an onrushing truck.

An hour later and several stone lighter, a bored-looking sentry ushered us through the gates and up a long drive that dissected the Braco Village golf course. There was a bumpy-looking football pitch to our right. Though this would be about the only facility the players used over the next few days, Braco was meant to provide the players with an oasis of luxurious seclusion – a treat after the monastic life of team camp in Kingston. A top-quality holiday resort was also the management's way of building spirits ahead of a potentially daunting trip to Iran.

It was not cheap so I decided to stay in Falmouth at the nearest hotel, a good inch away on the map. I'm sure the Fisherman's Inn is a very nice place but it was under renovation when I visited. After being told that the bar, restaurant and swimming pool were all under repair, I was shown to my room in an eerie silence. The beach was also off the menu as the boat that took guests round to the other side of the headland was not in operation. There was nothing for miles around, making it the Jamaican equivalent of a travel tavern. In the end, it was kind of the owner to admit that, yes, I was also the only guest in residence and, no, the cigarette machine did not work either. I checked in and out and returned to Braco with the taxi-driving prophet of doom.

Ten minutes later, I was driven to my ground floor suite in an electric buggy and managed to get my bags through the door, unpack and admire the 'tropical shower of petals' on my pillow as Ian Goodison, Ricardo Gardener and Gregory Messam emerged from the room opposite. 'Hello,' I offered brightly.

They did not seem overly impressed.

In the brochure for Grand Lido Braco – to give it its proper name – the 'island's finest craftsmen' are described as having 'recreated a genuine seaside village on Jamaica's north coast'. First impressions were that the Jamaican national team was trapped in a tropical version of *Prisoner*, complete with town square, cafes, shops and grand plantation-style houses in white timber. The only thing that was missing was the men in brown coats shifting the scenery.

It is the sort of place where honeymooning couples spend an idyllic fortnight. True, the sky is always electric blue, the palms are green and, just a short stroll from the hub of this artificial little community, there's 2,000 feet of white sand – but the only locals around are those paid to provide a bit of 'native culture' by serving drinks, preparing food or mowing the greens on the golf course.

It was very quiet and when they were not training, the players were holed up in their rooms. But while it was a slower pace than Kingston, the coach did not let up on his strict routine. The players were to be up for breakfast at eight and on the training pitch by nine for two hours' practice, followed by lunch, sleep and more practice in the late afternoon when the sun had lost some of its strength. Most evenings would be spent at functions.

It was my first day at Braco and Peter Cargill sat alone inside the Italian-themed pizzeria off the main square. I had spoken to him after the morning training session and he waved me over with a smile that broke out from beneath his permanently furrowed brow. He looked tired and admitted that it was hard being away from his wife and two young kids for ten months of the year. The routine was starting to take its toll.

Cargill had made his debut for Jamaica in 1984 but spent seven years in Israel after going on holiday and being persuaded by a Jamaican friend to try his luck on the outskirts of Tel Aviv. 'I went over for a one-month trial and I liked it. In Israel, the footballers are gods.' Fame had then come round a second time after the same friend urged him to go back to Jamaica and join the new programme. 'There is no point having fame if you have no house or car at the end of ten years' playing football,' Cargill said seriously. 'There are two sides to being professional – it is being paid for what you do and being responsible. You have to be responsible because it keeps the money coming in.'

In Britain, Cargill had showed himself to be the type of player other footballers appreciate. Watching him at work, gliding round in the space in front of Dixon, Brown and Goodison, it was clear that this was the band leader. He had the archetypal build of a stocky, midfield general but was beautifully lithe about his business. He conducted the youngsters and his ability to make himself available for any pass and to redistribute it with a quiet, authoritative efficiency was crucial in a team that lacked both experience and understanding of the tactical nuances at the highest levels of the game. It was an important job for a responsible person and Cargill's only concessions to 'flash' were his lime-green boots.

'Sure it's an important job,' said Cargill, looking grave, 'but I have always played like that – in midfield or as a sweeper, so I know what I have to do.' He seemed surprised that I had even mentioned it. 'Ever since I was a young boy, all I wanted to be was a professional footballer. I love football,' he explained plaintively. 'I've never played any other sport. I've never tried any other sport.'

A commotion outside heralded the arrival of Simoes. The coach had arrived a day later and looked preoccupied as he strutted past the fountain and flowerbeds towards the bar. Peter finished up his pasta and said goodbye, so I loitered outside the bar as Simoes treated the film crew to some more of his thoughts. An English newly-wed, who had been in the piano bar the previous evening, motioned at Simoes and whispered: 'They're rubbish this lot, aren't they? No better than a pub team, I heard.'

When he had finished talking to camera, Rene Simoes put his mobile phone on the table and said hello to a passing guest. 'You been talking to Cargill, eh?' he said, still looking over his shoulder at who was sitting round the pool. 'He is the grandfather of the team.' It was a theme that Simoes had touched on in Cardiff. Paul Hall was the team DJ, the man who would rap on the bus for the amusement of his team mates; Dean Sewell was the joker, a character known as 'Two Face' because one minute he would be serious and the next he would be up to mischief; Spider was the vibemaster and controlled the level of excitement, lifting the players when their heads dropped. The coach had studied the group, and worked out its dynamics and was now helping the players to cement their own identities within it.

'In this team there is a captain, a commander and a sheriff,' said the professor, spreading his palms. 'The captain is that guy who knows how to be involved in politics. He must be a politician to express the desire of the players. He must have the confidence of the players and good relations with them. That is Barrett.

'The commander is the guy that everything moves around. Cargill is the commander. Sometimes he plays so bad that the others play very well as a service to him. If the commander is not there, the other players who move round him will be dead.

'The sheriff is that guy whose voice you can hear very strongly when things do not go well. He is there to put his finger in the face of an opponent. Sometimes it is the right time and sometimes it is the wrong time, but he is the guy who makes a decision. If you need to fight, he will fight. I think so far, Goodison is my sheriff, he has the capacity for this leadership. I think also Fitzroy has this capacity. Leadership is something you are born with. You cannot teach leadership. You are born with that, you are not born to be under anyone else's control. But,' warned Simoes, 'if you don't drive the sheriff then he will start to fight for everything and he will get the red card. You must be smart.'

Simoes was a busy man. The Reggae Boyz were off to Iran the following week for a four-team tournament, followed by trips to France for a game against Saudi Arabia, England, to play Manchester City, back to Jamaica for 'Reggae Boyz Week' and a match with Santos of Brazil, on to South Korea and then to New York. The JFF had revealed that 'more money was needed to maintain the programmes put in place', prompting the government to donate JA \$10 million to help cover expenses. Part of the funding had gone on bringing a team of nutritionists in from Brazil to continue testing the players at Braco and a lot of it would go on flying Jamaica's jumbo touring party round the world. It was little wonder that Simoes' feet were fidgeting under the table.

'We try to improve many things,' he said. 'One thing we are doing is moving round the world so the players get contact and experience of different countries, football culture and how the medias operate. In the qualifying games I hide my team from the media. Now I give free access for the media because I want the players to know how to deal with this situation.'

Money was also being spent on sending the coach to spy on his World Cup opponents, to draw up the battle plans for the next psychological war. 'You have to understand the culture of the opponents,' Simoes insisted. 'This is what I have been trying to do. I went to Japan and I spent a week there. I walk in the streets, I sit down in some places and watched as the people returned home from their jobs. I went to a hospital there, I went to a game, I went to a museum so that I could understand as much as possible about Japanese people and their culture. If you know their culture, then you know how the players will react on field. You cannot say, "I express myself different on the field to the way I express myself in my life." What I learn about Japan is that when you look at statistics, you can see the number of students and businessmen who kill themselves. You can see that the Japanese people don't accept failures. What this means is that this is going to be hard time for them with all this pressure. Each time they fail, they will be in trouble.'

I asked whether he worried that some of the younger players would not take the opportunity to display themselves to their full potential in football's shop window. The Reggae Boyz were a tight-knit, almost impregnable, group from which only a few seemed willing to talk as individuals. Three sparkling performances at the World Cup would be the ideal way to generate that dream move abroad – and the money, prestige and trappings that would come with it – but while they were complete unknowns, gaining some exposure would help matters. Despite being placed in a room in the same part of the resort as the team and them knowing my face from the British tour, I could never even establish eye contact with the younger players. The likes of Durrent Brown, Linval Dixon, Warren Barrett and Andy Williams at least offered the odd 'Irie' but came no further out of their shells. It was a very private group.

'So far, we have stopped in 23 different countries around the world,' argued Simoes. 'Now they know how to exist in different situations. Like a house, you have to know how to build a player, a human being. A human being is a triangle and each point is different. One of the points is physical, another is psychological and the final point is spiritual. If you work on only one aspect the others will be weak and the house will fall down. We give the same importance to all three points and hopefully the players now feel very strong.'

All coaches are supposed to impart their knowledge but from what I had seen in Cardiff, the Brazilian assumed the role of an inspirational tutor cajoling problem students into taking masters degrees. He agreed that the huge psychological progress made by the Jamaican players had probably been the greatest achievement of his time in charge. 'Every time [a player] does something right I praise him. In the spiritual aspect, we make them believe that God has a plan for all of us. If you are given a talent you must use it in all capacities. The analogy I use is that if you have a son and you give it a toy, he might only play with that toy for five weeks. After that he won't want to play with it. It is not nice when you spend money and give the child a gift and he does not use. How does that make you feel as a father?

'[Jamaican fans and players] thought before that football is eleven players on the pitch who play the game, the fans shout at the players and the players must show how much they love the country. That is the background. I think now they show a completely different approach.'

Many people believe that Brazilian footballers have a genetic advantage, that their skills are a national trait. This ignores the fact that Brazilian football is among the most scientific in the world – the clubs are enormous, with in-house sports science facilities, coaching is intensive and the best players are snapped up young. Hard work has long been the equal partner to natural ability.

'Everything we do comes from Brazil,' Simoes explained. 'When I arrive there was no culture of coaching in Jamaica. I keep saying that and they go mad with me. You cannot say you are a journalist if you don't work 24 hours a day as a journalist. I think a football coach must be the coach, always. You coach the team and you take the risks. In Jamaica they are all part-time coach. They have their job which gives them money to live and then they have their hobby, which is to be a coach.'

The rhythmic warm-up routine was a popular pre-match, pre-training ritual, giving the players a chance to express themselves while going through the motions of mundane stretching. I asked Simoes to expand on the samba-reggae philosophy. The little steps, hand claps and rotations were essential preventative exercises yet the Brazilian seemed to make them fun. 'Everything in football is a rhythm and football is not a sport with only one note. When you play the piano you do not always hit one note, you make music, make melodies. You have alternatives and that is what makes music. Football is the same, you cannot always play in the same way.

'I didn't have any book I read so far – and I like to read books – that tells me that we have to work in a bad mood, tense and show that we are upset. My conception is that I like my players to enjoy every time; enjoy the training session, enjoy the game, express themselves as much as possible.

'In England, Fitzroy Simpson said something amazing,' he

continued. 'He said that the way you play with Jamaica is "freedom with discipline". I think it is important that you put freedom with discipline to give the idea of what is Jamaica. My view is that with freedom you don't need discipline. Freedom mean freedom. If you don't have respect for another person, that is not freedom. That is anarchy.

'It was good what Fitzroy say because it say that my team has a script. It is like going to the theatre. There are actors there but there is also a script. But at any time the actor can still be himself – he can show his qualities and express himself. That is what I ask my players always. The script is there but you have freedom to do what you want but not break the harmony of the team.'

His squad was like a collection of homes, he explained, and added, 'I cannot decide to listen to music at four o'clock in the morning very loud. This is not freedom, it is responsibility.' He said that he had only twice been allowed to listen to samba on the team bus. He chuckled and after checking his watch for the third time in as many minutes, made his excuses and got up to leave. I presented him with the book on Shankly but he had never heard of the legendary Liverpool boss.

That evening, I sat beside the training pitch with some of the hotel staff and spectators to watch the Reggae Boyz go through their paces. As Alfredo had them lapping the field to warm up, Simoes pecked at the pitch with a shoe, digging out stones and tossing them absent-mindedly to the touchline. He looked like a man lost in his own thoughts.

A short man with a pair of baggy shellsuit bottoms emptied some footballs from a net bag and rolled them towards the solitary figure in the centre circle. Simoes trapped the first ball to reach him, flicked it up in the air, bounced it three times on his head and brought it to a standstill on the instep of his left foot. A collective sigh was emitted from the touchline. 'Champs', the kit man, had seen it all before and continued laying plastic cones out for the first drill.

Further up the touchline, Denise Nicholls, the team's travelling physiotherapist, took some strapping out of a cold container. Having run her own sports medicine clinic in Kingston she now worked with the Reggae Boyz full-time and was waiting on clearance from Iranian authorities to travel with the rest of the team.

The Captain had initially been told that she would not be allowed to accompany the team to the Middle East but after threatening to withdraw altogether, secured entry for her on the condition that she kept herself well covered at all times. Life had been very different for both Denise and 'Champs' since being swept up by the Reggae Boyz.

Simoes called the players together and as the film crew circled, making sure that the levels on the coach's radio mike were set correctly, conveyed his point by jabbing his finger and punching his fist into his palm. Despite the obvious drawbacks of looking archetypically English, Mike and Dave – camera and sound men respectively – found it easy to blend into the background.

They had no interest in football and had come to the job fresh off working on *Children's Hospital* and *Pleasure Beach*. They were an amusing double act who brought a refreshing insouciance to the assignment. Dave was a small, dry Yorkshireman and Mike had an ale fancier's beard, white legs and wore a hat more associated in these parts with long days chasing cover drives to the boundary.

'Read the game, read the game,' urged Simoes, as he led an exercise that saw two defenders pitted against six attackers. The pitch at Braco had a generous covering of grass but that was where the comparison with Bisham Abbey or the French Football Academy in Clairefountain ended. It was bumpy and visibly undulated, the uneven bounce keeping Champs busy rescuing wayward shots and sliced crosses from the golf course. 'Attack the ball!' barked Simoes. Gardener's touch was wonderful and Whitmore looked alive and interested for a change. The first cross in six on target was met with a header that rippled the net behind Spider's goal. 'Amokachi!' boomed the chorus of approval.

It was amost pitch black by the time Simoes sent them off to shower. They had ten minutes before meeting back at reception in shirts and ties for yet another function.

I spent the evening trying to track down Captain Burrell. Four mobile phone suggestions and a number for his private office failed to throw up any new leads.

The players had the morning off and while some chatted to the the girls that worked at the resort, others lounged by the pool. A female compere was trying to whip up enthusiasm for a game of aquatic 'It's A Knockout' but there were no takers. It was just too hot. Inside, Theodore Whitmore sat slumped at the bar, wearing black shorts and a black Kappa T-shirt. An interesting footballer, he was known as 'Tappa' presumably for the tap-tap-tap of his dribbling style. And while he was very different to anything that I had seen in Europe and undoubtedly skilful, he did not look like a primed athlete with his shorts slung low over his hips and one sock up and the other rolled down. His long, spindly legs only served to make his feet look larger than they were. He was always good to watch, though. I chanced my arm and asked him what he thought of the game in Cardiff. He could not have looked more baffled had I addressed him in Welsh.

Warren Barrett rounded the corner and approached with a bashful smile. The captain of the team liked a lie-in and rolling up only 25 minutes late was quite respectable in the circumstances. 'Boopie' is something of a national icon. There are the wise men in the squad, like Cargill and Durrent Brown, the young bucks like Messam, Gardener and Goodison, the bad boys like Boyd and Lowe, the reformed characters like Malcolm, the good guys like Rudi and then there is Boopie. Extremely clean cut, he is the embodiment of the team's work ethic and a dignified leader. One description of him stuck in my mind for its additional – some might say, unnecessary – detail; it said he was a family man who 'lived with his wife and two young children'. Like Cargill, he missed them and conceded that being a Reggae Boy had become more than just playing football.

'Well, yes, we have activities outside of football where we attend functions, visit Golden Age homes, go to visit homeless kids or orphanages, so we do a lot of activities outside of the actual football,' Barrett told me in a warm, melodic voice. 'At times you don't mind doing that but there are other times when you are tired and you still have some things to do. But we know that most of the sponsors that have come aboard will want to stage some functions to really highlight their product or contribution to the team. In that case, it's not that we have a choice to go.'

Indeed, management were very conscious that the team was seen to be giving something back. 'Yes, that's right, we are. It's very important that we don't forget the people because they are the ones who have helped to put us in the position that we are in. We are careful that we try to give back to them as much as possible.

'I guess the way this country is is very different from most of the established football countries in Europe. But here we are in the public's eye almost every day. Maybe it's the type of people we are and our approach to the game. Most people, especially in the rural areas, have only seen the national players on television so when we are in their part of the country they come out in their thousands to meet and greet and talk to us. The pressure from the public is more dominant now since we qualified. Wherever you go you are noticed and you hardly have time for yourself. Whenever you hit the streets, everyone notices you or comes across to say a good word or get an autograph. I don't mind that much.' He too looked tired.

Barrett was working in the Holiday Inn in Montego Bay when Brazilian captain Dunga hoisted the World Cup in 1994. I reminded him that in a couple of months he would be one of only 32 people in the world with the chance to emulate Dunga. The beam that made Jamaican grannies go weak at the knees broke out all over his face. He shook his head and took a sharp intake of breath through pursed lips. 'It's an incredible feeling. I'm just glad that God gave me the opportunity to represent my country and to lead them into the World Cup.'

I had spoken to all the Jamaicans I could find at Braco about the long days and nights of partying that followed the home draw against Mexico in November. Most whistled wistfully at the memories. Barrett was one of the people responsible for the biggest 'bashment' the island had ever seen and recalled spending an hour on the pitch after the game amid music and champagne, and then signing autographs by the team bus for what seemed like an eternity. 'We climbed into the coach and then we drove around the city waving flags and shirts through the windows. Everybody on the streets was calling to us and it was a great atmosphere.

'Right after we went up to look for Andy Williams because he had a broken collar bone,' Barrett explained. 'We went up to his house and we wanted him to know that we had not forgotten

him, that he was a part of us. He was happy to see us and I could
see it in his eyes that he was kinda surprised. We just wanted him
to know that we love and care for him, just like all of our other
team mates. I guess that's the kind of family atmosphere we have
where we look out for each other. In good times and bad times.
When things are going bad we know that the public will criticise
you and want to kill you but who do you turn to then if not your
family?'

That lunchtime, a special ceremony at the side of the field –
hosted by representatives from the SuperClub hotel chain –
unveiled Braco's bumpy pitch as 'the official training ground for
Jamaica's national football team'. Simoes and Carl Brown sat
behind a long table while the players, in sponsors' T-shirts, took
up the block of seating opposite the invited guests. Simoes said
Jamaica was a 'wonderful country' and went on to talk about the
lowliest waiter being as important as the boss of the complex
before sitting down to polite applause. Four younger members of
staff then delighted the assembled guests and local press with
some suggestive bogling before a rapping chef emerged to steal
the show. The biggest cheer, however, was reserved for Champs,
who accepted an award for 'nation-building' on behalf of the JFF.
At the unveiling of a colourful plaque, coach Brown removed his
distinctive Rayban Aviators and sang the national anthem like he
meant it.

As he walked back towards the plantation-style blocks, I
jogged alongside him. He looked more human without the
glasses. Less sinister, I ventured. He laughed. 'I like to do a lot of
observing and I like to see things. I know that people don't like
that when they see you looking at them; they don't like that when
your eyes may follow them. The sunglasses allow me that privilege to look directly at them even when it might appear that I am
looking somewhere else. It's part of my personality. I like to get
into the National Stadium when we have a team visiting, and I
stay under those dark glasses so no one will recognise me.'

Watching the team train day in, day out, it did appear, as has
been suggested, that Brown was marginalised by Simoes. He was
always first out, wearing a black zip-up training top and stretching out the muscles that had served him in hundreds of games,
but during the sessions his input was restricted largely to encour-

agement. However, he was too proud and had too much integrity to talk about his reported difficulties with Simoes.

'I still want to do the things that I started doing when I first got into football,' he said, side-stepping the indirect reference to his diminished coaching responsibilities. 'My main objective is to stop these youngsters from losing their way, slipping up, losing their focus. I will have to pull them back in if they do that. I always want to be there for them. I always want to be there to give them one reason to go on. I know it can get tough; I know about the pressure of the whole expectancy from the public and from the world. This is a role I have always wanted to play; it is the reason I have been in football all these years, that I have remained in it. I don't believe that will ever change. My whole coaching role has somewhat been altered because of the presence of coach Simoes but I believe that my real role here will never change, and that is to motivate these youngsters.'

From Trenchtown, Brown shared a similar background to 90 per cent of the Jamaican-born members of the squad, and is born again. 'I got saved,' he explained. 'It helps me stay humble, helps keep me real.' He certainly seemed contented, even if Simoes was making him swallow his pride on a daily basis, and did not mind confessing that he half hoped that he might still get the nod to play in France: 'I always keep myself fit just in case and because I love to play still with the guys.' Living an opportunity he never had through the Reggae Boyz, Brown was looking forward to the World Cup perhaps more than anyone.

Lamenting the lack of proper training facilities, Brown reminisced about the cream of his generation who, he argued, could have shown the present team a thing or two. 'This current crop of players we have now could easily fall outside the top twenty of all-time Jamaican teams,' he stated. 'In terms of sheer talent they would fall at the bottom of the twenty. The talent in the past was amazing to see. This is no form of exaggeration but we have really produced some incredibly talented players. We just didn't get any opportunity to express it.

'When you get a group of thirty to forty youngsters out there,' he went on, pointing to the hills outside Braco, 'no one wants to score a goal. They want to do some sort of magic. This is what our crowd grew up to understand. We grew up to love the Peles, the

Garrinchas, the George Bests. You might have heard the conflicts about Walter Boyd but this is what he can do and this is what the people have missed. This is what the people want and he is very, very skilful. You see Theodore Whitmore and he is smooth; Ricardo is too and this is the sort of thing Jamaicans have been brought up to appreciate.' It was interesting to hear Brown talk about Boyd unprompted. I could not imagine John Gorman arguing publically that Glenn Hoddle should have picked Paul Gascoigne.

Alfredo Montessa had been working with the nutritionist all morning. The shock of discovering that so many players had worms had focused his mind and he now had to effect major physical improvements in a short space of time. Younger and fairer than Simoes, it had taken some bottle to pack up his job back home and take a chance on the strength of the affinity he felt with the coach. The two were now close and when he spoke, it became clear that he had attended the professor's School of English.

'When I came here I had to adjust myself because the culture in Jamaica is a little bit different to what it is in Brazil,' Fredo told me. 'In Brazil, they fight for their right, for their place. Every time they are in competition. If a big player for Corinthians in Sao Paulo give his place to a guy in the Under 20 side, he will have lost his place because you have many, many good players there. In Jamaica they don't have the habit to fight for the right to play because there are not so many good players as there are in Brazil.' He stopped and considered for a second. 'They have other things to fight about.'

If Simoes had any difficulties settling into his new environment, he at least had his authority to fall back on. The coach could command respect whereas Fredo had to go in and work physically with the players. And he was younger than Peter Cargill and Durrent Brown for starters, so could not draw on a wealth of experience to pull him through the initial stage. How difficult had he found it to become accepted?

'I had to fight for respect,' he said, looking very serious. 'We were strangers, foreigners. The first time I came to Jamaica I didn't speak nothing in English so my language was only Portuguese. I had to get their respect and work and train them with and give them some knowledge. I think it is important that we share these things.'

I asked him how he felt when he got the results from the training camp in Brazil. Fredo shrugged his shoulders and tried to look philosophical. 'We adjust our programme to do what we need to reach World Cup in good shape. We now have a special diet with a lot of carbohydrate for energy reserves which we will need in the competition. We want the players to have a fat level of ten to twelve per cent so they have a reserve of fuel in the game. In Brazil we find that the level was only five or seven per cent. This is much less than what we need.'

Fredo was due to attend one of the coach's epic team meetings and as the sun dipped over the horizon and darkness gathered across Braco, the players were locked in the equivalent of the Braco town hall. There they were forced to sit through a video of their match against Wales – a surefire cure for insomnia – before being canvassed about whether Onandi Lowe deserved to be sent off.

A bit of a loner, Lowe is a giant with a small face permanently screwed up in anxiety. One of the hotel's waiters, who claimed to know him, explained that Onandi had always been a large boy, growing up to be 'extroverted'. He came from the ghetto community of Rockfort, a dusty township set in the shadow of an ugly cement works, where people 'throw their weight around'. He had learnt how to look after himself at a young age probably because he and his brother, who also played for Harbour View, were driven hard by their 'strong-willed' father. By the time Onandi was a teenager, 'him a tek bak no chat'.

Simoes had thrown Onandi off the programme after the débâcle in Mexico but the touchline experts at Braco felt that he had been treated very harshly, arguing that the administration had needed a scapegoat for the whole fiasco. Onandi had not walked off, they said – he had been substituted. Jamaican fans loved a conspiracy: mere mention of the name Walter Boyd was enough to start a full-scale row. Lowe's supporters had even blocked the road during their man's enforced exile, trying to head off the team bus as it took the players on another foreign tour.

There were others, however, who felt Lowe should have been

banned for life – he should never be forgiven for deserting his team mates. However, they supported the coach's decision to make him seek psychiatric help before allowing him back into the squad. It could be argued that Simoes was 'playing God' but the widespread feeling was that Lowe's natural aggression, and his habit of saying whatever he wanted, could not be allowed on the pitch. In this new age of discipline – a quality that Walter Boyd's critics harped on about – red cards could not be tolerated.

They explained that after the first game against Mexico in the qualifying rounds, Lowe got an offer to play in Mexico. He went out there, didn't like it and was back within two or three weeks. Simoes wanted to tone Onandi down but the assorted experts argued that his game had suffered as a result. Against Wales, Simoes got the old Onandi Lowe. Unleashed from the bench, the striker responded to his shirt being tugged by ramming his elbow into the face of an opponent. He took a good minute to leave the pitch and was reportedly in tears when he got to the dressing room. He had not meant to hit the guy, he claimed, and after the group watched the rerun during the team meeting, Simoes asked the other players to decide.

In a typical show of solidarity, Lowe was backed by all his team mates, who said he was innocent and did not deserve a red card. Simoes said he was disappointed by their decision and stripped Lowe of his match fee. The players had to learn that there could be no justification for lashing out like that.

The film crew bundled out of the town hall, smiling conspiratorially at all the quality footage now safely in the can. They were desperate to tie down a filmed interview with the reluctant, troubled Lowe and explained that Fitzroy Simpson and Linval Dixon were the main characters from the team but they wanted back-up, just in case either of them got injured. Rene and The Captain both had starring roles and now it seemed Onandi was being lined up for a cameo part.

The players were also happy, exhibiting signs of demob fever as they spilled out of 'class'. They were to be given the Easter weekend off and after days of hard work at Braco, they were pleased to be able to relax for a while. Mobile phones came out; Spider sang at hotel guests as they passed. Andy Williams, an interesting character, stood to one side, out of the light of the lanterns that swung in the wind to give that 'genuine seaside village' effect. 'I'm too tired,' he had said to me one day when I asked for five minutes of his time. Stretching the fatigue out of his shoulders he had continued, 'Too much practice, too much training.'

The son of a former Jamaican international, Williams was one of few players in the squad from a middle-class background. He was born in Canada and grew up in leafy New England before moving to Jamaica and attending school. In 1994, he enrolled at Rhode Island University in the States and became the highest goalscorer in the college's history, twice coming close to making the All-American soccer team. Williams had played island football for Real Mona and attracted the attention of clubs in the States but had promised his mother he would finish college. Although the standard of the collegiate game was far higher than club football in Jamaica, his decision to finish college upset Simoes. The coach wanted him in the programme full-time.

When Thoedore Whitmore broke his nose in the Gold Cup, however, Williams was handed his chance to shine. He took it and signed himself over to Sunil Galati, deputy commissioner of the MLS in America. Galati brokered a deal with Columbus Crew and Andy had booked his ticket back to the States after the World Cup.

He was a boy with a bright future, different in some ways to many of his colleagues. The way his feet moved was far less unorthodox and he struck the ball cleanly. In a country where lighter skin tones usually signify better living standards, 'Bomber' is not as dark as many of his team mates. The contrasts are purely academic, however, because he loved being with the other Reggae Boyz, drowning the twang of American vowel sounds in his native patois and rediscovering the Jamaican pace of life. He was also suddenly a big fish in a small pond and got his fair share of female attention.

Andy rolled his eyes. 'You can't go out on the streets like you did before. Your profile . . .' He rolled his eyes again. 'They just recognise you easy. People are like, "Andy, what's up, man?" or "Andy this, Andy that" – and they're like people I don't even know. Just random people.' Random seemed like a preppy word to use. 'Sometimes it's annoying but, y'know...' He had experienced a little local fame by playing high school football on the island but nothing like being mobbed in the streets. He was a star but still sometimes liked to get away from it all by going back to Rhode Island to see his college pals. Besides, he couldn't get too carried away with the adulation: he had promised his mother that once the little matter of the World Cup was done and dusted, he would go back to finish his studies.

'They two different worlds but, y'know, I'm used to it. I'm quite happy but I'd be happier if I was making a lot more money.' His mobile phone went off and he slipped out of east coast Stateside straight back into Jamaican.

'Irie, irie. Hold on a bit; call you back in ONE minute.'

Our conversation continued for about half an hour but, listening back to the tape, he said very little. He revealed that he only knew about five of the players before joining the squad in 1996 and that playing with the English-based players had taught him about 'giving heart and soul and getting paid'. I sensed that he was not comfortable being seen talking to a reporter in front of his friends.

Did he think the Reggae Boyz should be paid more?

'Mmm, yeah, personally I think so. But it's better than it was.'

Cargill, however, seemed a lot more relaxed. 'I just feel mellow, you know. Sometimes I'm in a happier state of mind but today I'm cool, y'know. I'm low key and just keeping it cool.' We were both being bitten alive and Peter wanted to get off to the party going on on the beach. Did the other players realise how Jamaica have captured the imagination of the footballing world? I asked. Peter paused and then laughed. 'It's nice, real nice.'

The next morning, I watched Rene Simoes give a masterclass in beach foot volley and beat all comers at head tennis in the swimming pool. He was obviously not suffering from the effects of a long night charming the other guests round the piano. He had said that you could become a countryman through what was in your heart and that he now felt very Jamaican, and it showed. He looked comfortable in his environment, safe in the knowledge that he had been taken to the country's heart. I wanted to know whether he believed the country now thought the same about the English-based members of the squad.

'I think there was a very, very good blend between them,' said

Simoes rubbing the sweat off his face with a towel. 'Nobody can
convince me that Paul Hall, Fitzroy and Deon are not Jamaicans.
I can tell you that these guys are really pure Jamaicans. They came
over for trials, a week of trials, so they said, "We are Jamaicans,
we want to play." It really is a good blend between the Jamaicans
and the players from England. I had doubts because I don't know
if they are Jamaicans who are born in England or English who
had Jamaican blood. I didn't know what they are.'

The nation was still on a high after the draw against Brazil and,
after qualification, the result in Miami had represented the next
major step forward. What had that match taught him about the
spirit of his players? 'I think that this team has a mission,' said
Simoes. 'If you remember the war between Iraq and Iran in the
1980s. Iraq has much better weapons, they are better equipped.
But you know what happened when they started the war? The
Ayatollah made that war a mission for the people of Iran. I was in
the United Arab Emirates and I saw some of life of Iran people. It
was unbelievable. There is mines in the fields. There are people
who walk into the mines so that the soldiers can come behind.
Iraq could not win the war because they had the machines but
Iran had the people. Missions make people different.'

While Simoes prepared to make the transition from Trelawny
to Tehran, I was bound for Kingston to continue the vain quest for
The Captain, kick a football around and sample the faster pace of
the capital. Devon Chin, a photographer who had introduced
himself at Braco, offered to show me the sights. He had followed
the team for years and knew many of the players.

Kingston looked dead flat as the film crew's 'Praise Tours'
minibus clattered into the city. It was dusty, in an advanced state
of disrepair and only two modest tower blocks in the centre interrupted the skyline. The Wyndham and The Pegasus were the
highest buildings in town and tourists were advised to stay at
either one or the other. Located side by side in the relatively affluent district of New Kingston, both had been designed to face
away from the ghettos near the port to the south. From the
windows, guests were afforded a view that took in the expensive
houses in Beverly Hills – where The Captain and Simoes had
their homes – and the National Stadium to the right. I had seen

confined areas of zinc-topped 'housing' crammed between buildings on the way into Kingston but even from the eighth floor of
The Pegasus, they played no part in the wide sweep of the
tourist's vista.

Captain Burrell could not be traced so alternative arrangements had to be made. The name of a football writer in *The
Gleaner* had grabbed my attention and a few enquiries later, it
emerged that Audley Boyd was indeed the brother of the great
Walter. I contacted him at work and he told me that he would be
playing football with his work mates at the RJR Sports Club on
Thursday evening. I invited myself down for a game.

Devon pulled his car out of a long queue of cars with dark
windows and wonky bumpers and navigated a rough path up
the side of a modest, one-storey building off the main avenue.
The RJR Sports Club did not boast a swimming pool or gymnasium – it did not even boast a football pitch, for that matter.
Instead, behind the long bar room that served as a club house,
there was a patch of rough ground about the size of a tennis court.
It was enclosed by mesh fencing on one side, a wooden house
painted blue on the other and bushes at each end. It sloped uphill
away from the club house and thick undergrowth marked the
touchlines.

Audley arrived wearing a red and black striped Arnett
Gardens strip, and the family resemblance was immediately
evident. He had played National League football for Arnett
Gardens, based in the PNP-run garrison, up until a couple of
years ago and it was the team that his exiled brother now turned
out for. After joining the other eight guys kicking the ball about,
Audley invited his sheepish-looking guest over.

Jamaican kickabouts, or 'scrimmages', are best enjoyed with
shinpads. It was a game of clattering legs and few goals although
on either side there were players who had the touch to tame a
fearsome bounce. Carl Brown's words circled my head as I was
sent lunging into the vines for the umpteenth time by a middle-
aged opponent with snakelike hips. These boys could play and
what was also interesting was that the game was set up to make
do with limited space. Small goals and rough ground made for
deft passing and close control. They did not encourage high balls,

long kicks or 25-yard pile-drivers. I tried them all the same –
English style.

We lost 3–1 but afterwards, like Robbie, I felt a sense of relief.
In the time it took to work up a sweat and graze both knees, we
went from not saying much to sharing beers and chatting about
everything. Football had broken the ice. During the evening, I
joined the Jamaican equivalent of going down the pub to talk
about football with mates. We talked about Walter, the state of
Jamaican club football and about the JFF. It became clear that
Audley was one of the professor's critics although it should be
said that his opposition was not purely driven by family ties. I
asked him whether he thought Captain Burrell had political
ambitions.

'He has a close alliance with P.J. Patterson because P.J. has been
supporting the programme in a major way, not only in terms of
cash,' said a wry-smiling Audley: 'They help to get practice
matches with other countries. The match against Zambia in 1995
was a straight-on government thing ... I don't think Burrell
would want to jeopardise that kind of assistance from the government.' He also confirmed that people in Jamaica had started to
question where the money was going. 'Every time they want
more money,' he said. 'When they play in Kingston the stadium
is full and when they play away they take eighteen players and
something like sixteen officials. Now they shouldn't be complaining about the money.'

A Friday night out in Kingston was called for before my return
to London. Devon took me to an open-air reggae sound splash. I
was introduced to his friends, among them reggae critics who
had come down to judge the show. Reading write-ups on concerts
and bashments in the papers, they were described in a similar
way to football matches in British newspapers. After the eye-
popping spectacle of a five-way bogling contest, Beenie Man
made a surprise appearance. The current king of the dancehall
went down well but ultimately could not match the girl who had
spent five minutes back-thrusting a wooden pole while doing a
handstand. Despite the sea of appreciative pistol gestures from
the audience, Beenie was susbstituted before the end. Devon, a
man who seemed to know everyone, tried to say hello to Beenie
but was lucky not to be trampled to death by the stampede of

security guards rushing him from the 'area'. In Jamaica, the exits are more important than the entrances.

At the island's main nightclub, the giant sweatbox known as The Asylum, Devon managed to avoid the queue by ducking under the ropes and ushering me up the steps. Mine was the only white face on view and no matter how nonchalant I attempted to look, it was impossible not to stand out. As my chaperone limboed between the bodies on a guided tour round the perimeter of the enormous, seething dancefloor, those standing at the edge did double takes when they saw who was with him. Audley had talked about how close the contact still was between the players and the public and about how Walter liked to go out to a club or have some food in town. This was a rare break for the players still in the programme and on my second and final lap of the club, I bumped into Peter Cargill. The look of surprise on his face when he saw me was worth the plane fare alone.

Twenty-fours hours later I was back in England. There had been no takers for *Dalglish* but, on the bright side, I hadn't been shot either.

9

Counting Down to France

DANIEL

There was just over a month before Jamaica's first game in the World Cup finals when Captain Burrell swept through the doors of a small conference room in the bowels of the London Piccadilly Meridien and gave a flamboyant welcome to the smattering of reporters. He was in town to bang the drum about the forthcoming friendly against freshly relegated Manchester City at Maine Road.

'I will be looking forward to seeing a very ... large ... turnout,' he warned. 'Why Manchester City? We have already played a game in London and we think the people in the northern United Kingdom should be given the opportunity to see their favourite players. I understand there is a large Jamaican and West Indian community in that area. We will be hoping to see the stadium packed to capacity.'

Flanked by Horace Reid and Carl Brown (in shades), The Captain was also in London to tie up a few loose ends – and satiate his lust for shopping.

The assembled media did not seem to have much to talk about. There had been some interest in Denise Nicholls becoming the first woman to set foot on a football pitch in Iran but a disappointing two-game jaunt to the Middle East was neatly side-stepped. The Reggae Boyz had not enjoyed themselves, producing a couple of half-interested displays. At the team's first hotel in Iran, Captain Burrell moved the party out *en bloc* after being told by the management that they were prevented by law from switching the air conditioning on. Had Iran not heard? The Reggae Boyz were preparing to go to the World Cup.

Simoes was furious at the performance in an opening defeat to Macedonia, who were late replacements for Ghana. To add to the humiliation, the lowly stand-ins had taken the pitch after a last-minute flight and three hours' sleep. QPR's Danny Maddix made his debut and Paul Hall, Fitzroy Simpson, Darryl Powell and Marcus Gayle were all thrown on, having arrived after the main party, but could do little to repair the damage done in a totally lacklustre first half. Jamaica lost 2–1 and then went down again in the third and fourth place play-off to Iran. The draw with Brazil seemed a long time ago.

I put my hand up. Burrell whispered to Horace Reid, who then asked me to declare which 'media house' I worked for.

'Is Jamaica's qualification the biggest thing since independence?' I asked.

'Well, definitely,' boomed The Captain. 'I don't think there can be any question at all about this phenomenon. It has impacted on Jamaica's people in a tremendous way – positively that is. This has to be regarded as the single most important factor in life in general in Jamaica in recent times. You only have to go to Jamaica to a game and anyone who has witnessed such an event will tell you that before, during and after the football game they have never experienced anything like it. This has to be one of the biggest events to have happened in the history of our country.'

Burrell harked back to how his Jamaican Davids had tamed the Goliath of Brazil in Miami. 'It tells me that football is a very democratic sport,' he professed solemnly, 'and if you go there mentally prepared, you can do well.' The Captain looked around the room and puffed out his chest. 'Jamaica,' he said, had the potential to 'shake up the world'. The phrase was Ali's although The Captain was more like George Foreman.

There was an uncomfortable silence in the room.

'And, Captain, where do you get the energy to do two such high-powered jobs?'

'Where do I get the energy to combine two jobs?' A chuckle rumbled deep in his throat. 'I find it very difficult to keep quiet, so to speak. I like challenges and I saw Jamaica's qualification for the World Cup finals in France as probably one of the biggest challenges I've faced in my life. Therefore, the energy comes from the challenge. Indeed –' His face swelled with pride, '– if you go to the most remote village in Jamaica you will find the smallest child coming out to greet Captain Burrell and that in itself is another motivating factor. It shows that you are involved in nation-building and that has to be the hallmark of the development of a country. When that concept of nation-building reaches even the smallest of childs that gives us the purpose to push even harder.'

The man was a politician waiting to happen.

The task of integrating new recruits into the Reggae Boyz' philosophy was proving more difficult than the coach had anticipated. Rene had said that The Captain had 'prescribed a four year medication' and that he had to provide the right dose. The measures of Brazil, Jamaica and England had been perfectly balanced for qualification but the cocktail had been poorly shaken since.

All the ingredients were swilling around at the team hotel on the day of the match in Manchester. Meetings were being conducted in huddles on sofas, papers were juggled in the wake of suited officials and walkways chirped with the bleeping of mobile phones. In one main room, the boys were being fitted up for their World Cup suits and being coaxed into posing for the photographer. A showbiz reporter from one of the tabloids was happy just to sit and drool as harassed stylists and PR people ushered a succession of fit young men in and out of sponsors' clothing. An already expensively attired Frank Sinclair lounged back on a red couch trying to look calm. Darryl Powell could not contain himself and burst through the double doors, shaking his head. 'We've got a game in three hours,' he said, wincing. 'This is madness.'

All it took was a word from on high, however, and the madness would be brought to a halt. Rene announced that the players had to eat and sleep and would not be available for any more 'medias'. Then he stalked off to the area of the dining room cordoned off for the visiting Jamaicans and helped himself to a plate of food prepared by the team's travelling chef.

Since qualification, the coach had maintained that Jamaica were going to the World Cup to play seven games and win.

Although the odds were listed at 250-1, Simoes insisted that while there was one hope, that is what Jamaica would reach for. It was a dogmatic approach but Rene had stuck rigidly to it as he toured the world acquiring a cult status and list of famous doppelgängers – Super Mario and Inspector Clouseau being just two. He had revelled in being the coach of the world's unlikeliest underdogs and all comers underestimated his side at their peril.

In Manchester, though, he admitted that playing mind games on opponents might be more difficult at the World Cup. There would be no switching the kick-off to midday or blocking the coach in at France '98 and Simoes was suddenly facing the bald facts of his team's deficiencies. With time running out, they was now only so much he could do.

'If Argentina play a hundred per cent of what they can play and Jamaica play a hundred per cent of what they can play, we will lose the game,' stated the coach. 'The same for Croatia and for Japan, or maybe we get a draw.' It was the first time he had publicly acknowledged the prospect of defeat. Iran had clearly given him a dose of bitter reality. It had been reported that he had exploded in the dressing room at half-time during the Macedonia game and I now wanted to know whether he thought the players had grasped the significance and magnitude of what they were about to face.

'Now that we have played games around the world and met the press, the Jamaican players understand how big will be World Cup,' he replied, before warning that the Jamaican public did not. It was a theme that he would return to in just over a week.

The players had shown their inexperience in recent games, yet to my knowledge no one had highlighted the fact that the coach did not boast much of an international pedigree himself. I wanted to know what happened to him as a player and how it affected the way he managed. 'I could not make myself wake up because I already knew what I would be doing [at the club]. I hate routine. You must use your imagination. We did not so I started to contest the coach. As a player I didn't have the chance to talk or give my own opinion. Every time I say to my players, "No matter how good I am, no matter how brilliant ideas I have, you have to go out there and put the ideas on the field. If I don't convince you with my ideas then you have to tell me." '

Fitzroy Simpson had wanted him to change things at half-time in Iran but the coach had said no.

'At the end of the game he said that I was right,' Simoes quickly pointed out.

'Sometimes if you are winning the game you go mad and shout and are very angry because when the team is in a good psychological spirit you can do that. Sometimes if the team is losing, you cannot go in there and kick them for they are like orphans, they don't know nothing. They need somebody to tell them what to do. That is when you keep cool and tell them to listen.

'Players respect the chance to make mistakes,' Simoes continued. 'What makes the players sometimes so confident is when they know they can make mistakes. When they know they can make mistakes, they make less mistakes. I don't like it when a player makes a mistake and he start to blame himself. I will go against him if he do that. I say to him, "What do you think? You are Pele?" '

Like all great men, Simoes was a parcel of contradictions.

Pele would be waiting for the party when they returned back to Kingston for Reggae Boyz Week – a calendar of special events culminating in a match against Brazilian club side Santos at the National Stadium. The greatest player in history would return to Jamaica – he played exhibition matches there in the seventies – to lead the delegation from the club that will forever be associated with his name. It promised to be a hectic, moneyspinning week but first there was the dubious delight of a match against doom-struck Manchester City.

Not many people turned out on a filthy night in a deeply depressed corner of Moss Side. City had been relegated the previous weekend and the fine mist of rain that slanted across the beam of the floodlights could have doubled for a cloud of despondency. Jamaica's fans tried to brighten the occasion but the football matched the mood. Simoes picked a largely home-based starting line-up and they did nothing in 90 minutes to trouble a team that was preparing to face the misery of life in Nationwide League Division Two. Another 0–0, on the back of an undistinguished 0–0 draw on the French Riviera against fellow qualifiers Saudi Arabia, made life that bit harder for the Jamaican spin doctors.

At the post-match press conference, Simoes shrugged off his side's inability to find the net in their last three games, preferring instead to use the referee as a smokescreen. 'In England the football is very different,' he argued. 'The referee allows contact and the players are holding each other. It was amazing. At half-time I went for referee and said to referee, "When someone hold the jersey of another player it is a foul." '

Apart from the obvious financial considerations, playing City was meant to give the boys a flavour of the physical confrontation they could expect from Croatia in Lens. Davor Suker would not have been flattered by the comparison.

The coach also explained that Danny Maddix's World Cup adventure was over almost as soon as it had begun. 'There is no time to bring any new players now. I discussed the matter with Danny Maddix on the telephone. I didn't have time to meet him in person but I am a professional, like he is, and I said that he must be a good player and I saw some quality but I have no time to adjust him to the philosophy. It was unfortunate because he was the first player who report to me an interest to play for Jamaica. Two times I came here, he was injured and then when I call the players for trials he had some particular problems and could not go there.'

Robbie would go to France, the coach said, whether he was injured or not.

A reporter asked whether the poor turn-out had been a disappointment. 'I was surprised that it was not a full stadium,' mused the professor. 'Maybe it was a bad game.'

Burrell visibly bristled under his cashmere overcoat. 'It is ridiculous to state that the low crowd has anything to do with Jamaica not scoring goals.' The Captain glared at the reporter who tried to protest that that was not what he meant. Sensing that the mood had changed, notebooks were snapped shut and chair legs scraped on the floor as reporters got up to leave. The Captain ushered the coach towards the door while continuing his attack on the journalist who had asked the offending question. It was clearly a touchy subject. The JFF would not have made much from a crowd of 10,000 – certainly nowhere near the £85,000 they were reported to have banked from the game at QPR.

Despite their below-par performance, the boys held court back at the team hotel as two Jamaican heroes came by to pay their respects to the men of the hour. Looking tall and lean, cricketing legend Courtney Walsh had recently been made a special ambassador for Jamaica. He sipped from a bottle of beer and chatted with Cargill and 'Tatti' Brown in a corner. Elsewhere in the lobby, the intermittent explosions of laughter and high fives suggested that Beenie Man was 'vibemaster' for the night. The King of Dancehall was a prestigious title in Jamaica and the man in the red gangster Trilby and immaculate dog-tooth jacket certainly looked 'bad' enough for the job. Beenie was fresh off a couple of sell-out gigs at Brixton Academy and would be headlining the fund-raising 'Rise Up' concert – one of the main events in Reggae Boyz Week on the team's arrival back in Jamaica. For now, The King of Dancehall seemed happy to be sunning himself in the warm afterglow of the football team.

Spider collapsed into a sofa and offered his fist. He looked pleased after a good night's work deputising for the injured Warren Barrett. I commented that the hotel lobby had turned into a Jamaican reunion party. 'That's what it is in Jamaica,' he croaked in a voice hoarse from shouting. 'You have the artists and the cricketers that come around us and it's good. Everyone link together and try to get something going, y'know. Togetherness is there, y'know: DJs and cricketers, track and field – everyone come together. Everyone follows in someone footstep and that's the way it is in Jamaica. Everyone like to do something and come together.'

There seemed to be a better vibe than at Braco now that all the British-based players had returned to the fold. 'It make a difference when they come in,' agreed Spider, looking over to where Robbie stood chatting. Not able to play because of his toe injury, he had wanted to see the boys and talk through some details with the Federation anyway. 'They been here a long time and it's one happy family. It's supposed to be like that. All the players are important, everyone is like big family and there is no bad feelings or difference like some people say. Whether you're playing or not playing, it doesn't matter – everyone play a big role. You have DJ, entertainer, people like myself who can give you a few riddims and ting like dat. The vibesman get everyone going. When we all over the world we keep the vibes going.' Spider looked tired but relaxed. The travelling had been hard work but he maintained that the spirit was good within the camp. 'Everyone is on a level right now,' he said. 'We're like one unity, one family – that's what bring us here, y'know, the unity. Unity is strength.'

Unity on the flight back to Jamaica did not extend to the party sitting together. The players were scattered across economy while the JFF officials and coaching staff enjoyed the bigger seats in first class. The Captain and co. might have got more leg room but they missed out on what Fitzroy called the equivalent of 'Oasis giving a concert in the air free of charge with the England team'. Beenie Man was up and out of his seat almost from take-off – flashing white teeth and wide eyes, chatting to keep the younger set hanging on his every word. Pouting impressively throughout, Ian Goodison was Beenie Man's favourite player. The DJ had paid tribute by incorporating 'Pepe's' trademark number five into several of his expensively tailored suits. For the crossing, however, Beenie wore his show clothes, complete with shop tags to show how much he had spent.

It was time to collar The Captain. There would be no better opportunity of commanding his undivided attention than being trapped together in a flying steel tube tens of thousands of feet above the ocean. My first request was politely declined: 'These nice ladies would be terribly offended if I did not participate in their exercise programme,' he explained, reclining back in his seat, shoes off. Since customary pre-landing aerobic routine was about to take place, it was a pretty good excuse.

Arms, legs and neck suitably relaxed, I tried again. Kneeling at his feet merely made The Captain appear more presidential than usual. He was the big chief and we were aboard JFF1 as it prepared to touch down for another key rally on the campaign trail. Horace Reid, Burrell's Dan Quayle, sat next door listening in.

I wanted to know just how proud he felt at the World Cup draw in Marseilles, hearing Jamaica's name being drawn out to the biggest cheer of the night. 'Just to see the name Jamaica come out alongside the great teams of the world, it was a very emotional moment. If I had tears I would have shed those tears.'

The Captain explained that he had never cried in his life. 'I don't know why,' he said. 'Maybe my tear glands are blocked.' I asked what he did to relax. He looked nonplussed for a second: 'I don't know what I would do if I had time to relax.' His face creased back into a smile. 'I think that community service is one of the greatest honours that you could be involved with, doing something for your people, your community and the country. I take great pleasure in doing all of that. It is in fact so pleasurous it is maybe why I find it satisfactory to just work and not to think about anything else.'

Perhaps money was a better subject – like how much had been raised. It was not really a question that I expected The Captain to answer but after offering a vague, 'Difficult to say but millions of dollars,' he turned to Horace Reid to get confirmation on the party line. 'Approximately US$12 million has been expended to date on this very important programme,' he finally said and Reid nodded. 'But when you observe the results and what those results have caused in Jamaica – in terms of the confidence of the nation, the *esprit de corps*, the whole camaraderie that has been enhanced by our success, that is one thing that money can't buy.'

Did he invest himself? 'Oh, yes, many, many times I went into my pocket and invested millions. I demonstrated my commitment by, at times when the programme has been in trouble, dipping into my own pocket or securing loans using my own private collateral. I would hand that money over to the Federation.' The bootleg trade in Britain had alerted The Captain to the money-making potential of official Reggae Boyz merchandise. 'I was amazed out of my mind,' he said. 'This is one area that we will have to properly tap into once we qualify for the World Cup 2002.'

The pressure in my ears had made The Captain's voice sound like muffled bass. The landing lights were on. ' "When" not "if"?' I asked. 'Oh yes, yes. I never pass the baton backwards, I always pass the baton forwards.'

Apart from the JA $5,000 a plate gala dinner starring Pele, the first half of Reggae Boyz Week was not much to write home about. Kingston continued to suffer from World Cup fever although the locals were getting edgy now that the date for announcing the final squad for France was drawing near. Walter Boyd was still out in the cold and many were upset that the likes of Marcus Gayle, Darryl Powell and Frank Sinclair had not yet played in Jamaica.

Reggae Boyz Market at Devon House sounded more interesting because the local papers had billed it as an amnesty for bootleggers. In return for legitimately cashing in on the Reggae Boyz, a slice of their profits would be donated to the 'Road to France' programme. It had promised a bonanza for collectors of memorabilia but walking round the parched grounds where Jamaican newly-weds traditionally have their picture taken, most of the stalls seemed to be rented by sponsors of the Reggae Boyz rather than vendors of T-shirts and tacky souvenirs. The best effort came from a man who said he was selling Reggae Boyz chilli peppers.

'We're counting down to The Boys,' hyped the compere from a clearing between the trees. 'The Reggae Boyz will be in the place in just five minutes.' A cheer went up from those packed in front of the rickety wooden stage. They had been told the same thing 45 minutes ago and the grounds of Devon House were swarming. People had climbed trees to get a better view and when the selector unleashed the popular 'Playground' rhythm, the crowd responded with whistles and air horns. Foreign film crews jostled for position. I could see Devon trying to brace himself in order to hold his place in the crowd. 'Can we move back now, people?' urged the compere. 'There are people getting crushed at the front.' The stage creaked as more people tried to clamber over the back for a sight of their heroes.

The players were introduced one by one and huge roars greeted Bibi, Pepe, Tatti Brown, Spider, Gregory Messam and Paul Hall. The throng had developed a motion of its own and handkerchieves were held to faces as the dust rose in a cloud and people coughed theatrically. 'The Reggae Boyz will not be able to perform unless we move back, people.' There was nowhere to go and as the stage dramatically gave way at one end, the compere reluctantly conceded defeat: 'The Reggae Boyz are now going to leave.' It was time for another spectacular exit.

Little more than the tip of Bibi Gardener's fabulous new Tina Turner-style hair could be glimpsed above the fans that engulfed him. Elsewhere in the stampede, Pepe was being swept along by his band of loyal followers. 'This is fucking crazy,' barked Fitzroy as he attempted to brush through the tangle of pens and paper being thrust in his face. 'It's dangerous, man.' Behind him, Paul Hall was grinning, while at the back, Simoes dripped in sweat and tried to free himself from a sea of Japanese autograph hunters. The Japanese loved The Reggae Boyz.

As the players spilled though the gates and made a break for the bus, the crowd poured out on to the road behind them. Women screamed hysterically as fans attempted to clamber aboard the bus, hanging off the window frames or perching precariously on the bumpers. The front windscreen shattered and outstretched arms pleaded for shirts, shorts and training tops. Ten minutes later, the shriek of sirens heralded the arrival of the police. Somehow, the bus was freed from the crowd and the Reggae Boyz were sped through a succession of stop lights to the National Stadium for training. It was a miracle that no-one was killed in the stampede.

Afterwards, Fitzroy Simpson and Paul Hall sat down to dinner in a a glass-sided restaurant at the Wyndham Hotel in Kingston. They both loved being treated like pop stars when they were in Jamaica but the events of that afternoon had been quite frightening.

'Football is bigger than music now,' said Paul quietly. Fitzroy shook his head and admitted that although he would like David Beckham's money, he could do without that sort of hype every day of the week. 'In Jamaica, you've got superstars in their own right,' he said. 'People like Ricardo Gardener and Ian Goodison. Where they live is where the support is. It's at ground level. Nothing can happen to them; no one can touch them.'

Less than a year before, the two of them had set out with Deon Burton on a voyage into the unknown. They were a tight-knit group of friends who had come together at Portsmouth in the summer of 1995. Hall had been at Fratton Park for two and a half years and Deon Burton had just broken into the first team squad when the cocky Simpson swaggered in from Manchester City. Hall and Simpson hit it off immediately and took the impressionable Burton under their wing. They were three very different characters who called themselves 'The Clique'.

Fitzroy had shone briefly at Manchester City after emerging under Glenn Hoddle and then Ossie Ardiles at Swindon. But he did not feel that he had fulfilled his potential. Hall had never hit the heights of the top flight and had already given up one promising career by the time he signed his first professional contract with Torquay. He had been a rapper in a band called RME that was good enough to win a recording contract back in the late eighties, but he had elected to stick with his football, heading for the English riviera while RME took off towards bigger things on the Continent. His skills on the mike had made him a popular member of the squad and his chatting can be heard on the Reggae Boyz record that The Captain was so keen to ban. At the 'Rise Up' gig, he achieved the ultimate by matching Beenie Man in a good-natured showdown on stage. The shaven-headed Simpson was this double act's talker while Hall was a man who liked to observe and listen. His team mates had nicknamed him 'The Ninja' because he was stealthy, deadly and dark.

Brought up in Handsworth's Jamaican community – speaking patois, eating traditional Jamaican food and listening to reggae, Hall had dreamt of playing for Jamaica since taking a holiday on the island in 1993. His letters to the Jamaican Football Federation asking for a chance to try out for the team had got no reply. It was the arrival of Simpson, a kindred spirit brought up in a similar West Indian environment, that provided Hall with the extra impetus he required. The pair made phone calls and wrote more letters.

In 1996, Hall and Simpson came into contact with a Canadian named Ed Oldbrook, who indirectly knew Horace Reid. 'To be honest, they didn't even want to know,' said Simpson of 1997. 'They were being told that guys like us could help their programme but we didn't hear anything so I booked my holiday with my wife, my son, Paul and his girlfriend. The phone goes two days before we were due to go away, telling us that, by the way, we had a trial. I had to drop everything.' Burton felt a bit left out as the three normally went everywhere together so Simpson lent him the money for the flight, telling him that the training would do him good.

At the time, Hall had just enjoyed his best season to date, scoring fifteen goals after carving a niche playing just behind the main striker. Simpson, too, had starred as Pompey enjoyed a good cup run that included taking the notable scalp of Leeds United at Elland Road. Burton, who had started as first-choice striker after scoring seven goals the previous season, lost his place and had been out on loan at Cardiff. He was not a naturally confident person yet had the knack of scoring important goals. In his first full season at Pompey, he grabbed the winner away to Huddersfield in a match that saved the club from relegation to Division Two. Alongside his two older sparring partners, Burton arrived in Jamaica not knowing what to expect.

'Fucking hell. Have you ever been to Beirut with suntan cream?' Fitzroy threw his head back and laughed. 'No one knew of us in the whole country; no one even bothered to find out about us or what we'd done. That had no value to them at all. All they'd done was to invite Robbie and Marcus on the strength of being Premiership players with names and reputations behind them. They didn't have to go through the trial process; they were already in with the big press conference to announce it. That didn't bother me but we got thrown in the lion's den.' He didn't have to prove his commitment to me.

'There we were – I'd never been to Kingston before in my life – and [the JFF] were an hour late meeting us off the plane. We were like three stooges stood there. No one was saying nothing to us. It was one of them when your mum sends you on the train to London for the first time wearing a placard saying, "Just arrived. Don't have a clue what I'm meant to be doing." '

Fitzroy's eyes widened. 'We were put in this house where the fridge didn't work and you would think the lock on the door had been kicked in every night when a new tourist came in. There we were, man. Deon had to sleep in the room with Paul because he was shit scared. They put me in a room by myself and I had to put a fucking chair behind the door. I didn't have a clue what was going on. I'd been to Jamaica once before that, on my honeymoon, but that time I went to civilisation.'

That is not to say that Fitz didn't end up loving his new home. 'Now that I know the island, I think that Jamaica is fucking amazing. They want to get westernised but at the same time they don't. They're scared to ask but they want to know, if you see what I mean. It is fascinating because when we first came out here for a trial you would catch them looking at us to see what we were doing. We could feel their eyes on us but they wouldn't ask. They didn't come over and ask how we were or anything but then they are quite reserved people.'

Fitzroy is a man who says what's on his mind and to hell with the consequences, a quirk that sometimes gets him into trouble. His trial for the team sounded memorable. 'I got a bit of advice off the cricketer Franklyn Rose,' he recalled. 'He said [the Jamaicans] would try it on for the first couple of days – giving you the cold shoulder and also giving you a dig on the football pitch. They forgot that I had come from England where that is all part of the game.' He smiled. 'So, after I got the first dig, I lined one up and gave the geezer a good old-fashioned Division One challenge. That was the end of it. They didn't come near me after that.' Despite putting one of his prospective team mates in Row F of the stand, the trial went well. The three returned to England and got the news two of them had been hoping for and the other one had never dreamt of.

And it could have been so different. 'I got a call-up to England Under 21s at the age of nineteen years old. We were due to meet up on the Sunday at Bisham Abbey but on the Friday at training I went over on my ankle. I never got called again. It's fate really, let's be fair about it.' The way he looked at it, 'Paul Ince got a bye.' He was only half-joking. 'If I'd have taken my chance, learned and progressed like I should have done, he might not be playing now. Instead of all the headlines going to a Paul Ince or a Paul Gascoigne – which they probably would have done anyway because they're great players – I might have been part of a nice little trio with them. As it happens, I'm quite happy with Peter Cargill and Theodore Whitmore.' The cafeteria echoed to the sound of his belly laugh for the second time.

'I've done twelve years in English football now and I'm look- ing to go abroad. English football is too regimented and I've got my eyes set on Milan.' Paul Hall choked comically on his food. Fitz elbowed him and continued. 'To be totally honest with you, when I got called up for Jamaica with the opportunity of the World Cup at the end of it, I took a basic decision to take a year out of domestic football to totally concentrate on the World Cup. If it hadn't paid off I might have shot myself in the foot.

'I really have got a point to prove and this is really what I want from the World Cup. I want to prove a point to myself and to English football that I can do more than talk a good game.' He could certainly do that. He referred to the 'little chap' who went from Scotland to Borussia Dortmund, Paul Lambert. 'The guy just blew up. He's got a Champions' League winners' medal! It says to me that there are a lot of technically good players playing at a shit level.' There would not be many players in France who did not play in the top divisions of their respective leagues and fewer still who played near the bottom of the second.

Paul Hall chose this moment to chip in for the first time. His Brummie accent was more noticeable than Fitzroy's occasional, and somewhat incongrous, West Country burr. 'What it is, right, is that in football, when you go from bottom to top rather than from top to bottom, you learn to appreciate it more. In football, you learn when you lose. The only time that we go forward with Jamaica is when we have setbacks. It's the same in your career. When you've made it from the bottom up, you know what it takes. There's values, man, certain values.'

It had been easy being away for so many weeks of the year, especially with Portsmouth rooted in the relegation mire at the bottom of Division One. I asked them what the reception had been like when they got back from playing across the world. Fitz raised his eyebrows. 'Do you want this straight on the line? If you were playing for Portsmouth, fighting for survival in the middle of winter and you had two players going off to Jamaica for a month while you're at home watching *Caribbean Uncovered* on Sky, how would you feel towards those people?' Enough said.

'This is the man who put it all on red,' he joked of himself. 'How can you play in front of 92,000 against Mexico and 48 hours later – 48 hours after talking to CNN, they send me –' He paused for comic effect '– to Bashley Town to play for a Portsmouth Representative XI? That means you can't even get in Portsmouth reserves, never mind the first team.'

'The pitch had a slope and the grass was up to your ankles,' said Hall, smirking at the memory. 'It was like one man and his dog . . .'

Fitz held his nose and made the crackling noise of a cheap tannoy system: ' "And number eight today is Fitzroy Simpson . . ." '

'And number seven is Paul Hall,' added his partner with impeccable timing.

Paul took up the theme. Less boisterous and less opinionated than Fitz, he is certainly no less ambitious. 'In eleven months I've made more of a name for myself than in the rest of my career put together. You can get ignored in English football and I was getting tired of it, man. Everyone is in football to be famous. The type of thing you want is for someone to hold the door for you when you walk into Harrods. I've become, world renowned, right, in a matter of months. If you asked every league manager in England they would say, "He'll never make it at this stage." But look at this. Look where I am all of a sudden. The whole lot of them are wrong and I'm now looking to shock the world.'

Fitz nodded. 'What has happened to me in the last six months is that I've gone from being a domestic football player in a domestic league to being an international who has played against the world champions.' He rocked back in his chair and laughed again, incredulous at his own good fortune.

'To be honest with you, we've took a gamble and it's paid off,' said Paul. 'We gambled the price of the plane fare over. We haven't had a week off football to recharge our batteries since that time we came over here but I am going to be able to tell my grandkids so many different strories.'

'I'll tell *you* a story,' interjected Fitz. 'I was in the Posthouse in London and they asked me my occupation on the form that you sign when you check in. They only gave me two or three boxes to fill in on the form but I said, "I want an extension." ' He put on a strong Jamaican accent: ' "Professional footballer, musician, director, model and chat show host, property tycoon, hotel owner . . ." '

Chat show host?

'I'm after Ian Wright's job,' he said grinning.

The Reverend Al Miller was already a major star. Grey-haired and moustachioed, he had a personality that bathed those in his company with a goodness that's hard to define. He looked you right in the eye when he spoke and his sentences were littered with positive phrases and buzz words. Despite being a spokesman for a set of values that had decreasing relevance in the late nineties, the Reverend retained an inherent cool. When a reporter had asked The Captain whether Jamaica would be taking an Eileen Drewery-style faith healer to France, the Reverend was described as the 'spiritual guardian of the team, a man the players loved like a big brother'. His presence needed no justification; whenever Al Miller's name was mentioned, the words 'top man', 'incredible guy' or 'special person' soon followed.

At the team's last training session at the National Stadium, the Reverend had been out in the middle of the pitch as Simoes held a lengthy meeting. The coach did not have time to discuss spiritual matters with the Reverend at length but did not underestimate his input. Indeed, the Reverend's was perhaps the most powerful Jamaican voice within the backroom team. He said that he had been working 'intensively' with the programme for the last three years but had been giving spiritual guidance since Carl Brown's appointment. 'The approach that I take is that I am not after converting the boys to become Christians *per se*,' he explained. 'What we share are principles of success and all principles of success –' He lowered his voice as if preaching '– come from the word of God.' I believed him.

'A lot of [the players] have had tough and varied backgrounds and as a result there are many hurdles to cross to work all that through – the changes, the adjustments and the transition that they all have to make. We all need help and guidance to get through that transition so that the best result comes out at the end. That is why I spend a lot of time working with the guys on an individual basis.'

He described the religious society that he came from. Records state that around half the adult population went to church regularly although commitment to the church had waned in the last 20 years. 'In this current generation,' explained the Reverend, 'those under twenty-five are not as "churched" as their parents and predecessors. I would say that seventy to eighty per cent of all Jamaicans over thirty are very "churched". They grew up in the church and had a strong religious background. The younger

One Love

generation is not as strong but are very God conscious, God fearing and sensitive to spiritual things because of their parents' influence.' The spiritual patchwork of the country was reflected in the religious make-up of the team, he said. 'I think they are all Christian denominations but it varies.'

Young sweeper Christopher Dawes was a keen student of Rastafarianism and rumours suggested that other members of the team held certain 'tenets', like not touching meat, tobacco or alcohol. Devon had told me that people did not like openly expressing their faith in Jamaica for fear of being persecuted, although growing 'locks' was usually a reliable indicator. When the veteran DJ Papa San announced his conversion to Christianity, it made the front pages in many of the island's reggae papers. Somehow I could not imagine the *NME* doing that.

Before going to the squad bungalow for the customary team session on the morning of the Santos match, the Reverend had to attend to his regular flock in Kingston. The Fellowship Tabernacle was an unremarkable building from the outside, and looked like a white-washed warehouse set at the end of a long dusty car park. The doors were opened at nine and a sincere 'Good morning, God bless you' from the smiling man at the entrance welcomed me inside. I sat at the the back of the hall, near one of the extractor fans. The 'house band' was playing soothing, background music and I watched as the crescent of seating arranged around the stage filled with a congregation made up largely of women and children.

'Let glory fill this place,' crooned the male singer as arms were raised and clapping broke out to 'Welcome the Lord'. The hall was almost full and as the music grew louder, 'hallelujahs' were offered up to the rafters and life stirred from those who had been fanning themselves with service sheets. A change in the drummer's beat signalled the arrival of the Reverend and he bounced onto the stage looking the consummate showman in a beige double-breasted suit. He took the microphone, flicked the lead professionally from under his feet and called out: 'Newcomers in the house, birthdays in the house, wedding anniversaries in the house – Allll-riiiight!' This church was something else.

The Reverend was certainly a master of the vibe. It was

Mother's Day and he wanted to make sure that the ladies in the place felt special. 'Anyone in the house have a baby last night?' called out the Reverend, offering JA $1,500 of groceries to the lucky winner. 'We have a PRIZE for the oldest grandma in the house,' he roared before handing over a gift certificate for the Rockport Mineral Bath to a little old lady in a black dress. 'OK, OK,' gasped the Reverend, mopping sweat from his brow; 'Let's have a prize for the mother who can show us a picture of all her children.' A reluctant mother of seven was pushed forward by her friends. 'How do we know they're all yours?' joked the Reverend as the band continued to build the atmosphere.

It was a wonderful mix of game show, community radio and cabaret. An overhead projecter flashed a message onto the wall to the side of the stage: 'Will the owner of BMW 2537AI please remove his car now. It is blocking the gates.' The Reverend broke into song, made announcements and gave 'big shouts' to members of the congregation before asking us all to shake hands with the person sitting on our right. He pulled his flock along, urging, 'Stay focused, people, stay focused' and asking them to 'present themselves to the Lord' . Once the brethren had been whipped into a singing, foot-tapping frenzy of supplication, the Reverend got down to the business of delivering the sermon.

It was evangelism with charisma, religion that people enjoyed – James Brown presenting *Praise Be*. The Reverend, who had a wonderful voice, needed no encouragement to break into song. He even managed to growl a line from Boney M's 'By The Rivers Of Babylon' in the course of preaching about the pain of motherhood. It was mesmerising and when the hall had come down to their seats again, the service was closed with a special prayer for the Reggae Boyz.

'God has used the national football team to restore a sense of hope and pride,' he hollered to a chorus of 'Amens', 'and it is unity they bring.'

By the end of that rollercoaster three hours, I did not know whether to clap, cry or be converted. A morning at The Fellowship Tabernacle was a truly magical start to matchday.

The Captain had not been exaggerating when he said a match at Kingston's National Stadium was like nothing else. Advised to arrive early, I walked past the bronze statue of Bob Marley and down towards the mound of parched, brown earth from which the stadium had been scooped. On the road leading to the covered grandstand, vendors sold watermelons and rum punch from bicycle baskets or from delapidated wooden carts. Heavily armed policemen glided between the crowds wearing mirror shades, nudging people with the butts of their machine guns to take their seats inside. The familiar raucous shriek of whistles had a disorientating impact in the heat and after being ushered through a gate near the players' tunnel, I skulked in the shade for a while to recover my senses.

'Make some noise for The Reggae Boyz bellowed the MC outside. The bleachers on the far side looked like a great bank of sunflowers shimmering in the heat. A huge, inflatable packet of Craven A cigarettes was moored behind the goal to the left and all manner of vehicles, mini marquees and stalls were set out on the running track round the pitch. The press box was a flat pen behind one bench, containing trestle tables and plastic garden chairs. It was set at pitch level and by the time the game kicked off, it was evident why visiting journalists had been advised to bring a hat. Behind us, a 'set' – turntables, PA system and copious record boxes – was being manned by a crew wearing Hilfiger bandanas. 'Squeeze me something nice from dem turntables,' urged the MC. The atmosphere was tremendous.

First out were the players' mothers, wives and girlfriends who were presented to the crowd and given huge baskets of tinned food. They lined up in front of the grandstand for twenty minutes while a boy band serenaded them for Mother's Day. A couple of the older women looked about to wilt under the heat of the sun and the weight of the baskets, so it was a relief when the MC finally announced the arrival of 'King Pele' to thunderous applause from what looked now like a near-capacity crowd. The distinctive Brazilian burst through a large posse of photographers and ran out into the sunlight on the pitch. After running around for a minute in his suit, waving to all sides of the stadium, he was introduced to the Jamaican team amid a scrum of cameras. The Captain led Pele back up into the box, the Reverend said his pre-match prayer and Rene stood on the touchline, palms held up to the heavens. It was show time.

Jamaica started slowly, looking strangely ill at ease on their own bumpy pitch. The ball was given away cheaply and Santos threatened to carve an early opening when Fitzroy sent a perfectly weighted 45-yard cross-field ball into the path of Ricardo Gardener. Cushioning the pass with the inside of the green Puma on his left foot, Bibi looked up and volleyed diagonally over the head of Pele's son in the Santos goal. 1–0! 'World-class goal, world-class goal,' proclaimed the Jamaican denizens of the press box as the selector plucked an air-horn sample from his box and scratched the stylus back and forth across the grooves. The stadium was still bouncing on all sides when an Air Jamaica jet buzzed low over the ground, throwing a huge plane-shaped shadow across the pitch. Back in the stand, The Captain was beaming.

Santos equalised soon after and an embarrassed hush descended on the ground. Rene paced the touchline, gesticulating and shouting instructions. The boys looked sluggish and when Spider could only parry a fierce, long-range free kick, Santos bundled in the rebound to make it 2–1. It would have been a major blow to have lost the long unbeaten home record in the final match at 'The Office' before France and the Reggae Boyz seemed to sense this. Andy Williams sent over a corner which Linval Dixon met firmly and Paul Hall scrambled over the line. 2–2. It was the first time in months that the Reggae Boyz had scored twice in a game.

The second half was perhaps more sprightly than either coach would have liked. Tackles flew in and tempers bubbled. 'Bibi' got involved in an altercation in front of the bleachers and as 'Pepe' came steaming in, bottles rained down on to the running track. The Selector revved things up with a snatch of bashment from the speakers but Simoes dashed across the pitch from the bench and called for calm – it would not do to have the game abandoned in front of Pele. Pepe laughed last, however, scoring the winner with a typically brave header to send the fans rejoicing into the night. It had been a wonderful day's entertainment, although not quite as momentous as some locals would have it. They insisted that the Reggae Boyz had just beaten Brazil.

*

General secretary Horace Reid was altogether more sober when he invited me into his small, ground floor office on St Lucia Crescent.

He sat behind a desk busy with paper and turned the volume down on a small transistor radio. Reid was not a man who smiled easily. 'So what exactly is it you would like me to talk about?'

It was a slightly defensive opening. There had been some sniping in the media about where all the money was going and this was the last thing he probably needed on a Monday morning. 'I'm a little disappointed that our memories don't go back to 1994 when you read some of the comments made in Jamaica,' he said. 'We have to remember where we have come from. Some people are letting their imaginations run away with them. They think that we are just going to go in there and beat up everybody at the World Cup.' Expectations had been raised – both of the team and of the Federation – and as the chief administrator and a man privy to key decisions, Reid felt the pressure more keenly than most.

He bridled at the suggestion that there were concerns about the JFF's accountability. 'When people see a private sector company making a million dollar cheque out to you and they see the government making a ten million dollar cheque out to you, they want to know what this money is being used for and whether it is necessary to spend it at international level. These are not things they can answer and not things they take time to research.' His voice did not waiver. 'If you look at the expenditure statements of the thirty-two qualifiers for the World Cup, we fall at the bottom of that scale. We might be spending money that seems a lot to Jamaicans but if they want us to be at a world level, there is a price to it. We have had to bridge that gap in four years and that costs money.' It was a fair point.

It was difficult to pin down exact figures on what the players were paid or who exactly they were contracted to. Like all international squads, their names were listed against club sides in brackets yet when it came to negotiating the move abroad everyone anticipated for either Ricardo Gardener or Theodore

Whitmore, who would be sitting round the table and which bank account would the transfer fee be paid into? If the JFF paid the players' wages, through the umbrella of the Adopt a Player scheme, and were responsible for making them attractive to foreign clubs, then surely the programme should bank the fee. As far as I could tell, though, the players were still registered to their clubs.

'Most of [the money and benefits] will go to the clubs and that is why it is important that the clubs understand their responsibility in supporting this programme.' Reid explained that the Federation was in the process of trying to restructure the domestic game, reducing the size of the Premier League and starting the equivalent of the English First Division below it. The British agent I had seen in Cardiff had been brought in to advise them on the 'best way to keep the funds in the sport' and Reid was on the frontline of the ongoing dispute with the clubs on Jamaica. Most of them were run by one or two people, and Reid was worried about how far the local infrastructure had to catch up in order to deal effectively with their potential new wealth. 'If they made a good transfer fee they could see that as their return on years of hard work,' Mr Reid remarked of the businessmen behind the clubs. 'They could take all of it if they wanted to.' Reid revealed that the Federation had been angered by making nothing when Andy Williams negotiated a move to the States.

Reid's icy demeanour almost cracked when I asked whether he thought there was a mischievous element within the local press. 'Mischievous is one word,' said Reid calmly, 'but I'd say that there is only a small minority – a clique, that is malicious. If their intent is to destroy then let me see how far they will get. I don't usually get emotional on these issues but I think it is important when you have results. We have demonstrated in four years what could not be done in fifty and we have done it with average cash.'

The malicious minority certainly got to Simoes. The coach had adopted something of a siege mentality with sections of the Jamaican media for over a year but was enraged and embarrassed when the *Sunday Herald* disclosed the size of his salary on the morning of the Santos match. He was on US $25,000 a month compared with annual per capita income on Jamaica of US

$1,700. It made him the highest salaried official on the island. Nine days later Simoes would point out that the story was in bad taste and that he would be the lowest-paid coach in France. He would also announce his intention to stand down after the World Cup.

10

Jamaican football idols – 'Skill', Johnny Barnes and 'Blacka Pearl'

DANIEL

'He's what I'd say was a very Jamaican player,' said Ray from Braco of the enigmatic Walter Boyd. When someone is called a British-style player it instantly conjures up an image of a brave, physical, whole-hearted footballer. Similarly, the Germans are known for being clinical, the Italians precise and the Dutch technically perfect. None of these mental snapshots provide an accurate picture yet they all contain elements of the truth. In Walter Boyd – the current keeper of the Jamaican flame – we have a player who can excite and frustrate in equal measures. 'Blacka' has a skill which appeals to Jamaicans' highly developed sense of aesthetics, yet all too often goes missing in games. Or just plain missing . . . Both Alan 'Skill' Cole, a legend in local football in the sixties and seventies, and John Barnes were great crowd pleasers who drew gasps with their tricks. These three totally different men embody Ray's 'very Jamaican player.'

I had heard of Alan 'Skill' Cole but never realised just how magical his qualities were. Audley Boyd stood in the gloom of the RJR Sports Club car park, flipped the lid off a bottle of cold Red Stripe and was about to tell me where to find 'the greatest Jamaican footballer of all time' when a pick-up truck rounded the corner and pulled to a halt in a cloud of dust. Out stepped a tall man wearing a stylish blue bandana over greying dreadlocks. He held his head high, as if on the look-out for the early pass or incoming tackle.

"Skill!' He was called over and introduced to me – he seemed to know pretty much everyone else round the car. Radiating raw charisma and leading with an infectious perma-grin, he then ambled over – he had that bandy gait of an ex-player – to spar with the guys who shouted greetings amid a typically raucous game of dominoes under the electric strip lights of the veranda. Audley advised me to pin him down as he could be a bit slippery when the mood suited him. Alan, it transpired, loved the gee-gees and spent most mornings down at the track either checking on one of his horses or picking up tips.

Carl Brown had talked about playing with the maverick Rasta – a legend in Jamaican football and long-time brother of Bob Marley's – and Peter Cargill was old enough to remember him fondly. John Barnes' father, Colonel Barnes, had been Cole's captain in the Jamaican national team. The name 'Skill', I soon found out, had an ice-breaking impact on any conversation in Jamaica.

When you mention his name Jamaicans ask whether you knew he was one of Bob Marley's best friends. But before the music of Trenchtown reached the wide world, Skill was already a local legend. 'He was like a goal machine,' Audley gushed. 'He was of those men who could dribble down the field and score. Jamaicans have always loved players like that. He was the first Jamaican, as far as I know, to play out in Brazil but he left because of his locks, his hair. He coach in Ethiopia too. He likes a smoke as well but all dreads love to smoke the ganja.'

When this infamous character had finished nodding his head and offering his fist for 'respect', I arranged to meet him the following day.

Skill, a light-skinned, striking man, eventually strolled in approximately 45 minutes after the appointed hour – bang on time in Jamaica. At first he seemed vague, the magnetism of the previous evening missing. The sandwich on the table was distracting him and it took no more than 30 seconds before we were interrupted for the first time for him to acknowledge a waving fan. As he gradually got more comfortable in his chair, the long pauses between questions, mouthfuls and answers subsided.

'Yeah, mon, I was de star attraction,' said Cole, grinning as he wiped mayonnaise off his impressive beard. 'They used to call me the football idol of Jamaica.' He had been born in Vineyard Town, a poor district of Kingston to the south of the National Stadium, and had first burst into the national consciousness as a gifted college player. His full international debut came at the age of fifteen, the youngest player to do so in the island's sketchy football history. And the nickname? 'As a youngster, I started playing liccle boys football at the age of ten or eleven. I played with all dem big guys, top Jamaican players, and it was dem dat gave me the name. I was about ten ... and I played scrimmage with dem big guys.'

Charting his own progress from crowd-pulling feats of ball juggling on street corners to making headlines in the papers, Skill proceeded to tell a story about how he single-handedly ended the domination of the Manning Cup by two colleges. 'I became a legend in ball after dat,' he added as a footnote.

Despite insisting that he was good enough to make his international bow some years earlier, Cole first played at the National Stadium for Jamaica that same year, at the age of 15. 'I was pretty small,' he remembered, 'and the coach told me that I had to wait for the right time. I had to wait until one of the big guys got hurt and I tell you, the first game was against a Brazilian team. Can you imagine that? Don't ask what I did, believe me.' He leant back and grinned. 'The rest is history. The guy whose jersey I took never got it back.'

Audley had grown up watching Alan play for the Jamaican club side Santos. 'When you have a player that talented it is always interesting to find out who they modelled their game on but he had everything,' said Audley. 'He was good at free kicks, he could dribble and the fans used to love to see him, if anything, just because of his skill.' He was a Brazilian-style player and after, in his words, rejecting an offer from Matt Busby's Manchester United – 'I was scared of England den' – and playing professionally in the States, Cole secured his place in Jamaican football folklore by signing for Brazilian club side Nautica.

It is no coincidence that the Jamaican word for the best individual trick is a 'Skill' or a 'Pele'. 'The Jamaican people love excellence,' explained Skill, 'and if you're somebody who is a performer they love you. People down in the Caribbean love dem Brazilian players. The Brazilians are very fresh and when you are doing it at the Brazilian level people know that you are a serious ball player.'

According to Skill, it didn't take him long to make an impression in South America – he scored ten minutes into his debut. He mimed the act of controlling the ball on the chest, flicking it down onto his knee, gliding to the penalty spot and volleying the scoring shot between two defenders. As we both followed the trajectory of this imaginary ball, he rapped the beat of the manouevre – 'Bop, bop, BOP!' – and rocked forward. 'Riddim, right?'

'I was a big star round there,' he insisted. 'I was well loved down there, man. If I go into town there was a problem. I had to jog in and jog out. I remember in Brazil the team doctor took me down to the bank – they had to get me out through the back door and give me a police escort to drive me home.' Alan shook his head at the memory, the beads woven into his dreads bouncing off his temples. 'Jamaica is different because Jamaican people have a different culture but people in Brazil could identify with me because of my big hairstyle.' His dreadlocks reached down to his waist at that time.

After a successful first season in which, according to Cole, Nautica made 'good money', he was sacked for what the club described as 'his unnacceptable Rastafarian lifestyle habits'. 'De club got a new coach and he want me to cut locks,' is Cole's version. After a protracted falling out with the authorities, he left under a cloud. There were no regrets, he said, but I could not resist teeing one up for him: did he think he would now be regarded as one of the world greats if he had grown up in Brazil?

'Weeeeell,' he exhaled. 'My coach in Brazil told a reporter that he compared me in midfield to Gerson. They say I was the best passer of the ball they saw in that part of Brazil. One of my assets was passing. I pass very well, I don't know if anyone tell you. Did anyone tell you about my passing?'

Er . . .

The 'greatest natural talent the island has ever seen' now

does the odd bit of coaching at Arnett Gardens, although his role had recently been changed from team coach to a rather more comfortable fitting 'technical director'. The move 'upstairs' (if the Arnett Gardens club had an upstairs) left him more time to appear as a football pundit on Jamaican TV and do what he loves most: being with *his* people on the streets of Kingston. It was where I met him for the second time.

The timing of his appearance was as magical and mysterious as the first occasion. It was the Friday lunchtime before the weekend of the Jamaica v. Santos match and a group of journalists were waiting in the air-conditioned cool of the JFF reception area. They wanted to find the person dealing with accreditation for the media circus that had arrived in town for the game. I had just been talking about Cole who did not believe that the efforts of past players were being recognised in Reggae Boyz Week. A gala dinner, featuring Pele as guest of honour, was taking place at the Prime Minister's official Vale Royal residence that evening, but Alan was not on the guest list. He brushed off the snub, saying that he would have boycotted the occasion anyway. Suddenly the door swung open and in bounded Cole, flanked by a couple of friends. Dressed in his customary knee-length denim shorts, sandals and bandana, smiling but clearly aggrieved, he asked where he could find 'my brother, King Pele'. Something about the episode was rather saddening.

Since last meeting Cole, I had tried to find out more about him but his career was hard to plot, regularly disappearing into the cracks between urban myth, the lack of accessible, reliable records and colourful anecdote. Pertinently, one of the latter relates to a match in 1971 when Pele led the Santos team over to play a Cavalier Invitational XI. It was just a year after 'King Pele' had inspired the greatest side in World Cup history to glory in Mexico, and his arrival for the showdown with 'Skill' Cole saw tickets sell out in days.

Outside the JFF's offices, a man selling dog-eared magazines from a cart showed me a picture from the match. As we looked at an out-of-focus black and white shot from one of the ancient issues he had in stock, the man said that there had been a 50-50 ball which Pele and 'Skill' both went for. The Brazilian had the slight advantage but Cole won the duel. Legend has it that he distracted Pele by rising up to his full height and shuffling the waistband of his shorts. 'Boom!' shouted the man, evoking the sound inside the stadium. After the game, Pele dubbed the precocious Cole 'Boy Wonder'.

Skill is a man of the streets, a fact clearly demonstrated when I met him later on and we walked two blocks of the relatively plush Knutsford Boulevard. From preppy kids in glasses and businessmen in suits to shoeless street urchins and police officers, Skill was given 'respect' by absolutely everyone. He seemed to bask in an almost universal public affection. He walked so incredibly slowly, not just because it was hot and he was cool but because he did not want to miss out on one single greeting of, 'Respect, fatha Skill.'

We finally came to a halt in the queue for food at the memorably named Kenny Rogers' Roasters in uptown New Kingston. 'This is a nice franchise, yeah, a nice franchise,' he mused, before revealing that he had thrashed out a veterans' match on the Sunday as a curtain-raiser for the main event against Santos. He seemed satisfied; the game would see a few dollars find their way into the pockets of hard-up ex-players. Even though he was approaching 50 years of age, Cole still operated, as Peter Cargill put it, a strictly 'no pay, no play' policy. 'I didn't cause no problems when I was a player,' said Skill defensively. 'The only problem we used to have was when the Federation don't pay me. If they don't come with the money at the time that we agree at, that's where we had a problem.' Once a professional, always a professional.

'I am physically still good enough to play with dem guys,' he assured me. Cole rarely plays any more, however, having hung up his ancient Pumas in 1990. 'I was killing dem – even at the age of 40 – but one guy got vexed and jumped right in me foot.' He showed me an ugly scar on his ankle. 'That guy wilfully did me. I didn't even have the ball. It was because I still kill dem at the age of 40. I came back to teach dem a lesson. After that, I thought Forget it.'

He had learnt from the Jamaican Football Federation that Pele would appear for the invitational XI against the team led by Cole. This had not registered with Pele at the press conference but Skill was nevertheless relishing the prospect of facing the great Brazilian again. 'We were confident of having a good game,' he recalled of that game in 1971. 'We were not going out there to lose.' In addition to Pele, Santos fielded four other full Brazilian internationals. They were, in Cole's words, 'a bitch team'. Santos took the lead but the Jamaicans equalised when Skill – who else – scored from the spot. 'That was a good team yuh nuh, boss,' he said of his team mates. 'The whole of them, man, dey did know football.'

Alan, it turned out, was much more than just a footballer. He had managed the Wailers in the early days and says he was a co-founder of the famous Tough Gong record label. 'We started from the days when nobody knew Bob Marley,' he explained, underlining the fact that unlike most people who claim to have known the singer, his 'brotherhood' was genuine. 'I met Bob when I was a teenager. His mentor was a famous Rastafarian out of Trenchtown, very popular. He was one of the Rasta rulers in those days. I used to go Trenchtown quite a lot and I started to get very popular because of my football. That's when I met Bob, he was a football fanatic.'

The pair had Jamaica at their feet for a while and Cole treated himself to the first of what were to become regular sabbaticals from the game. 'We had the studio and the record label but it was easy for me to play league games. I was really a far cut above the other players so there was no pressure on me. We used to know how to get away in the night times and where to go to hide,' he admitted. 'Sometime we definitely had to sneak away. I didn't have a problem with going out the night before league games, but for international games I lived like a professional.'

Outside Bob Marley's old home on Hope Road (now the museum) there is a small, concrete 'scrimmage' pitch on the drive. The statue in the front garden has Marley standing with a guitar round his neck and his foot on a ball. The fresco on the wall contains images of the band enjoying a kickabout on tour, Marley wearing a funky red tracksuit. Inside, two rooms are wallpapered in newspaper cuttings. In the corner of one room, visitors can see a picture in *Record Mirror* showing Skill playing alongside Marley and the Wailers in London during the seventies.

Alan had spent five years coaching and playing in Ethiopia
when he hooked up with the touring Jamaicans in Paris. He had
got out of Africa just in time to miss the revolution. The brothers set up house in Hammersmith: 'Touring was always exciting
with Bob,' is all that Skill offered on a topic he has probably
discussed a million times. He did say, though, that when they
left, the Jamaicans were not missed by their neighbours. 'We
were together every day,' he said of Marley. 'We live like brothers for years.' He said that he had met the Rolling Stones, Stevie
Wonder, 'everybody, everybody', with Bob. He looked downcast for a moment. It is rumoured that the cancer that finally
killed Marley developed after he stubbed his toe playing football in Battersea Park.

I asked him whether, as a figurehead for football in Jamaica,
he has ever been formally asked to work for the JFF. 'I never
been approached by none of dem,' he replied indignantly. 'I
don't know why. People are always asking me the same question. I never been approached. Maybe it's got something to do
with personality, that's all I can say. Maybe it's personality. I
know most of the current team but most of dem has never seen
me play, that is one of the setbacks.

'I've never been a part of dem. My style of life is probably
different from theirs. My style of life is easy, easy, easy, outgoing.
I live with the people; I'm the people's . . . what do you call it?'

Hero?

'Yeah, the hero of the people. I'm here and everywhere, I can
go anywhere in Jamaica. Those are the type of relations I have
with the people. I go where the politicans can't go, do you
understand? I can go everywhere. These are some of the reasons
why I never been asked, I never been invited to be a part of the
programme but I don't let it affect me none.' I couldn't imagine
'Skill' in a suit alongside The Captain and Horace Reid anyway.
'Weeeelll, I believe it's my style of life,' he puffed. 'My style of
life is different from those that are involved. I have been a football idol. The people love football and they love me too. I just
live with it.'

Pele sadly declined the invitation to renew his rivalry with
Skill and instead sat in the shade of the stadium's one grandstand, eyes, one suspected, trained on nothing but the

waistband of the tall Jamaican's shorts. To confuse matters, the Jamaican XI were wearing the kit of Jamaican Santos, the colours of Brazil. Alan was one of the club founders – a club that was very successful on the island in the early seventies when Alan played for them. Somehow, he looked right in the famous yellow shirt, blue shorts and white socks. Inevitably, I ran into him again in Kingston after the match and complimented him on a good performance. I asked whether he wished he was in his prime now.

'I'm thankful for the time I came in history,' he said philo-sophically. 'It was something designed that way and there is no way you can try to change that.' As he ambled off up the street – stopping to talk to anyone and everyone, occasionally waving to the drivers who slowed down to shout his name over the pounding reggae on their car stereos – I reflected that at least the news was out at last: Pele's nemesis is a Kingston Rasta.

Just weeks before Jamaica's first game in the World Cup finals, the large reception room at the Jamaican High Commission in Kensington seemed a long way from Kenny Rogers' Roasters in Kingston. John Barnes apologised to everyone for being late and kissed two female members of the Commission staff before taking a seat. Colonel Barnes' boy was such a charmer.

At first glance, John Barnes would appear to be a very differ-ent kind of Jamaican footballer – a household name who has won every honour in the game and a well-spoken example of what can be achieved through hard work. He is a huge star in Jamaica and played for Captain Burrell's Jamaican Defence force side and in exhibition matches during summer holidays in the mid eighties. Anyone who fouled him on home turf, he joked, ran the risk of being lynched by the crowd.

Despite living in England since the age of 13 and playing for the country, Barnes is a Jamaican football hero. His accent, though never sounding less than honeyed, is distinct from many on the island. He grew up not far from Vineyard Town, but the disciplined environment of the army base at Up Park Camp was a world removed from the communities on the other side of the National Stadium. His father, Colonel Kenneth Barnes, is a man of some standing on the island and took a strong hand in his only son's upbringing. John was made to attend school and take his exams. He was enrolled at a well-known Catholic secondary school in Kingston a year before his father was posted to England as miliary attache to the Jamaican High Commission. His father believed that discipline was character building.

'Apparently he wasn't the most talented player,' said John, smiling, 'but being an army officer I think he probably picked himself! He was the captain of the team, but of course he was disciplined and that's what he tried to instill in us as children, and that's what he tried to instill in the team. Dad played with Alan Cole. Obviously, Alan Cole played for ever and my dad didn't, so we know which side the people are on!

'I think my father would have been an ideal person to get involved in some way, because he liked to see the result and the discipline.'

As well as being a former captain of the national team, Colonel Barnes sat on the JFF committee for many years though as far as John remembered he had not had much contact with Captain Burrell.

The Colonel initially encouraged John to take up swimming. 'My father was a very dedicated man,' John explained, 'and he used to say. "Whatever you are going to do, you do it properly." My earliest memories are walking off our camp to the national stadium where we used to swim. I used to stop off and play football and I remember saying to my sisters, "Don't tell Daddy".' The two Commission ladies visibly swooned at one end of the table. 'That's my earliest footballing memory because [my father] said, "If you are not going to go swimming training every day, don't swim." I would tell my sisters that I would catch them up in few minutes. I never used to make it. And that was right by our house. Ever since I was young – and not just me but all my friends – we grew up playing football.'

In 1976 the Barnes family moved to England and John was enrolled at a respectable grammar school in north London. He was introduced by his father to Stowe Boys Club in Paddington and spent much of his spare time indulging a passion for football. Although he was brought up to be a respectful, well-behaved young man, John enjoyed instant celebrity among his young, black peers off the Harrow Road. A 13-year-old with a curious accent, Barnes nevertheless represented the genuine article for a group of friends who looked to America and the Caribbean for their cultural leads. 'He was quiet and a bit shy,' remembers one of his Stowe contemporaries, 'but he was a fantastic ball player. He got the ball and just ran with it.'

The young Barnes got over his homesickness when he fell into a 'comfortable groove' with a group of friends on the under-age club circuit. In the mid to late seventies many black teenagers in London spent Saturday afternoons sipping blackcurrant and lemonade and dancing at the 100 Club on Oxford Street or Crackers in Wardour Street. It was innocent and safe – a far cry from the experiences of many of his contemporaries in Kingston.

John was strong and adaptable and did not take long to settle into his new environment. He listened to advice, never talked back and did what he was told. These qualities were recognised by his early coaches, and despite starring in a Stowe team that won every game by at least ten clear goals, teenager John was mature enough to shackle his own natural attacking instincts for the greater good of the team.

The first time I met Barnes, when he was still at Liverpool, he talked about those times. 'Everyone wanted to attack but I played centre back for four years because I was that bit more responsible and could be relied on not to be caught out of position. I would have rather stayed up and got all the glory,' he added. Simoes would have given his right arm for a player like Barnes.

'Simoes . . . tries to get away from individuals and we could all talk about the goals that Deon Burton scored but that is really something we have to get away from,' argued Barnes at the High Commission. 'We have to look at the collective effort of all the team because Jamaica for too long has idealised individuals and not really recognised so-called lesser talents. I remember way back, playing in Jamaica, the attitude of some of the players was incomprehensible to me. In training, if they considered a player to be lesser than them they wouldn't pass the ball.

'I have seen Jamaica play a few times on television,' he said. 'I haven't been there to play for a few years now so I don't know much about the current group of players. I know that there were

wonderfully gifted players in the past and I think that the players maybe eight, nine, ten years ago, even going back as far as
Alan Cole, were probably individually as skilled, if not more
skilful, than the team now. But this team now has got a collective spirit and team work. Although they may not have the
talented individuals of ten years ago this just goes to show what
is needed in team sports like football. In the past I probably
would have feared for Jamaica in a World Cup but now I have
no fears whatsoever. I am sure they will do themselves proud.'

Barnes could have been the greatest Jamaican player of all
time but that would have meant giving up on over 80 England
caps and a place in the Anfield Hall of Fame. It is tempting to
judge him against a historical backdrop of heroes like Alan
'Skill' Cole but only because they were born in the same city.
The life of a Rasta would have been anathema to Colonel Barnes
yet it is interesting to speculate what would have become of
John had he been born into a similar background as his dread-
locked predecessor.

'When I came to England at thirteen I fully intended to go
back to Jamaica,' admitted Barnes. His father had been posted
for four years but just three months before the family packed up
and moved home to Kingston, John was offered professional
terms by Watford. Modesty permits him from saying that his
break was down to anything but chance – a scout watched him
play for non-league Sudbury Court and he was lucky enough to
get snapped up. He was playing for England by the time he was
19 and the rest, as they say, is history.

'Although football in Jamaica had always been big, there
wasn't really the opportunity for any of the top players in 1982,'
continued Barnes. Peter Cargill and Paul 'Tegat' Davis were the
top players back then and both played in Israel. Others carved a
living across the United States or in Central America. Barnes
considered going back even after his family had returned but
there was nothing to return to. If he had been the same 17-year-
old in the same situation in 1998, however, he admitted the
decision would be less clear cut.

I remembered asking Audley Boyd and Devon whether they
thought the best Jamaican players had a tradition of under-
achievement. 'Definitely,' both said. They believed Jamaican

players had under achieved because Jamaica was not recognised as a football nation. 'Sometimes I think the only way you can measure the advancement made by any nation as a football power is the amount of players that are playing in big leagues across the world,' said Audley, 'in Europe, or South America, you know. If you're not having any players playing in those top leagues then trust me, you have not got very far.' It is not surprising then that the achievements of John Barnes have been celebrated on Jamaica; indeed, he is recognised as one of the island's favourite sons.

I wondered whether Barnes would have been such a huge star back in Jamaica had he played as a defender. Audley had tried to encapsulate the appeal players like Skill and Walter had for the public and came up with broken images: 'They will get the ball and take maybe four touches from the halfway line . . . past three players . . . not necessarily by pushing the ball in a straight line . . . powerful and very accurate in either foot.' They were words that have been associated with Barnes in a career that saw him ignite English football for the best part of a decade. In his pomp at Watford and Liverpool, Barnes was the consummate athlete, a thing of rare beauty. He had the tricks, the power and the capacity for the unexpected – a Jamaican idol through and through.

Walter Boyd is a man guaranteed to stoke passions in Jamaica. Enigmatic, elusive and troubled, my picture of Walter was built up through the opinions of others and the way people would suddenly become animated and excited; angry, even. Walter was a national debate: should Simoes forgive him and take him to the World Cup or was the coach right to ignore him? He was either the embodiment of pure evil or the footballing messiah. It depended on which side of the divide you stood on 'Blacka Pearl'.

He would not remember our first meeting which took place after the friendly against Santos. I was trying to leave the press enclosure on the concrete cycle track at the National Stadium when I suddenly became aware of being caught up in a large crowd. As too many people tried to squeeze through a small gate, I glanced to my right and saw the spitting image of Audley looking into the sea of faces in front of him. People were waving paper at him to sign or trying to touch him. 'Pearl', 'Blacka', 'Fartha'. I noticed a colossal brown stone set in a gold ring on one of his fingers and that he had small, dark scars on his face.

Walter had not been invited to the game but had, I was reliably informed, gone down to the stadium to be with his people and to make a point to the coach. As luck would have it, I was wearing a retro Jamaican shirt with the number ten on the back. Since being thrown off the squad for the last time in March, no-one in the team had dared pull on the shirt that 'Blacka' had made his own. I gave him a pen and he signed it before the wooden fencing collapsed and we all ended up in a heap on the floor near the tunnel.

Ray, a waiter at Braco, had said this about Boyd: 'He really is the best footballer in the Caribbean right now. Everybody from Barbados, Trinidad, Tobago – everybody asks, "Where is your number ten, Walter Boyd?" He is a number ten from the heart. Like in Brazil the best player always wears number ten. Even in the club sides, when you see the number ten you know that this is the special player. Before the English-based players come over Boyd was scoring goal after goal to put us where we are. But just before they come over he don't score a goal in like ten matches. People was wondering what had happened to him. That was the time he started to get hyped up, he miss training, he turn up late. At his club level that is OK but then he found Rene Simoes was serious and he was sent back.'

Walter had got stuck in the programme, Devon said. He was hard on himself and he hit the self-destruct button when he was not performing up to scratch. He was 'extroverted' as a player but quiet off the pitch. Devon also reckoned that because Walter could 'dismiss' any player on the training field, he got bored; he dropped down to the standards of the others rather than them rising to his. He was top dog in the squad because of the respect he had as a player.

In his home town of Nannyville, on the outskirts of the National Stadium, Walter was seen as a ruler because when the guys on the corner were hungry and had nothing to eat, Walter put his hand in his pocket. 'Most players come from ghetto areas and are godfathers in their communities,' said Devon, 'Blacka's popularity is because of that and also because he's come up trumps for Jamaica at crucial times.'

John Barnes was typically diplomatic on the subject of Boyd. 'Jamaica has got where they are on a collective effort,' he said. 'I don't know the situation with [Simoes] and Walter Boyd or any of the other superstars, as they were, but he is looking for a team and he doesn't want anything to disrupt that team.' It was a neutral stance.

It was impossible to get away from the fact that Boyd was Jamaica's star, the most prolific scorer in the qualification rounds (if you measure it on goals per game) yet he had been in and out of the team in the year before the World Cup. His supporters pointed to the fact that Walter gave up a relatively lucrative contract with the Colorado Cubs in the States, that he flew back for early games without the assent of his club and that he was prepared to dedicate his time totally to the World Cup programme. Walter was reported to be easily the highest paid player in the programme.

Paul Young and Altimore Butler, who both returned from the States, allegedly signed contracts with the JFF that guaranteed they would be paid the full amount even if they were dropped from the squad before the end of the qualification. When Walter was axed, however, he discovered that his contract was worth nothing. 'They dropped Walter out of the team a little after he left his club in the States and came back to Jamaica,' explained his brother. 'That started this controversy with Simoes. Simoes says he does not want any stars in his side – and that could be it. Walter is a star.'

Audley believes that people who love to rule with an iron hand normally confuse discipline with autocracy. 'The general perception in just about any society you visit is once you are not in favour with management or the people at the highest level, then you are indisciplined. A lot of the time then the public are not going to weigh up the circumstances, they are more likely to side with the management and the ones in charge. At the end of the day it is the person in charge who has the handle, and as long as you hold onto the handle then you can't get cut. Sometimes it's a funny kind of position.' It was the sort of defence Walter could expect from his brother. It was also the opinion of a respected journalist and perennial thorn in Simoes' side. I imagined Audley was among the critics that Horace Reid had been talking about when he had almost got emotional in his office.

Rene Simoes had looked rueful when he talked about one of the 'problem' players in his squad beside the pool at Braco. 'Onandi Lowe is a great player but he still has to discover his new way and how to approach the game because before, the way he play here was totally wrong.' When he moved onto Walter, however, the Professor visibly seethed.

'Unfortunately Walter Boyd did not understood what it means to be a professional because his world was so small. He just concentrate only on the island. He is so popular because of the way football was in Jamaica. Here, if you make one piece of skill against an opponent the ovation is much bigger than it is for one goal. He did not understand that this is not a circus. Before, they played like seals with the ball on their nose. We change this.' Walter was not used to being likened to a fish-gulper.

The official reason given for Walter's latest ejection from the programme was his failure to attend the Carreras Foundation Awards Ceremony that saw Deon Burton crowned Jamaican Sports Personality of the Year. Boyd had only just been re-instated for the Nigeria game after missing the Gold Cup through injury. He came on as substitute to a standing ovation but made little impact. It would be easy to say that after being the star for so long, Walter was reacting petulantly to his mantle being publicly stolen by a light-skinned stranger from Reading, England. Either way, he was dropped for the tour of the UK in March.

Walter is a man of few words. In the JFF's 'Road to France' booklet, he lists his 'most admired personality' as his mother, Rhona Campbell. His hobbies were spending time with his daughter and his 'favourite Jamaican persons' were his sisters and girlfriend. The film crew had boasted of paying a fee to a 'businessman' in Nannyville to secure an interview with the reclusive star. In it, Walter is portrayed as Bad Boy Boyd, a man in a small house full of modern appliances. His admission that he saw a friend shot dead beside him as they walked back from training does not tally with the unassuming hero who just wanted to 'try and win for my country'.

'But also,' added Simoes piquantly, 'I don't remember any time that Walter Boyd was the top scorer in Jamaican league.' It was a direct reference to the fact that Boyd had gone off the boil in an alarming way since the early qualifying rounds. The comments he had made about the coach wanting to 'play God in his life' in the summer of 1997 while at West Brom had been in response to Simoes relying too much on the whip to extract more effort. Invoking the almighty, however, was not the best way to mollify a coach that already suspected Boyd of running to the press every time something went wrong.

'In West Bromwich [Walter] was saying it's good that there isn't one person who is in charge like there is in Jamaica,' said Audley. 'Walter was saying that in a professional system you have your agents, your lawyers and your representatives and people have their right to say what they want.' The idea of a personal staff juggling mobile phones and striking deals appealed to Walter. 'In Jamaica, if you say something, it is used against you,' continued Audley. 'He said that in Jamaica Rene wants to be in his life. That was the comparison that Walter was making.'

Before his comments got back to Jamaica, Walter had been hopeful of a contract with the Midlands club. Audley estimated that he was set for a £500,000 transfer when West Brom's interest suddenly cooled. After two weeks, Boyd was back in Jamaica where Simoes asked him to explain his outburst before he could consider readmitting him to the team. It was reported that Simoes insisted on three conditions for discussion: that Boyd would be fined, make a public apology and admit that he had been 'stupid'. Boyd refused, before finally making a public apology a day later.

'After having a long discussion with my manager Mr George Phang, I would really like to apologise and say I am sorry for those statements that I made. This is to the football fraternity, the players, the JFF, the coaching staff, the technical director, my family, my sponsors and especially my fans,' said Boyd. He tried to reach the coach by phone for the reporters' benefit but could not get through. Even taking into account his apologetic version of an Oscars acceptance speech, Boyd did not appear in a Jamaica shirt again until the tour of Brazil in January 1998.

He was recalled for a hastily arranged friendly against Haiti in October 1997, however, but the story surrounding this 'incident' says a lot about how the programme was being run just a month before qualification. It also says something about the high-handed way Simoes liked to treat Boyd.

The team were training at the Tivoli Gardens field when the coach noticed that Kevin Lamey and Steve Green had injury problems. It was the night before the team was due to travel and at 7.30pm the professor, as he later wrote in the *Gleaner*, spoke to Pepe, '. . . who is Boyd's best friend, and who would have been able to find Boyd anywhere in Kingston at that time, to inform him that I, coach Simoes, was inviting [Boyd] for rejoining the squad.'

Goodison is said to have spoken to Cargill, who informed the coach that Boyd has been contacted and would meet the team at the Arnett field the next morning. Meanwhile, team manager Cranston Boxhill was instructed to speak to Boyd when he had been found. The nature of the call-up did not impress Boyd so he failed to show at the appointed hour, leaving Simoes apoplectic once more.

Not playing much in the early months of 1998, Boyd sank into a depression. Even when he did play, controversy seemed to dog him at every turn. In December 1997, Arnett Gardens played Waterhouse in a National Premier League match. The match had to be abandoned ten minutes into the second half after a fight involving Boyd prompted a shower of missiles from the crowd. In April, he was involved in a fracas at Jarrett Park after a semi-final match away to Seba United. Theodore Whitmore scored the only goal of the game but at the end, spectators swarmed onto the pitch and one fan attacked Walter with a bottle before bolting for safety. It makes Matthew Simmonds' goading of Eric Cantona seem like child's play.

Audley explained me what kind of life Walter had as the biggest name in Jamaican football. 'It's pretty different here,' he said. 'Walter will still go out but he knows that every move he makes is up for public scrutiny. The stars are very much in touch with the public right now. We have not got to that level yet where the national players cannot go out. He go out, he might go out to a club, you know, or go out for something to eat. Wherever he goes, a lot of eyebrows are raised and the heads are turned. He gets a lot of attention when he goes out.'

As the World Cup neared, the numbers of English-based players being drafted into the squad became a hot topic. Some people felt that Walter was being held up as an example of what could not be tolerated in order to ease the way for more recruits from across the Atlantic.

Ray was not one of them. 'Most people know that Simoes knows what he is doing. People try to find out why Walter Boyd is not in the side but Walter Boyd know that Walter Boyd had his chance and he blew that. Simoes says, "You give a man a job to do, let him do his job." Walter Boyd was put in the side and he didn't do his job . . . It's up to Rene Simoes. If Rene Simoes says he not going to use him then he would be out. If he is not playing for his country then there is nobody who is going to want him. He's still going to play for Arnett Gardens but you've got to look back and see that Boyd has no discipline and that's why Simoes don't want him.'

There were others who held out hopes that he might get a last-minute reprieve. 'He is hopeful, you know,' Audley said in April. 'He has had offers, you know, and the reason why he has not taken care of any of them is because there is still that expectation that he will go to the World Cup. The latest offer is from Germany. But he is still keeping his options open. He is no longer paid by the JFF and that is a major part of the contention. It's really mixed because you have some segments of society who are bitterly against Walter.'

As far as John Barnes was concerned, he believed Walter could have an impact and admitted that the striker had certainly not been the first Jamaican footballer to bridle at authority. 'Walter Boyd can have a team spirit because as far as I know he's a likeable lad and he's a nice guy and everything. But as well as that you need to have team function. When things are going well and Walter can get the ball and be fast and score a goal, fine. But that's not going to happen for the majority of the time. So for the other 88 minutes of the game you need a pattern, you need a function. I will always equate it to David Ginola at Spurs.

There is no point David Ginola playing so well and winning Man of the Match every week for Spurs and people saying he should be in the French team, and then Spurs nearly getting relegated.' Barnes added that by giving himself to the team, making self-sacrifices, Walter could mend the bridges. 'And I think that's what Simoes is talking about. Instead of having a team of stars, he wants the team to be the star.'

Carl Brown let his opinion on the matter slip when he summed up his views on great Jamaican footballers of the past. 'We've always been able to produce that one player that people always talk about. There was Syd Bartlett before Alan Cole came along and then Alan Cole was really something. He was fantastic but Herbert "Dago" Gordon rivalled Skill Cole in terms of talent, he worked magic with the ball. These were the type of players coming through and Boyd is probably the last of that line right now. I believe a lot depends on what Walter wants. I'd like to see him go because I think the team needs a player like him. I believe deep down that Simoes would like for him to go.'

In just a matter of weeks, Walter and the rest of Jamaica would find out.

PART THREE

© SIMON BUCKLEY

A pensive-looking Peter Cargill and 'Spider' lead Jamaica out for their farewell home match before the World Cup.

Rene Simoes prowls the touchline in his familiar T-shirt. Substituted is Steve 'Shorty' Malcolm.

© SIMON BUCKLEY

League football in Kingston: why pay when you can watch for free?

An early Simoes squad line up before playing Guatemala in Kingston, March 1996. Ian 'Pepe' Goodison (back row, fourth from left) makes his debut. He is flanked by the 'bad boys' of Jamaica football, Walter Boyd (to his right) and Onandi Lowe.

Ricardo 'Bibi' Gardener: an outstanding talent and one of
Jamaica's best performers in France. Displays like this, against
Japan in Lyon, earned him a £1 million move to Bolton Wanderers.

Diego Simeone of Argentina skips away from Theodore Whitmore in Paris but it
was 'Tappa's Day' in Lyon. He scored both goals in Jamaica's closing 2-1 win
over Japan.

Done it! Qualification secured, the squad assemble in the middle of the pitch to 'remember where they came from and who they have done this for'.

© EMPICS

'If an election was called tomorrow, Rene Simoes would win'. The coach is chaired from the pitch amid chants of 'France, France, France'.

© EMPICS

Another Jamaican
football idol, the
walking
controversy
Walter 'Blacka
Pearl' Boyd in
action at the
World Cup.

The one and only
Alan 'Skill' Cole
outside the JFF
offices in
Kingston.

THE BATTLE OF GIANTS
THE STORY BEHIND THE COSMOS JAMAICA VISIT

The Montego Bay quartet. From left to right:
Stephen 'Shorty' Malcolm, Durrent 'Tatti' Brown, Theodore
'Tappa' Whitmore and captain Warren 'Boopie' Barrett in El Salvador.

'The Fab Four' and original 'UB40s'.
From left to right: Robbie Earle, Deon Burton, Paul Hall, Fitzroy Simpson.

Everyone in the squad has a different role to play. Here, team DJ Paul Hall does his stuff on stage as the Boys look on.

Braco Village on the north coast. The team poses for the film crew as Devon (far right) closes in for another picture.

Aaron 'Spider' Lawrence, the team's reserve goalkeeper and all-important 'vibe master'.

Another good friend and room mate, the experienced Peter Cargill.

11

Last-Minute Nerves

ROBBIE

As people got up in Jamaica on the morning of the match against Santos, I was back in England watching Wimbledon complete a successful battle against relegation. I had been out of action since my season had ended rather abruptly at Southampton on Easter weekend. A broken toe completed an unfortunate injury hat-trick for the year after a troublesome knee had hampered me in my early games for Jamaica before Christmas, and then a torn thigh muscle away to Huddersfield in the Cup put me out for two months at the start of 1998. The broken toe was the last thing I needed with the World Cup looming.

I have been fortunate in that I have only had two really serious injuries during the course of my career but it was still gut-wrenching to think about what I had missed out on. Playing Brazil at the Gold Cup in the USA would have been an experience and the coach had told me that he wanted to make the team more flexible which would involve me having a bigger role. I did not feel that I had been able to show my true form for Jamaica and despite scoring a trademark header at Loftus Road, I had not appeared in the team since the match against Wales. It would now be an uphill struggle to make the squad, let alone the starting line-up, against Croatia.

More worrying, though, had been the downturn in Wimbledon's fortunes. As the season approached its climax, relegation had suddenly become a realistic possibility. I took it very badly that my beloved Dons were flirting with a potentially disastrous fall from the Premiership, especially as I had been able to contribute so little. We had pushed for a place in Europe and reached two cup semi-finals the year before – probably my best season as a professional – but 1997–98 had proved to be the club's toughest in the top flight.

It is ironic for a club traditionally shunned by international managers that the World Cup was one of the biggest contributing factors in our struggle. Apart from myself and Marcus Gayle playing for Jamaica, Neil Sullivan and Brian McCallister were called by Scotland, Kenny Cunningham and Michael Hughes were picked for Eire and Northern Ireland respectively and Efan Ekoku appeared for Nigeria. For a manager with a small squad, the price of the club's new international status was high and it meant that Joe struggled to field the same side two weeks running. The problem will only get worse when Neil Ardley and Chris Perry get their call-ups for England.

Having been at the club for so long, I cannot imagine myself pulling on the shirt of any other club side. I know how the system works inside out and it was extremely frustrating having to watch from the sidelines. Going away so much in the early part of the year and then picking up various injuries meant that I could not get into a run of form. I had developed a nice rhythm in training and going into games during the season before and that's important for achieving consistency. I don't think I played more than seven consecutive games in 1997–98, which meant that any excitement about the World Cup stayed firmly buried under fears about my own fitness and Wimbledon's Premiership survival.

Even if the toe recovered in time – which I was confident it would – the last thing I wanted was to go to the World Cup feeling that I had neglected my bread and butter at Wimbledon. I have always tried to do right by the club and knew there was no way, for instance, that I could have played as many games as either Paul or Fitzroy. Coach Simoes had attacked English managers for not releasing players for Jamaica internationals but I could see both sides. A home friendly in Kingston would inevitably mean that a player was away for at least a week. Before setting off for France, my top priority was to ensure that I would be starting the next season in the Premiership.

Unfortunately, all hopes of being able to finish off the season to get a bit of form under my belt bit the dust at The Dell. I got my head down to do all that I could to get fit and despite the pains that shot through the fourth toe of my right foot, it was hard not to let my mind wander off to scoring the winning goal against Argentina on 21 June in Paris. I was in and around the club throughout the recuperation period but I made a conscious effort to keep all thoughts of the World Cup to myself. The prospect of relegation was one factor, and another was that some of the other internationals in the Wimbledon squad might not have wanted to hear me harping on about France. Kenny Cunningham, not only a great player but a fantastic character in the dressing room, had missed out on qualification with the Republic of Ireland and Efan Ekoku, Brian McAllister and Neil Sullivan were all sweating on their places.

I should have known better than to worry about Wimbledon, though. When our backs were against the wall, the boys came through and we stayed up with something to spare. We went away to Leeds on the last game of the season with our Premiership status assured and played out a meaningless 1–1 draw.

That Sunday night, I got a telephone call from Mr Reid in Jamaica to inform me that I was requested to join the team in South Korea for a two-game tour of the Far East. The flight left London Heathrow at 10am. I had missed out on Reggae Boyz Week because I was having treatment on my toe and trying to take care of matters at home, knowing that when I left London, I would be gone for at least seven weeks. Needless to say, a phone call to tell me that I had until the next morning to tie up all the loose ends did not go down too well in the Earle household.

A few hours later Mr Reid phoned back to tell me that I was not to go to South Korea but travel direct to Jamaica for treatment and continued rehabilitation. I would meet up with the team when they returned from the tour. Muttering under my breath about last-minute arrangements, I rewrote my baggage labels and went to bed, rather naïvely as it turned out, because a third call from Mr Reid in the early hours of Monday morning informed me that things had changed again. I was now heading for Sao Paulo in Brazil to the Santos club.

Rene Simoes had an excellent working relationship with the famous Brazilian club and I was told that my end-of-season holiday would comprise a week's intensive rehab in South America. Not wanting to take anything for granted, I elected not to rewrite the baggage labels for the third time. I finally left England, bound for Brazil, on the Tuesday morning.

But if you think that was bad, spare a thought for Frank Sinclair, my Jamaican team mate who was at Chelsea at the time. Frank had been carrying a groin injury for the last month of the domestic season and was in the same predicament as me, except that his team had the small matter of a European Cup Winners' Cup Final in Stockholm on the Wednesday. Frank travelled to Sweden with his club side, picked up a winners' medal and then arrived back in London in the early hours of Thursday morning – on the back of a decent celebration, no doubt.

On JFF instructions, Frank stayed in the airport so that he could get a connection to Frankfurt at 7am. From Frankfurt he headed out to South Korea, arriving after a gruelling flight on the Friday evening. He spent one day in South Korea having discussions with the coach and it was then suggested that he travel on to Brazil to join me on the treatment table. He left Korea on Saturday morning and, thanks to the different time zones, arrived in New York at exactly the same time! It was definitely a case of *Groundhog Day* for poor old Frank.

His travels did not end in the Big Apple, however, and from New York he flew on to Brazil. By the time he touched down in Sao Paulo on Sunday, he had been in the air for nearly 36 hours. If he hadn't needed rehabilitation before, he did now. This was an example of Jamaican administration at its unpredictable worst and although it might not have been great for his mind and body, Frank could console himself by thinking of all those air miles.

We spent a week in Brazil, working with Dr Marco and Dr Rosanne at the Santos club. They were long days taken up with a combination of treatments that included massage, hydrotherapy, electrotherapy and laser treatment. The level of care was second to none and we both felt the benefit. Frank acquired a nickname while we were there. One day, we were both linked up to a Cybex machine, a device used by top physicians and sports science clinics to gain an accurate measurement of body strength. Both of us fared well on the endurance section of the test but when it came to measuring body strength, Frank's reading shot off the top of the scale. Dr Marco's mouth fell open when he calculated just how well he had performed and the only word he could muster from his limited English vocabulary was 'horse'. Frank's leg strength surpassed anything the doctor had seen in all his years of testing the elite of Brazilian soccer, Roberto Carlos included.

Five weeks after the original injury, my toe had started to show real signs of improvement and I felt more confident about playing. A British specialist had told me that the double fracture would need minor surgery at some point to fuse the damaged joint but that was something that could not be considered until after the World Cup. Nature and the magic of the Brazilian doctors would have to be allowed to take their healing course. I resigned myself to playing in some discomfort but in all honesty, I would have had the toe amputated if it meant I could go to France. At 33 years of age this was most definitely last-chance saloon.

At the end of our week in Brazil, Horse and I were posted to Jamaica with the rest of the squad. The boys had lost the first game in the Far East 2–1 against a less than full strength South Korea. The only plus point was that Darryl Powell had scored his first international goal. The second game finished goalless. Having flown round the world and back again in the last few weeks, the players were glad to be at home for a few days, although we were escorted to Montego Bay which meant the relative luxury of the Holiday Inn rather than the team house in Kingston.

A lot had happened while I had been away. There had been another bust-up between the Coach and Carl Brown in South Korea. Brown had not gone to one of the games and there was some unrest within the camp about the number of Brazilians now on the payroll. The Jamaican papers were also full of the professor's decision not to renew his contract after the World Cup. The politicians had got in on the debate, arguing that Simoes had boosted the economy and promoted Jamaica in a way that would normally cost millions. The coach was indignant, pointing out that he was poorly paid by Brazilian standards, and he was furious at the insinuation that his salary could have been better spent on housing and hospital beds. The Captain and Mr Reid both came out strongly in support of Simoes, declaring that they would have to 'consider their positions' if he was to leave.

Simoes seemed as focused as ever although his position became more precarious in the final days before announcing his squad. Never before had I heard of a national coach receiving death threats from people demanding the inclusion of a particular player but passions ran high about Walter Boyd. The Boyd v. Simoes debate had been raging since the squad reassembled on the island and everywhere we travelled in Jamaica, men, women and children had 'Blacka' on their minds. I gauged that public opinion was running 70-30 in Walter's favour although Simoes was adamant that Boyd had received his last chance.

The coach was advised by police to wear bulletproof body armour: a death threat from Nannyville was not something to be dismissed lightly. Simoes refused, saying that he was quite happy to leave his fate in the hands of God. Despite having a bodyguard assigned to him, Simoes wanted protection to be kept low-key and seemed defiant that gun law was not going to interfere with his final selection.

The switch from our usual base, he told us, was because we could be away from the hustle and bustle of Kingston and also so the people at the other end of the island could get a good look at their heroes before we flew off to France. I had a sneaky feeling it might have had something to do with the fact that roads had been blocked in Nannyville. Although he was unlikely to admit it, perhaps Simoes was trying to get as far away as possible from the eye of the storm.

Tension was also beginning to surface within the group as the time approached for the coach to reduce his party of 28 by six. It might even be seven now that it looked possible that Walter Boyd would get a dramatic, late recall. It was also my first week of 'real' football training in a long time and I was more than a little apprehensive about coming through unscathed. Another bad knock at this stage would leave me with nowhere to go.

Along with my notepad and laptop computer – which became a source of amusement among the English-based players, prompting references to Gary Glitter – my other prized possession was the medical bag that Wimbledon physio Steve Allen had packed me off with. I was determined to leave nothing to chance and carried round enough padding to fill a mattress. There was some discomfort at first but I was determined not to show it and my confidence grew as the week went on. By the weekend I was doing everything but tackling and striking the ball flat out. That could wait until game time.

I was not the only one with injury headaches. During that last week of training, the anxiety level shot up when Linval 'Rudi' Dixon fell awkwardly in an aerial training manouevre. He badly twisted his knee and was whisked straight to hospital to have his worst fears confirmed – there was extensive ligament and structural damage.

Rudi was an important member of the squad, having been part of the 'Three Pillars' during qualification, alongside Ian Goodison and Durrent Brown. Our excellent medical staff advised that it would be best to take action as soon as possible. Rudi went down for minor keyhole surgery to remove some foreign bodies and to clean up the joint. The knee swelled up and he was now in a race not only to be fit for the match against Croatia in three weeks' time but to make the squad, due to be announced in four days.

Softly spoken Rudi had suffered just the kind of bad luck that we all subconsciously feared at this late stage. He is a good player – someone I always felt would be successful in England. It shouldn't have happened to someone like him, a warm, engaging individual with a good sense of humour. The poor surface we were playing on had not helped the situation and I wondered again why the decision had been made to travel to Montego Bay.

During a long-distance telephone conversation with my wife, I learnt that another one of the good guys had fallen foul of the injury curse. Ian Wright's damaged hamstring meant he was to miss out on England's World Cup and his chance to appear in the finals.

After the last training session, we prayed as a group for Rudi's full recovery before the start of our historic campaign. At the end of this team prayer, a regular feature of life in the Jamaican squad, I said a quick word for my mate Ian so that he too might make a miraculous recovery.

The injury to Rudi was a blow but it did serve to pull us all closer again. Everyone was desperate to be in the squad but nobody wanted his place by default. The bond between players was tight and the spirit was strong. Everyone was focused on the football – an encouraging sign after everything else that had been going on.

There was more drama on the plane to New York for the final

warm-up game against a Caribbean All-Stars side. As we waited on the runway for clearance, Walter Boyd casually strolled on board and took a seat. Not a member of the official party, it looked like he had swallowed his pride and decided to plead forgiveness from Simoes in a last-ditch bid to make the final 22. Someone said he had even paid his own air fare.

Having watched Walter once in the flesh, seen video clips and heard about him, he would be best described as the Paul Gascoigne of Jamaican football. I was told that he had upset the harmony at times because he always wanted to be different. A couple of the lads said that if there was a team meeting at three he would make a point of not turning up until 3.15. If the bus was leaving at 12.30, he wouldn't get there until 12.45. As I understood it, it was the players who ousted him last time, not the coach.

For the record, we went down 2–1 in our last warm-up match against a team starring Dwight Yorke, the most expensive West Indian footballer in history. I managed 45 minutes in front of a crowd which made it feel like a home game in Kingston. It was my first taste of competitive action in six weeks and although I didn't play well, at least I had come through.

The plot thickened on the flight back to Jamaica. Simoes walked down the aisle and handed each player a piece of paper and a pen, asking us all to fill out a secret ballot form on whether we wanted Boyd in the final squad. The same man who had categorically stated that Boyd had played his last card was now canvassing our opinion on whether he should be picked.

The result of the ballot saw three-quarters of the players voting in Walter's favour and many of those who didn't vote for him preferred to abstain. Despite everything Walter was popular with many of the Jamaican-based players and perhaps they thought he had been punished enough.

Simoes accepted the outcome but insisted that his word would be final. He then pulled me aside for a chat near the cockpit and described how he had had serious discussions with Walter in New York. The coach had detected a change in his attitude and claimed that Boyd had looked him in the eye for the very first time. He had even been in tears at points. For a man like Walter, going to Simoes on bended knee must have taken some doing and I wondered whether other forces were at work behind the scenes.

The coach asked me how I had voted and I told him that I had voted for Walter. Simoes seemed surprised, assuming that the English-based Jamaicans would have been among the ones who voted against him. I voted the way I did for a couple of reasons: from what I had seen he was undoubtedly a great talent and I had no problem with his 'so called' reputation. More important than both, Jamaica could not afford to leave a potential match-winner at home.

Simoes stressed that he had given Boyd no verbal assurances about being selected because he wanted to see how the striker would react once we were back in Jamaica. On previous occasions, Simoes had been angered by Walter's willingness to go running to the media, complaining of victimisation. Boyd had put Simoes's nose out of joint in the past and the coach wanted to find out whether the new 'Blacka' was for real.

I was curious to know why the coach had suddenly had a change of heart. Maybe he felt that by indulging wayward Walter he would ease pressure on the forwards. He said that he had always maintained that Boyd was an exceptional talent and felt deep down that if he could get him to France, away from the bad influences that are attracted by his cult hero status in Jamaica, then maybe they could work together. I also suspected that Simoes wanted to show the sections of Jamaican society in uproar about the size of his salary that he was capable of forgiveness by picking Walter. If we went to France and got beaten with Boyd on board, the Jamaican public would have less ammunition.

It also crossed my mind that Simoes could be preparing a way for leaving his options open after France. Having stated that he would definitely quit following the story in the *Sunday Herald*, he might have been having second thoughts. Taking Boyd to France would win over some of his critics, regardless of the team's performance.

Simoes could not have many justifications for not picking Walter, which led me to believe that his mind was made up before the vote had even taken place. It all seemed rather stage managed. After all, there was no way Simoes would make a public climb-down and beg Walter to play. Another theory was that the secret ballot was rigged – but I doubted that very much. Simoes knew that the Boyd admirers among the Jamaican boys – the players who knew more of his legend – would have enough strength to vote him in.

It would be my guess that The Captain was involved somewhere along the line. Although Burrell liked to play the 'big man' I previously thought Simoes held the real power. I sensed that The Captain had not quite appreciated what an engine for change Simoes would become and what a big say he would have in decisions. There weren't many people on the island who could issue The Captain with an order and expect it to be carried out and that was one of the reasons why Burrell liked to keep the Brazilian very close.

If Burrell had reasserted his authority, gone above the head of the coach and engineered a situation where the prodigal Boyd could be recalled to the fold, it represented a telling shift in the balance of power. Perhaps the Jamaican members of the backroom staff – coach Brown, the Reverend, Denise Nicholls – had also played a part. It was intriguing stuff but as we touched down in Jamaica, I would have put my house on Boyd getting the nod for France.

Sure enough, when a relaxed-looking Simoes faced the Jamaican media on 2 June, he announced Walter Boyd's name among the 22. Such had been the speculation over the last couple of weeks that few were shocked by the news. Personally, I had never really doubted my place although it was still a special moment seeing my name confirmed on the list that was faxed to FIFA. Gregory Messam, Anthony Waugh, Donald 'Foley' Stewart and Steve Green were among the unlucky ones to miss out.

On 3 June we stopped off on our way to the airport so that the Prime Minister could wish us luck and then boarded a plane to Miami. After that, it was all change for France.

Before the story reaches its final stages, I feel it's important to describe some of those people on board the flight that touched down in France at 10.55am on Thursday 4 June. It was a remarkable set of individuals and the little things often said a lot about them. A small scene that took place as we waited to board the plane taking us from Jamaica to New York spoke volumes for the relationship between Warren Barrett and Spider.

I don't need to say much more about Spider, other than how proud I am to be godfather to his son. He performed superbly while deputising for Boopie, who missed the games in South Korea with a thigh injury. In one of his team meetings, the coach said how pleased he was that Spider had improved so much since working with his rival for the goalkeeper's jersey. Boopie could have been worried that Spider might take his place – but instead he beamed with pride.

As we reached the airport gate before departing for the USA, I noticed Boopie filling in the customs form for Spider, who had problems reading and writing. Boopie, who was well educated, handled the situation with the minimum of fuss. If that had taken place in England, Spider would have been ripped apart. Sure there was competition between the two keepers but there was also a deep well of mutual affection and admiration.

Warren Barrett was a big family man and a fine captain, and his communication skills made him an ideal spokesman for the group. He had a huge knowledge of world football and I had no doubts that he had the technique and character to handle the move to Europe that he hankered for. It was ironic that the Holiday Inn we stayed at in Montego Bay before flying out to France was the very same hotel that Warren worked in as a waiter and I was informed that he was still on the payroll some four years later. His was definitely a case of local boy made good.

Another Mo Bay man was the quiet Theodore Whitmore. Popular with the ladies, Tappa was very Jamaican in his outlook which sometimes made him a hard person to read. He is blessed with fantastic individual ability and I thought that he should use the World Cup as his showcase. He was hoping for a move abroad and had already signed up with the British agent hired by the JFF but I wasn't convinced that England would suit his game. I felt he might have a better chance of success on the Continent.

Durrent 'Tatti' Brown, or 'Maestro', was a very old-looking 34 year old and as Jamaican as they come. He had been a great sweeper for the country over the years and must have wished that he was 15 years younger. In all probability, this would be his last year on the international scene and he had not been 100 per cent since the car crash at the start of the year. The other players seemed convinced that he was back to his old self and ready to play again, but I suspected that Simoes was taking him along as reward for long service.

Tatti was more thrilled than most at being awarded the land to build on and was looking forward to starting work on a four-bedroom villa when he stopped playing full-time. I could see him going into coaching or maybe even taking up a position within the national football programme with one of the younger age-group sides. He was a quiet, God-fearing character but he commanded a lot of respect – until, that is, we caught him eating Kentucky Fried Chicken. We all thought he was a disciplined vegetarian!

Despite the warnings, I liked 'Shorty' Malcolm a lot. He had a very dry sense of humour and a big, infectious laugh. He was perhaps the most 'Jamaican' member of the squad – and certainly the most patriotic – but had no problem with any of the English players and seemed to like having us along. With Shorty it was a case of still waters run deep, and I think that's why we got on well without having to say much to each other. He could be very reserved at times but his hard expression did not always convey how he felt inside. I remember someone asking him what was wrong once and Shorty replying, 'I don't laugh if I don't find something funny and I don't think I have to be talking to show I'm happy.' I could relate to that.

Rudi wasn't from the western tip of the island but tended to tag along with them. He worked hard to look after his family and was a popular member of the squad. Tragic though it was, he probably knew that he wouldn't be fit enough to play. There was no way we would have gone without him though.

Peter was not a member of the Mo Bay crew – or any other crew for that matter. 'Jair' was a man who could move in any circle and he became a close personal friend in the time that I knew him. He was knowledgeable, communicative and interesting and was the one player that all the others looked up to.

Like Tatti, France '98 would probably be his farewell as an international as there were some exciting youngsters waiting in the wings. Peter insisted that he would consider another couple of years abroad if the right offer came along, although I suspected that he would be one of the front runners for Simoes' job if the coach carried out his threat to stand down after the World Cup. He had ambitions in that line of work and was well respected inside the JFF.

Cargill was another family man who was looking for this last big occasion as a player to secure his future. There were already various business options open to him and he would never want for work but it was for people like Peter that we had campaigned for the players' pool. It might just have made him enough to reward all those years of service. After watching what an example he was to the younger players and having spoken at length with him about the game, I would be very interested in getting Peter involved in any future management positions I might get offered.

Despite both being so young, Ian Goodison and Ricardo Gardener were strong characters. They were difficult to gauge because they could be friendly one minute and not want to know the next. Neither seemed particularly relaxed with people of different races and at times they could be distant towards the English-based members of the squad. I would like to think that this had more to do with their manner and the way they carried themselves than any personal grudge.

Pepe was not as frightening as he looked. He had influence within the group but that was probably because his personality matched his build – big. He had six brothers, four sisters and a whole community behind him but unlike Shorty, people were not afraid to answer him back. Underneath the rap star attitude, Pepe is a good man to have on your side and an excellent footballer.

Bibi was the baby of the squad and one of the heartthrobs. He tended to follow in Pepe's footsteps and they looked out for each other. Bibi had a strong personality but he never showed it much while he was in Pepe's company. He is a bright boy with fantastic ability – probably the most exciting prospect in the squad – yet I worried that he might not handle being on his own in a different culture. Peter put me right, telling me that he had come into the Jamaican squad as an unknown 17-year-old alongside local legends like Paul 'Tegat' Davis. He made his major league debut in Jamaica at the age of 14 so he already had a good deal of experience under his belt.

Dean Sewell, Andy Williams and Christopher Dawes were also part of the younger set. Dean was the team joker. Christopher Dawes was very quiet and heavily into Rastafarianism, which meant he did not eat meat or join in the team prayers. He was an excellent player who just lacked a bit of belief in himself. Andy was quite manipulative in that he could slip between English, American and Jamaican whenever it suited him. He was one of the most gifted players in the team but needed to be at the right mental level to perform. His attitude seemed to have dropped by the time we left for France.

Though they both had the bad-boy reputation, Onandi and Walter were not as bad as they had been painted. Onandi was a daunting prospect to look at, not known as 'Big Man' for nothing. He was not to be messed with although I always found him to be quite a funny, relaxed type of guy who was more intelligent than he liked to let on. He never seemed to get nervous before games – unlike some of the others – and he was very close to Walter, which surprised me at first. I had been led to believe that there were big problems between them.

From my very limited experience, Walter seemed like a quieter version of Paul Hall – funny, good natured and happy.

And finally, to my English-born Jamaican team-mates. Fitz, Hally and Deon are all very different. Fitzroy is upfront and in your face and I'm not sure whether that's to do with his upbringing or a reaction to the way English football had treated him. He speaks his mind, sometimes rubbing people up the wrong way. As I got to know him, I learned that that was just his manner. Fitz is larger than life and because of that people probably have more opinions on him than any other player from England.

I didn't get to know Deon that well as he is quite a bit younger than myself. Unfortunately, since winning the Jamaican Sports Personality of the Year, Deon went off the boil and his place now looked under threat from the likes of Marcus and Walter. After scoring all those important goals during qualification, he now had to prove himself all over again. Finding some form in training must just give him the kick-start he needs.

Paul Hall is much more confident. He is a popular, funny lad with a similar outlook on life as myself. Before he lost his place in the squad, a player called Paul Young used to be the MC. He would stand the middle of the group (on the mike) to introduce the players individually. Each player would then have to do a turn and Hally always got the biggest applause for his 'chatting'. He would pen a few lines on the coming match and ask for some 'UK stylee' from the English-based players and then some 'Jamaican stylee' from the home boys. He would have been a star if he had stuck with his music.

Marcus and Frank went out to the Gold Cup, enjoyed the success and fitted in well. Darryl, particularly, impressed the other lads with his enthusiasm and pride in playing for Jamaica. Unlike his better-known Derby team mate, Dean Sturridge, Powelly won a lot of friends with his attitude at QPR. Sturridge's agent had angered the coach by asking for special treatment whereas Darryl just wanted to be given a shirt and told what to do. The 'UB40s' (English reggae band – geddit?), as we were known, now numbered seven but the level of support and the warmth of the welcome in west London, Cardiff and Manchester had given us a bit more credibility in Jamaican eyes. Having been over to England and seen us in our professional environment, I also think the Jamaican players had a lot more respect for us by the time we touched down in Paris.

There was of course a cultural and professional gulf between us. The humour in an English dressing room is unique in the world of football, and I always felt that we had to be wary of becoming too vocal in case any of the Jamaican lads took the ribbing to heart. In England, if a player has a bad day in training he knows he will be forced to wear the yellow jersey or get the laces of his boots tied together. Insults are like water off a duck's back.

It was not quite the same in the Jamaican dressing room. Two players once had words during a training session and were still not talking to each other by the evening. One of the younger players who did not make the final squad also got upset over being nick-named 'brown girl'. He was light skinned with soft features but felt the other players were calling his masculinity into question. He took it so badly that the coach had to pull him aside and have a word with him. There is a big bravado among male Jamaicans and being top dog is as important in football as it is in everyday life.

Coach Simoes was always emphasising the team mentality and declaring that there were no stars. We were all pieces of the same jigsaw and he liked the fact that we had specific roles to play. Mine was probably as the talker, the man who represented Jamaica in press conferences, although I intended to broaden this out to include being a starter in the team. There were others who could get up at dinner and sing or tell stories that would make the whole bus laugh. We had an amazing variety and balance within the group, not to mention a burning desire to 'shake up the world'.

12

World Cup Blues

ROBBIE

4 June

After a 15-hour round trip from Jamaica, we step off the plane and are shown into a separate room to have our accreditation photos taken. The boys are a bit tired but in good spirits, wearing sunglasses and tossing beach balls about. Some have left the tags on their suits and the younger ones get the hump when a couple of us try to pull them off. Two and a half hours later, our 37-strong party arrives at World Cup base camp in Chaumont. The Chateau Arc en Barrois is a small hotel in a wonderful setting and team Jamaica has taken over the whole place for the duration of the World Cup.

It's a relaxed atmosphere but the players turn their noses up when they see what kit sponsors Kappa have supplied for the biggest show on earth. We have all travelled light, expecting a sackful of training kit and leisurewear to be waiting for us on arrival. Much to our horror, World Cup gear comprises of two shirts, two pairs of shorts and a tracksuit. In Jamaica, appearance is everything and comments are made during the stretching session on the hotel's front lawn.

Coach Simoes comes up with one of his famous analogies – apparently, our deal with Kappa is like a marriage. 'There are times that your wife does things that don't please you,' he says, 'but you either divorce her or work things out.' We are told to put the disappointment of the paltry kit quota to the back of our minds and focus on the job in hand.

It is the first time some of the players have had personal contact with Walter Boyd and after all the commotion in Jamaica over his selection, I can sense a lot of eyes are on him.

Everyone retires to bed at approximately 10pm and sleeps soundly.

5 June

We get down to some serious training – physical work in the morning and game practice in the afternoon. I am mildly surprised that Simoes has proposed a change in the team shape by going to a flat-back four which means an extra place in midfield. In training, match situations are always split into green and yellow bibs and green more often than not means a place in the first team. I am given a green bib for the first time! Having only played a bit part during qualification, I must admit to getting an extra buzz at the prospect of starting against Croatia.

After dinner we are locked away to study videos of our opponents. Everyone is starting to get a feel for the occasion.

6 June

The technical staff are keeping a close eye on Walter and he is told off for not wearing the right T-shirt to breakfast. Simoes does not like anyone to be different, although in Walter's defence, he did not have the right T-shirt to wear in the first place. I tell him to come up to the room afterwards and give him a couple of mine, just so he cannot give anyone an excuse to have a go at him.

Morning training is especially demanding with a lot of sprint and physical work. We are watched by a large contingent of locals who get their first look at the national team. Many come wearing Reggae Boyz T-shirts and waving flags. There are probably very few black faces in this quiet little village yet there are 500 people firmly behind an all-black Jamaican team.

After lunch a serious meeting takes place with Mr Reid and Captain Burrell. With just eight days to go before our opening World Cup match, the JFF has not worked out a payment structure for the tournament. Captain Burrell goes through the usual opening gambits – they have to pay the players' salaries and have forked out on new offices – and then reveals that the Federation is not in a strong financial position. The Captain says they can only afford to pay the players an incentive.

The same players' committee that faced him in London insists on match fees in addition to the incentive system on offer. Captain Burrell is adamant that this is impossible, reminding me of that one-way 'discussion' when he flatly refused to allow a players' pool to be set up. The best-paid players in the Jamaican squad are probably on no more than £400–£500 a week and if we get beaten in all three games they will go home with nothing extra for starring in the World Cup. Just imagine the bonuses and spin-offs for the likes of Ronaldo, del Piero and Shearer. It would be nice if we could make even a tiny fraction of that – or anything at all, for that matter – but as usual Captain Burrell opts for the big stick method of bargaining.

The players have been well paid throughout, he says. It is true, playing for the national team has made some of the boys rich in comparison to the people living round them in Jamaica, and The Captain reminds them of as much by harking back to the days when they had to walk home after matches, before they could afford cars.

However, the balance of power has changed since that late-night 'discussion' in London because anyone who doesn't see things his way this time cannot be dropped from the squad. The players' pool is coming back to haunt Burrell because we told him that generating our own additional money could take the weight off the JFF.

We press ahead with the demand for match fees and query where the revenue from all those games round the world, sponsorship money and FIFA bonuses have gone. Despite some frantic last-minute bartering by The Captain, we manage to clinch the deal. Players will receive a fee of US $8,000 for starting and half for coming on as substitute.

Simoes holds a meeting of his own before afternoon training and slams into us for our discussion with Burrell, disappointed that we requested a match appearance fee rather than settle for the incentive. He turns the situation on its head, accusing us of being scared of not winning any points and not believing that we can reach the second round. In the past, we have always felt that the coach has been totally behind us, but this outburst is alarming to say the least.

I don't like what he has to say or the JFF's policy of incentive only. We are Jamaica, the smallest country ever to qualify for a World Cup finals, and we are up against the likes of Croatia, Argentina and the heavily funded Japan. Some of the boys have given up two or three years of their lives to get here and they have done it for their country.

All any of us want is to come out of the tournament with some guaranteed figure. We have been waiting since November for payment of agreed bonuses and cannot be blamed for demanding something in writing from the JFF.

Not surprisingly, training is fractious and people vent their anger with some pretty crude tackling. The coach pulls me to one side, wondering how he can lift the players and get them refocused on the job in hand. Morale has clearly been hit by the coach coming out on the side of the JFF and true to form, there are whispers about the 'white man' not being with us and only being interested in protecting The Captain and his employers. Some of the players wonder whether he is on incentive only. In the light of the recent publication of his JA $8 million a year salary, they are very sceptical.

8 June

The players complain of tiredness after twice-daily sessions. Since our arrival we have been working really hard. Most of us assumed that training would have been stepped down considerably by this point – at this rate, we won't be feeling fresh for the match. We have also been travelling, playing matches, training and attending functions for what seems like months. Simoes takes our feelings on board and lightens the morning session a little.

In the afternoon Simoes sets up match scenarios for the game against Croatia. It looks like he has definitely decided on changing the team shape, going with a flat-back four, four or five in midfield and maybe just one up front. Myself, Marcus Gayle and Frank Sinclair are added to the first team but it goes badly. The second team try exceptionally hard to prove their point and it looks as though the coach's starting line-up has caused quite a lot of resentment.

After the session Simoes looks distinctly unhappy. It's not surprising: training has been a mess and there is bickering and back-biting within the group. He tells us that he is going to call a 'clear the air meeting' tomorrow to see what the problems are and to establish whether the group wants to go back to the tried and trusted 3–5–2 system. Talking to Spider I sense a feeling of unease in the camp, especially from the Jamaican players. He inadvertently tells me that some of the players are saying that it is only Jamaica who are *not* represented in this World Cup!

There are also voices inside the camp complaining that this is turning into a second England team. Myself, Frank and Marcus getting more practise time with the first eleven has not helped and I would say that Steve Malcolm and Andy Williams are among those unhappy with the way things have panned out since we have been in France.

But it's not only the English: the Brazilians are also here in force. Alongside the coach and Alfredo, Chicko Santos, the goalkeeping coach, Walter Gamma, who compiles dossiers on the opposition, Dr Manos, a foot doctor, and Jose, the roly-poly masseur, all speak Portuguese and talk animatedly in their mother tongue during meetings, making the players suspicious. By the end of the day, the unrest has spread. Tomorrow's meeting could have a big bearing on Sunday's outcome.

My guess is that Simoes will back down and revert to a 3–5–2 formation. It would go against everything that he has planned but maybe he senses that he is losing control. The Jamaicans are unhappy about the money situation and now seem to be flexing their muscles about team selection and tactics. If he does not restore the old spirit soon, we are in real trouble.

9 June

At the meeting, Simoes summons an appropriate analogy from his large repertoire. He talks of a teenager who thinks he knows everything and constantly argues with his parents. When the teenager reaches the age to have children, says the coach, he realises his parents had been right all along. He tells us we are acting like teenagers and it is time for us to listen rather than make our own judgements. We stick to the coach's 4–4–2 and the session goes remarkably well. One-nil to Simoes.

The coach and Peter Cargill go to watch Croatia in a practice game against a local side, so Carl Brown takes the evening session. It's a rare chance for Carl to be in charge and show his worth to the watching audience. It is a light-hearted couple of hours – one of the most enjoyable sessions so far, and we have our first press call afterwards. TV crews from all over the world have come to speak to our cosmopolitan group. We seem to have struck a chord from America to Japan; so many people are thinking of Jamaica right now. It is inspiring in one way but adds to the already mounting pressure in another.

After training we meet up with eight of the lads who missed out on the final squad. They are staying 2km from our hotel but don't have much contact with us, which makes me wonder whether flying them over in recognition of their efforts was a promotional stunt by the JFF. They feel a bit like prisoners because food has to be despatched from our hotel and there is so little to do in town. We are feeling a little enclosed ourselves, security is so tight at the Chateau. No press or civilians are allowed in and we are not allowed out. We have been living in each other's pockets for nearly four weeks and tempers are starting to get stretched. We need a change of scenery but most of all we need the games to start.

10–11 June

The twice-daily training sessions are becoming tedious and the players break the boredom by watching a variety of videos or by taking their lives in their own hands and playing pool. Shorty completed evening training without any difficulties but is seen a few hours later with an enormous ice pack strapped to his right foot. Rumour is rife that Malcolm was watching a game of pool when one of Deon Burton's 'power breaks' caused the cue ball to hop off the table and land on his foot. Denise Nicholls ruins a good story by revealing that Shorty actually leapt down a couple of stairs and sprung a ligament in his foot. It is the small things that are keeping us amused.

Rudi is making progress under Denise's expert supervision although I have picked up on some more unrest, this time from the physio. The Brazilian contingent are forever trying to get Rudi to do things like jumping, ball work or stints on the vibration machine which Denise does not feel he is ready for. Rudi is the sort of person who just gets on with things, but when his knee flares up it is Denise who is left to look after a depressed player. She is having to play agony aunt as well as physio and I understand she confronted Alfredo and said that only when a player is medically ready is he allowed to start the fitness work. I imagine she feels undermined by their constant intrusion.

It is yet another worrying example of friction between the Jamaicans and the Brazilians on the staff. Many of the Jamaicans feel that their positions are duplicated by Brazilians and it does appear that they have the final say. This is not lost on the Jamaican players, who have a lot of respect and affection for their Jamaican counterparts.

12 June

We travel to the hotel in Lens which takes five hours on the bus. I wonder whether we could have flown or gone by train but I say nothing to the coach. This is definitely his baby.

The hotel in Lens is lovely but remote. The general opinion is that we still don't feel part of the World Cup because we have hardly seen any fans or sampled any of the colour and excitement. It's like being a theatre-goer who cannot buy a ticket for a show but can hear the performance going on in the distance. We need some cup fever but it is 9pm when we arrive, meaning there is only enough time for a quick meal before bed.

13 June

Today is supposed to mirror the day of the first game so we stretch at 11am then take a rest period before going for our last training session in the Félix Bollaert stadium in the centre of Lens. Simoes looks almost certain to stick with his 4–4–2 and I am quietly confident of starting the first game.

Training goes remarkably badly. It is pouring with rain and the second eleven continue to cause us all sorts of problems which creates a bad atmosphere within the group. The awful weather might persuade Simoes to play more of the English-based lads than expected – which certainly won't help matters. Influential Jamaican players like Cargill are not happy about changing the formation when 3–5–2 served us so well in the qualifiers. Jamaicans don't like change and in football as well as life, they tend to stick with what they know. The bad feeling degenerates to such a point that a running feud develops between Onandi and Fitz as we shower.

Fitz appeals for Onandi to 'grow up' and take criticism once in a while. It is not the most intelligent thing to say to a man who stands like a six foot three wall of muscle and has a famously short fuse. Onandi is ready to 'stamp on Fitz's head' but Brown steps in to restore order.

It is at times like these when Brown is at his best. He is totally respected by all the players and has a fantastic relationship with them. He talks calmly and quietly to both parties and restores the peace, although there is a look on Onandi's face that says all is not forgotten.

Before we leave the players' area, Simoes calms us down. It is probably due to nerves, he says. He hadn't needed to chip in however. Carl had already sorted the problem out and it was the one occasion Simoes didn't need to have the last word.

DANIEL

Devon's dreadlocks are unmistakable across the fast-emptying press pavilion. There are smiles and 'respects' because we have done what we said we would: met up in Lens for Jamaica's historic first match in the World Cup finals. The last time I had seen him, Devon was still waiting to hear about accreditation but his situation was not helped by the fact that the postman did not always deliver to where he lived. In addition to his trusty camera, the man who has been following the Reggae Boyz 'f'way back a long time' is now dragging a vast zoom lens in a coffin-sized box. He tells me he managed to blag it off Nikon in Paris.

The impressive media centres at France '98 are staffed by volunteers working for the CFO and, in Lens, all the green shirts seem to have congregated round the Jamaican press contingent. If the team has captured the imagination, then so too have the reporters. Simoes had criticised the Jamaican press for not travelling enough to cover the team but there is a hardy crew in France – Nodley Wright, Earl Bailey and Tym Glaser the Aussie football writer from the *Gleaner* among them. Each of us wears the laminated badges that guarantee access to all the World Cup venues. It is like owning a membership card to the United Nations and the amount of foreign media representatives that come by to say hello suggests that the world is happy to see Jamaica being represented at the table.

Devon (who looks about 28 but is actually nearer 40) seems to have wangled a commission as the team's official photographer and is travelling back to Chaumont with them after the match. His friend Evon Hewitt, sports correspondent for Irie FM, is at the end of one of the long tables, looking pensive. He is trying to send a report back to Jamaica on the mobile phone he has hired for the tournament. Devon tells me that they have not seen much of the team so far and that Chaumont is very quiet – unfortunately for Devon, a man who likes to get out and about. Over the next couple of weeks, he will cut a distinctive figure in the scrums of photographers down at pitchside or perched behind a goal grappling with his gargantuan lens.

Braving the monsoon conditions, I leave them cursing the weather and make the short dash to the 'Mixed Zone' at the entrance to the main stand. Security is extremely tight at France '98 and the only access to the players in the stadium takes place in the lobby area between the changing rooms and the team bus. In each of the tournament's eight stadiums, zig-zagging wooden partitions have been put up to create a warren for the players to walk through while, on the other side, reporters elbow and rabbit punch each other to get the best position for the all-important interview. The spots where the players stop to 'chat' is arranged beforehand with England but there is no need tonight because less than 20 reporters have turned up to talk to the Reggae Boyz on the eve of making history.

After about 15 minutes, Marcus Gayle pops his head round the corner and ambles through in a black Kappa tracksuit with 'Reggae Boyz' splashed across the shoulder blades. He grins sheepishly and says that Chaumont is decorated in black, green and gold and that he will be having a trim tomorrow morning.

Fitz, Paul and Deon mooch through next. Fitz has a distant look in his eyes like he's 'in the zone'. I wish him luck. 'It's my show, you know that,' he says and walks on. Hally tells me he's in the best shape of his life and is looking sharp, 'very sharp'. Security is tight at the hotel but Paul is impressed that the French authorities are making such a big deal of protecting the team's privacy. It is almost exactly a year since he went out to Jamaica for the trial and he says he's buzzing on being only 24 hours away from playing in front of the world. Alfredo breezes past as we're talking, squeezes my arm and weaves out into the rain.

The Reverend loiters in the corner wearing one of the black tracksuits and a Reggae Boyz baseball cap, capturing the scene on a video camera. I ask him what he has been saying to the boys during the build-up. 'It's a matter of dealing with anxiety and just how to cope with that. Yes, it's the World Cup but you've,' he puffs, 'kinda got beyond the World Cup blues. We've got to stay in control and maintain the good discipline that we have endeavoured to cultivate.

'It's a matter now of focusing. We been telling the guys, "Heeey, accept it in your stride, relax, take it easy, it will come." They are raring to go. They are hungry for it and when there is a hunger for anything you devour and consume what you want.'

What would he be telling me at 8.30 tomorrow night if I was playing for Jamaica, I ask. He laughs. 'I can't let everything out. But I'd be saying, "Hey, guy, stay calm, give your absolute best. If you never had it in you, you would never be here. It's proof enough that you've got the goods and if you've got the goods, deliver the goods." ' His voice slips seamlessly to a lower octave and he raps out the final, killer line: ' "Now go, get on stage and perform." '

It is what the Reverend does best. This beguiling mixture of Jesse Jackson and Luthor Vandross is a far cry from England's spiritual adviser, a suburban housewife with magic hands.

An excited-looking Rene makes a point of saying hello to all the female reporters. I wasn't surprised, having already seen what a charmer he is at a press conference in Kingston to welcome 'King Pele'. Tonight, his eyes are dancing and I ask him what he has up his sleeve for Croatia. 'You know I am a reader and I remember the Gulf War and the strategy the Americans use.' The first war reference is clocked at five seconds. 'Surprise is the principal tactic, the principal weapon. Let us try do something that Croatia don't expect from us.'

As he seems to be in a jovial mood, I push my luck and ask him what happened to change his mind over Walter Boyd. 'Every time Walter Boyd was sent out of the camp was because of his own attitude and the attitude of some other ones. People always make apology for him, never him. He must take the attitude that it is eyes to eyes, face to face, man to man. He call me many times and I did not reply or answer the phone to him. I wait for him to take the right attitude.

'And he did. He bought a ticket and fly in the same flight to us to New York. He come to me to beg me and implore me but I said, "Sorry. You are out." He call my hotel and spent more than one hour and I said, "Sorry. You are out". After the game he came to the hotel and he sit at the table. It taught me two points. It was the first time that he had talked to me in my eyes. The second thing is that people come to have autographs from him and he was crying. I think it must have been hard for him.

'It was a great attitude for him and he faced the problem and said, "I have to do something." I go to talk to the players and that attitude helped him. Before, only three players vote to him to return to the squad. Now it is fifteen. Before, he did everything that he wants and I did not like that. Then after, he came and try to do everything that I want and that was wrong too. Now he does what the team needs and what he likes. It is a short time to say that he is a changed person but he has made lot of sacrifice.'

There is no way Walter can be match fit after playing so little all year but it is unlikely Simoes will pick him to start anyway. Evon Hewitt had spoken briefly to Walter at Chaumont, and he had said he was going to 'score three goals for Jamaica'. When the news went out to Irie FM's listeners, there was no hint of doubt in Evon's voice that Walter would come through with the goods. At this point in time, the man himself is nowhere to be seen.

Conversation turns to the other big debate in Jamaican football: Will Simoes leave after the World Cup?

The coach cocks his head, rubs his moustache and gives his verdict. 'The attitude I take constantly is that I try to help the country because people have a very short memory. They don't follow my acts. The month before, I said, "Listen, I will not allow this World Cup to blind the people. The people must continue to talk about the problems of this country. We have many problems and like Brazil, it is a very unfair country because five per cent of the population has 95 per cent of the money of the country. It is not a poor country, it is an unfair country."

'What I say is that the citizen must be a shareholder of the whole country. They must decide the salary of the coach. My relationship with the country is that I walk where some people cannot walk, I face them.' He was talking about going into the ghettos and preaching how a philosophy for life could be found in his philosophy on football.

'I don't want to be there if they think, Hey, look at the salary of this coach,' he argues. 'I work in Jamaica for four years and someone puts in the paper that I have the highest salary in the country, not the lowest salary at this World Cup. I have lost a lot of money to be there so the people must discuss whether they need me. I think it will be very difficult to stay there and very difficult to leave there.' And with that, he says 'God bless you' and is gone.

ROBBIE

After a light snack back at the hotel, we return to our rooms, unable to think about anything else but our World Cup debut. Despite the problems in training, everyone is determined to make the most of this opportunity. We are also intrigued to see what the final cut of the Reggae Boyz documentary made by TransWorld International is like. Luckily, we can pick up Channel 4 from the hotel and we settle down to watch the last six months of our lives on screen. What better way to spend the night before our first game?

How wrong could we be? *Reggae Boyz* is a bitter disappointment, especially for the Jamaican players who are depicted in a really poor light. The makers go to some lengths to show how the affluence of the English-based players contrasts with the lifestyles of the Jamaican boys. Fitzroy is very much the central figure, one of the worst moments being when he takes the camera crew to his mock Georgian house, complete with showhome decor and convertible BMW parked in the drive. We next see him giving the crew a guided tour of the team house in Kingston, taking in the 'basic' toilet facilities, home of cockroaches and the 'dumplings and curried goat' are flushed away. He even lies on film, saying there is only one bathroom when there are in fact five.

Fitz, it seems, is lowering himself by playing for Jamaica. His other flippant remarks include references to all the Jamaican players having ten girlfriends each and how he would not allow his wife to use the bathroom in the team house. He comes across incredibly badly, swilling a couple of beers before catching a flight for a match and claiming that all the World Cup means to him is money. He is also captured questioning the Jamaicans' attitude, saying that they 'had better realise that this is the f***ing World Cup'. In short, the whole documentary focuses on the negative aspects of Jamaica rather than celebrating the incredible achievements of a remarkable group of footballers.

Judging by our reactions, it is lucky for the film crew that they have gone back to England. They had been staying in Chaumont and were hoping to make a follow-up film on Jamaica's experiences at the tournament. They came into the hotel to film us watching the opening match between Brazil and Scotland, which was all a bit staged because we were told how to act. It is easy to be wise after the event but when they interviewed me while I was having treatment on the broken toe at Wimbledon I was somewhat suspicious. They asked me to put on a sad face but I told them I could not be negative about my experiences with Jamaica. I believe in fate, and although I would have accepted not being fit to play, since first making the decision to join up I have always had a sneaking feeling that I would play in the World Cup finals. When the film crew got fed up with me not playing ball, we called it a day. Unsurprisingly, the interview is nowhere to be found in the film. I would advise Channel 4 to scrap plans for Part Two immediately.

14 June

Breakfast is strictly optional on the morning of the most important football match in Jamaica's history. Most players opt to stay in their rooms rather than poke their head up over the trenches dug in the night. I have not spoken to many of the boys yet but I can sense war is about to be declared. Simoes comes to my room, wondering what my opinion of the documentary is and what he should do about Fitz. I convey my disappointment. I don't feel that Fitzroy's TV misdemeanors should affect the coach's football decisions, though.

My opinions are not widely shared. Understandably the boys are furious with Fitz. They think he has too much to say about everything and has 'sold them out'. Peter Cargill says an hour's television has destroyed a year's hard work in smoothing the introduction of the English-based players. Fitz either hadn't seen what the documentary makers were trying to do or was paid enough to not care about the consequences. Onandi stirs up the feud that has been simmering since last night by issuing Fitz with a warning. It would be best if he did not return to Jamaica for a long time after the World Cup, he says. Team spirit is in tatters.

After lunch Simoes attempts to address the problem. Fitzroy is allowed – or instructed – to say his piece in order to repair the damage. He argues that the TV crew stitched him up, using only part of interviews, but it's a poor attempt to appease the players. Many nod while he's talking, but I don't feel he has won anyone over.

Outsiders cannot be allowed to affect the group harmony, Simoes tells us, and there must be none of the England v. Jamaica, Boyd v. Simoes divisions that the film implied. We desperately try to stay focused and pull together but the atmosphere on the bus from the hotel to the stadium leaves a lot to be desired. As usual, Spider is in a class of his own and is up and out of his seat, trying to get the boys going. However things will undoubtedly come to a head if we don't get a good result so Carl Brown is on standby.

This day is what I have dreamt about so many times since that day in November. I think back 25 years to smashing a ball inside two strategically placed sweaters and running to take the acclaim of the imaginary crowd in a replica No. 10 Brazil jersey. I called myself El Ray Pele. I never thought I would be lucky enough to play on a magnificent stage like this.

It is one of the first times in 16 years as a professional that I feel nervous arriving at a stadium and there is a massive knot in my stomach. The Jamaican fans are here in their thousands, turned out in yellow, gold and green to witness Jamaican history in the making. Women sporting a minimum of clothing dance to the reggae beat, intent on enjoying the event. Seeing the familiar things that you encounter week in, week out in the Premiership – the dressing rooms, the tunnel, the pitch – eventually settles me down and I slip into that 'just another game' state of mind.

DANIEL

'Progression. Upwards movement.' It's a pretty good stab at explaining what being here today means for Jamaica.

'It's gonna be one-love Jamaica. Trust me, it's like Bob Marley say.' The smiling Rasta with the waist-length dreads shakes my hand and walks off, soon becoming just another yellow T-shirt in a human palette of green, gold, black, red and white. The rain has given way and Lens, a town that would not look out of place in Lancashire, is bathed in a warm evening glow. There is a constant banging of drums and squawking of horns and I almost expect floats to go past or to turn the corner and find a sound system set up on the street. The scene is one of those that makes France '98 special: the eye-catching check of the Croatian shirts and facepaint set against the colours of Jamaica makes the northern-most city in the competition feel decidedly tropical.

'More visibility, strengthen economy, publicise tourism and the sport arena,' states an elderly Jamaican man as though he's reading the answers off a list. The younger woman with him has one of those whiney American accents. 'We are taken seriously now, y'know, really.'

There is a five-piece Blues Brothers band playing on a traffic island outside the stadium and a cacophony of whistles greets their wry version of Bob Marley's 'Jammin'. Gathered around the dark-suited five-piece are other people who have seen football used as a tool for nation-building: the exploits of Davor Suker, Robert Prosinecki and Zvonimir Boban have featured prominently in the early chapters of Croatia's short history.

'It's means a lot to us. This is history.' The accent is pure south London but the last word of the sentence is swilled round in the mouth for the full Caribbean taste. 'It's gonna be two-nil to the boys and Walter Boyd will score one and Deon Burton will get the other.' The man is from Brixton and his two friends lean in to give their verdict. 'It means everything to us; it's something we can all rally behind and all be proud of.'

A young woman guides the arm of what looks like her grandfather. They are from Kingston. 'Charlton road, right in the middle,' explains the gentleman considerately. 'Four-nil to Reggae Boyz!' shouts the girl, and her grandfather frowns. He is wearing his best suit for the occasion and scolds her playfully: 'No, she a bit ambitious.'

A couple of New York Rastas – 'via London and Mandyville' – confirm that it's 'gonna be one-love Jamaica'. The man with the shorter dreads, lighter skin and Jamaican headband declares: 'This means history. The football has united Jamaica. Before, the people used to fight against each other because of politics but now, no more. This is unity, it's a mystic thing. Last election there were no guns. Like Bob Marley say, it's gonna be one-love Jamaica.' It is a popular phrase.

ROBBIE

It is a very proud and emotional moment hearing the national anthem before the game, and I can't help but think of my mum and dad in their front room in Stoke-on-Trent. My mother, I know, will be beaming with pride, probably more so than if I played for England. After all the sacrifices they made for me, my brother and sisters, it is a fantastic feeling to be able to make them happy. And, suddenly, our troubles have been put to one side and there is a confidence running through the team.

DANIEL

As the sun sets behind the stand to my left, the clock has finally ticked round to 'showtime' in Lens. Simoes has gone for a 4–4–2 with Frank Sinclair and Ricardo Gardener either side of a centre back partnership of Onandi and Pepe. Robbie and Fitz flank Peter Cargill and Theodore Whitmore in midfield and the trusted, if recently goal-shy, Hall and Burton partnership is retained up front. Argentina opened Group H with a 1-0 victory over Japan in Toulouse and Croatia are expected to whip Jamaica. Suker takes less than 60 seconds to pot his first effort at Barrett's goal and tests the keeper a second time before two minutes are on the clock. Jamaica look hesitant and somewhat stage-struck.

A nice interchange outside the Croatian box brings a free kick and high fives but Fitz buries his shot into the wall. Suker dances round four challenges at the other end and it is left to Boopie to claw out a Stanic shot. A huge drum beat rumbles from the stand housing most of the Jamaican fans and the players start to slow the pace. Croatia are flooding the midfield and Peter Cargill gets dispossessed with alarming ease, while Tappa looks more spindly than usual. It's like watching friends playing at the World Cup and I feel two or three disapproving glances in the press box when I give one of Pepe's block tackles a standing ovation. Alongside him, Onandi is demonstrating the defensive qualities that Simoes has talked of.

Bibi has a minor scuffle with Asanovic and Jamaica force two corners in quick succession. Robbie and Onandi go up together and the ball is cleared to safety. But just as the Reggae Boyz get the fans up and interested, Croatia break away and win a corner. Frank Sinclair is flummoxed by a short-corner routine and the ball is clipped in for Stimac to drive a shot against the bar. It feels like driving over a hump-backed bridge at speed – the 'up' of the ball cannoning back into play is immediately cancelled out by the dull thud when Stanic buries the rebound. The Croatians in the stand behind the goal go mental.

Frank is limping after a tackle and I notice Tappa and Pepe are wearing wristbands in the Rastafarian colours. Croatia almost make it two when Soldo leaves the bar above Boopie's head, twanging with a powerful shot. The red and white squares of the Balkan midfielders are taking the ball off Cargill with ease now and Suker forces another good save from Barrett. Stanic is stretchered off and Simoes takes the opportunity to issue frantic instructions to the players nearest the touchline. Jamaica calm down and then Ricardo Gardener picks up the ball near the halfway line on the far side, pads forward a couple of steps and flights a perfect diagonal cross towards Robbie.

ROBBIE

Don't ask me how, but I knew I was going to score. When you have played the game for a while, you recognise the feeling and I was having one of those moments. As the build-up to a goal starts, I sense that I am going to get an opportunity. As a scoring midfield player, people often ask how you know when to attack the box and I always describe it as being like filling out a 'spot-the-ball' coupon. As the play builds up, you have a picture in your mind and it is then your job to get to that spot at the same time as the ball. I am not blessed with blinding pace so I have always relied on my innate sense of timing. The ball from Bibi is perfect and I don't have to break stride to make contact with my head. That is the essence of timing. All I have to do is concentrate on heading the ball. Maybe it's *déjà vu*, because I could swear I have headed that ball before. Maybe it's fate again. Either way, I believe that historic goal was meant to happen.

I sprint away towards the corner flag to perform the special celebration I discussed with Spider last night. The other lads call me and Gayley 'Coco' because they reckon we head the ball so hard, we must have skulls like coconuts. The little salute is a tribute to that.

We go into the tunnel on level terms at half-time. The Croatian players are arguing among themselves all the way back to their dressing room, which is a good sign. They are ruffled and I believe we can pull off a miracle. I find out that Frank was racially abused by Davor

Suker in the first half and Pepe had to restrain him. How sad that such a great player has to stoop so low.

DANIEL

Half-time is a riot. The stadium has erupted and TV screens in the press tribune beam pictures of two gyrating Jamaican women in the lower tier of the stand to my right. Devon had pointed out this pair of dancehall legends back in Kingston and tonight 'The Ouch Girls' are dressed to impress. The larger of the two is spilling out of her tight-fitting plastic top and the younger girl is wearing surely the smallest pair of denim shorts ever made. Both are bogling and grinding for the cameras. All round the ground, people are jumping up and down and roaring with head-splitting joy. In among the Jamaican flags are Scottish saltires, French tricolors and a St George's cross with 'Everton – Huyton Blues' emblazoned across the middle.

My face hurts from smiling but after the break the Reggae Boyz fail to capitalise, allowing Croatia to take an immediate stranglehold. Asanovic forces a corner and another short free-kick routine buys Prosinecki the space to look up and slice a cross over Barrett's head and into the net beyond the lunge of Onandi Lowe. It is a second soft goal.

From the restart, Paul Hall uses his pace to clip a perfect cross into the path of Deon Burton, lurking just outside the six-yard box. But the Midas touch has deserted the Derby County man because he somehow glances his header wide. Across the field, chins sink into yellow shirts.

It is the last Jamaica has to offer and Croatia threaten to run riot. Suker tangles with Onandi Lowe and the Real Madrid striker is about to remonstrate but then he looks up, sees the size of his opponent and theatrically crumples to the floor. Boos and whistles ring round the stadium as Suker is stretchered off with his head in his hands. He is back on within ten seconds of reaching the touch-line and inevitably, it's the dark-haired villain who then puts the result beyond doubt. The Jamaican defence is sliced open and Suker's shot deflects off Bibi's boot and over Barrett for the third.

Robbie is replaced by Andy Williams, a decision that baffles reporters in the stand, and Walter Boyd, wearing yellow Pumas, comes on for Paul Hall. The game is all but done and Croatia's fans – bare-chested, with scarves wrapped round their heads – sing through the final ten minutes. The referee blows for full-time and the emotions are a mixture of regret and relief. What might have been? It could easily have been five.

ROBBIE

Even after the events of the day, it is a huge disappointment to lose. Back in the dressing room, there is time to reflect on a match that mixed the ultimate high of scoring with the let-down of such poor defending at set-pieces. Our organisation was poor for the first two goals and it's an area of the Jamaican international set-up that compares unfavourably to football at club level. Joe Kinnear goes to great lengths to work on defending set-pieces and each player knows who they are marking and the sort of movement we can expect from our opponents. The fact that we do not concede many goals from set-pieces at Wimbledon is down to hard work on the training ground and I have been surprised that we have done so little in this area with Jamaica.

The coach had always talked of people having the responsibility to take control of a situation but Jamaican football does not really cultivate that way of thinking when it comes to defending. In any case, I believe most players like to be assigned specific jobs. Once given the job, good players see it through and expect praise for doing that. We have got to learn these lessons before playing Argentina in Paris.

I enjoyed the game and felt good considering the last time I started a match was two months ago. It was therefore disappointing to be substituted for Andy Williams, who did little to change the course of the game when he went on. Andy is a main rival for a midfield spot but has lost his appetite lately. The atmosphere in the changing room is pretty flat and Deon Burton is disconsolate.

DANIEL

The jostling begins early in the Mixed Zone and Croatian coach Miroslav Blazevic appears first, looking 'bookish' in a smart blazer and wire-rimmed spectacles. An English interpreter tells the room that Mr Blazevic is happy with the result and that he told his side they would not be allowed back in the dressing room unless they won three points. In the second half, Croatia's back four pushed up into midfield because they recognised Jamaica lacked the pace to trouble them.

Simoes is led on to the stage next and begins to perspire under the lights. He looks flattened by the experience and is struggling to find positive aspects to expand on. The second Croatian goal so soon after half-time had knocked the stuffing out of his side, but just when he looks as though he's said enough, Simoes perks up. 'Jamaica never lose, Jamaica always the winner because if you don't score more than the other ones then at least you learn more than the other ones. Every time you learn something, you are the winner.' It is one of his old favourites.

Paul Hall is absolutely gutted. 'Three terrible goals, weren't they?' Fitz walks straight past behind him. 'If Deon had scored that header it would have changed the game once again. Up until the time Deon missed it we really believed we could get something out of the game.' Admitting that the game was up when there were 20 minutes still left on the clock and only one goal between the sides does not sound right.

Tappa is further along the dividing wall and I grab the opportunity to talk to him for the first time. He has been watching the tournament on TV and says Japan were unlucky against Argentina. 'We weren't trying to prove nothing, we just go out there trying to do the best for our family and for our country. But some goals scored against us tonight . . . and at this stage we cannot afford to give up goals like those.' The standard response sounds more interesting drawled to a Mo Bay rhythm. I ask him how the boys are going to pick themselves up before facing Argentina in Paris. He half smiles. 'We be fine, we never give up, y'know.'

Darryl is looking as serious as ever and is adamant that Jamaica should have got something out of the game. He moves off to shake hands with Igor Stimac, his club mate at Derby. Warren Barrett is smiling ruefully. He had a mixed night – making a number of fine saves, being at fault for the second goal and taking a full-blooded shot 'right in the private parts' in the 70th minute. 'I didn't think they were by far better than us but we need to create some more scoring opportunities. We were not over-awed by the occasion and the luck was with Croatia today.' As Davor Suker passes behind him, Boopie pulls out a small insta-matic camera and asks him to pose for a picture.

The Jamaicans are the last out of the press centre for the second night running. There is much sucking of teeth at the performance they have just witnessed. Theodore Whitmore and the strikers come in for most of the ever-ready team photographer's criticism – 'They were real bad, no fight' – and Devon is inconsolable.

ROBBIE

In some ways I get the feeling the group is happy to have got the first game out of the way. We have been waiting an eternity for it to arrive and the pressure and anxiety have grown by the day. Simoes talks about how proud he is of us but I sense this is a hollow statement. I think he really expected a little more from us. His standards are higher than that.

13

From Bad to Worse

ROBBIE

15 June

We hit the ground with a bump. It's good to finally feel part of the World Cup but the realisation has dawned that last night's game was a missed opportunity. Add a bit more belief in ourselves and eliminate those defensive lapses and we would have had enough for a point. A draw would have left us in with a chance but we now know that we will be out unless we can take something from the match against Argentina. Predictably, the critics don't give us a chance against Daniel Passarella's side, and watching a video of the Croatia game on the five-hour bus ride back to Chaumont does little to convince us otherwise. In fact, it seems to add another couple of hours to the journey.

On arrival at Chaumont, Simoes gives us the evening to ourselves. We have been constantly cooped up and some of the boys take advantage of the time off and stroll into the village. The local press have dubbed Chaumont 'The Jail' and this is a bit like giving the prisoners a quick walk round the yard. Spider and I retire to our room, believing our colourful conversation to be more entertaining than anything Chaumont has to offer.

16 June

Apart from Simoes and his staff, the dining room is empty for breakfast. Most of the players decide to take an extra 30 minutes lie-in rather than face the ackee and saltfish today. We feel really isolated in Chaumont and the boys are getting bored. As I prepare for the 9am session I am told by the general manager, Mr Watt, that morning training is cancelled and a meeting has been called in the video room.

We had expected to watch a video of Argentina but instead Simoes rips into us, saying that we have lost our discipline since the match in Lens and are mentally preparing to go home after the third game. He has picked up a rumour about some players saying it is now impossible for us to qualify and makes reference to the financial package we struck with The Captain. We are selling each other and the dream short, he tells us.

He talks of the 'true Jamaican team' having a great spirit that makes it unique and the only way of progressing to the next stage is to rediscover that spirit. The documentary crew will 'win' if we allow the film to interfere with what we want to achieve. If that happens, he says, something special will have been broken. Mending spirit is easier said than done at the moment, however.

The coach's method of refocusing us is to crack the whip and he demands that everyone is on time from now on and totally committed to the cause. Anybody stepping out of line will be hit with a $100 fine. Anyone not training to their maximum will be asked to leave immediately. We sense these are not idle threats. Simoes is animated at the best of times, but when he is very angry he has a funny method of using his bottom lip to push an already grand moustache further up his face. His face becomes all eyebrows and moustache, which is not a pretty sight.

Todd and Rupert, the main guys behind the documentary, make an appearance at the hotel but are run off the grounds after a meeting with the incandescent Captain Burrell. Bobby Smith, Head of Security for the Jamaican team, tells me that he warned them to get off the premises quick because if the players caught sight of them they would get ripped apart. The JFF are also said to be looking at the possibility of taking legal action.

True to form, the evening training session is based around workrate and running but nobody dares give anything other than 100 per cent. Simoes is watching everyone from the sideline – not saying a word, and his moustache shows no sign of returning to its normal altitude. The coach is a man who likes to wallow in his moods and some of the players feel he has been bearing this grudge a little too long. It is time to move on. Training is so tough it is bordering on pre-season level and is not what I expected in 'tournament conditions'. Someone quips,

'Can someone tell me when the World Cup is starting?' which just about sums up the mood of the players.

When we watch the Brazil v Morocco match on TV we see that the England squad are at the game. We have barely been allowed to venture off the Chateau grounds yet England are allowed to go to watch matches – and probably have a McDonalds, a few beers, a night out. The jokes go on and the gallows humour is one of the only things that is keeping us going.

Peter Cargill and I both feel that this is a time when we should be able to talk to the coach and tell him how we are feeling, physically and mentally, but we don't feel we can at the moment. There is a crying need for more things to do to keep ourselves occupied as people have taken to spending most of the time locked in their rooms, talking in small groups or watching games on TV. The fact that many of Simoes' Brazilian staff have their wives in a nearby hotel does not sit well with the majority of players.

17 June

After two hard training sessions there is an open press conference. The major topic on the lips of the media is the effect the documentary has had on the group. I have already gone on record and slaughtered the programme makers in the press. Even Simoes admits that he has had to work hard to maintain harmony in the camp.

On the way back from the training ground to the hotel I realise that the volcano is about to blow. From the back of the bus – the domain of Pepe, Bibi, Onandi, Tappa and all the 'lively' Jamaicans – come some choice comments made in the broadest, quickest patois you will ever hear.

Fitz is labelled an 'informer', which is perhaps more derogatory in Jamaican life than elsewhere. You never sell out your own and Pepe and Onandi accuse him of making money on the back of the players.

Fitz tries to stand his ground and things get heated. Understandably, his comments have upset a lot of people, especially the one about the toilet in the team house not being fit for his wife to sit on. Fitzroy's wife is white, which some of the Jamaican players seize on to make offensive remarks. Fitz challenges anyone who has anything to say to come to the front of the bus and say it to his face. The reply comes back that if he goes to the back of the bus, he might just get his head stamped on.

The 'reverse racism' from some of the Jamaican lads cannot be justified but there have been many times when I have been the only black person in a place. My life has been shaped by racially motivated experiences and some negative situations in my youth made me bitter that I had to do twice as much as my white counterparts to achieve what I wanted. To be born in Jamaica is to have a different mind-set, where you never have to feel uncomfortable about being black. In many ways I envy them this privilege.

Peter Cargill and I look at each other, sensing that things are rapidly getting out of hand. Peter confesses that he knew this would happen – the Jamaican players would not just stand by and do nothing after what Fitz said. It would be better for Fitz to stay quiet but Peter and I fear that he's just going to get himself into further trouble.

18 June

The volcano is bubbling again after an early breakfast. As we get ready for training, there is a discussion going on in one of the player's rooms. We have been banned from meeting like this since the initial talks with The Captain but this is a free-for-all about the outstanding monies owed by the JFF and the payment structure negotiated by the players' committee. Onandi seems to have enlisted the support of the players who have been forced out of the starting line-up and is arguing that a flat match fee should be paid to all members of the squad. It goes to a vote and is carried, which means we have to go back on the agreement we fought so hard to strike with Burrell.

There is also a sum still to be settled from qualification. Fuel is further added to the fire with the rumour that a certain player within the group has been given a loan by the JFF to purchase a new house and car while others have still not got a penny of what they are owed. And what the documentary did reveal – apart from the true feelings of Fitz – is that the JFF received a substantial sum on qualification, unaccounted for as yet.

Such is the mood that some players even turn on Peter Cargill, saying that he is seen talking to staff too often and is not doing his job as group spokesman. After the unrest over payment, the documentary and the boredom in Chaumont, it looks like the good ship Jamaica is now breaking up and about to sink.

It is not the best time for a visit from Prime Minister P.J. Patterson and his delegation, yet whether planned or not, it helps to ease the situation. Jamaican sports minister Portia Simpson senses all is not well in the camp and gets the low-down from one of the players when she arrives at the Chateau. After lunch, she gives one of the most moving, emotive speeches I have heard, talking about our commitment to the people of Jamaica and how Jamaicans all over the world are monitoring our every step. Whatever we did as Reggae Boyz, she says, would further enhance the perception of Jamaica in other people's eyes.

We must put all the difficulties to the backs of our minds until after the Argentina match on Sunday, she says, but then inadvertently opens a can of worms by stating she will be personally responsible for making Captain Burrell, Horace Reid, P.J. Patterson and Rene Simoes deliver on their pre-tournament promises. Captain Burrell's face is a picture and his uncomfortable expression is shared by Simoes. The coach is obviously a little surprised that Portia Simpson is so forthright and I'm sure he will get to the bottom of this episode. He will feel betrayed that a player feels more comfortable talking to a politician than him.

Over lunch, Peter Cargill asks me whether I think he should tell the coach how the players are feeling. We want to be paid the outstanding money before Sunday's match so I tell him that he should. I am interested to see what Simoes' reaction will be, and how Peter handles the situation. The group leader is looking vulnerable at the moment and his relationship with the coach has cooled because of his opposition to changing the formation. He has not been playing in the first team during training for Sunday's game at the Parc des Princes and is frustrated that the coach has not picked up the mood of the players. After the match in Lens, Simoes said to Peter: 'You have not got the same vibe that you came with. It means you are not the same player.' Cargill told him that he cannot just switch the vibe on and off, he has to feel it. He is not bitter at being dropped and has said that he'd rather give someone else a chance than do badly and let Jamaica down. After everything that Peter has done, it is sad to see him like this.

19 June

After breakfast, an ashen-faced Simoes calls a meeting in the hotel lobby. He tells us he is disgusted that we had more discussions with Captain Burrell about wages and bonuses and states that he is over-ruling all previous agreements. Simoes is basically saying that he has the power to void decisions made by the president of the JFF. He has all the players' passports and travel documents spread out on a table and instructs anyone who is not committed to the cause or worried about financial arrangements to take their documents and leave. He is prepared, he insists, to go into the game with 15 squad members if that is what is required.

Eyes flick nervously at each other to see if anyone will make the move towards the table – but nobody does. We are then ordered on to the bus to travel to Paris for our date with Gabriel Batistuta and Argentina. There is an unnerving silence throughout the three-hour journey to our next hotel on the outskirts of the capital.

After arriving at the Hotel Ermitage des Loges, we train using the 4–4–2 system. Personnel has now changed, though, and I am disappointed to be given a yellow bib after scoring the goal against Croatia. This has less to do with my toe injury than Simoes' game plan, which is to play two man markers in midfield to combat the threat of Ortega and Veron, hence limiting the supply to Batistuta. Having studied the early matches in the tournament and consulted his own computer data, the coach has noted that a lot of goals are being scored late on and explains that he wants to use me as a sub when the game opens up in the latter stages. I believe that the best form of defence is attack and you have to pick a system that suits what your team is about. The coach, however, believes he can spring a surprise on Argentina.

20 June

The players are now moaning about just about everything. Rooms in the new hotel are small and have no air-conditioning but these complaints are only surfacing because of dissatisfaction in other areas. Our problems on the pitch are directly linked to the problems off it and this is demonstrated when we go to train at the Parc des Princes in the afternoon.

When we arrive, Argentina are finishing off their regulation 45-minute session and we have to wait in the changing room. The Argentinian players are still loitering on the sidelines when we take the field so Simoes calls us together and says it would be a great psychological advantage if we could show our opponents what camaraderie there is within the Jamaican squad. He suggests we hold one of our 'impromptu' singing sessions.

He calls for Bibi and Paul Hall, the team DJs, to select the vibe. Both stand silently, pulling faces. Alarmed, Simoes asks for the ever enthusiastic Spider to lay down a beat for the rest of us to pick up but none of us feel the vibes. I have never seen the group disobey Simoes before and there is an awkward silence that seems to last for hours. It is like the dog that has cowered after repeated beatings finally baring its teeth and growling at its master. When we sing, joke and have fun it always comes from the heart and it is certainly not a trick that can be trotted out on demand. We are not puppets who perform when the master pulls the strings.

Simoes walks away in disgust, muttering in Brazilian under his breath.

DANIEL

The Rene Simoes who takes the stage in the Mixed Zone after the training session is a different man to the bundle of energy I had talked to before the match against Croatia. Wearing black shorts, short white socks and a white Reggae Boyz T-shirt, when he stands behind the microphone it looks like he is about to sing the blues. (I heard him sing at Braco and know he has a terrible voice.) He looks strained and drawn and his voice is flat as he hints at the problems that have beset him. They are made worse by Croatia's 1-0 victory over Japan in Nantes, which means Jamaica now has a straight fight with Argentina for the second qualifying spot.

'We had a problem on Saturday which I think affect the team but I don't want to comment on this too much,' says Simoes. 'In the first game, our team only makes twelve fouls, it is the team that makes less fouls in the entire competition. The team was not with the fight and spirit in them. I tell them that the statistics prove that and the spirit of Jamaica is not there.' Rene always maintained that his greatest professional achievement was leading Brazil Under 20s to the South American Championship in Argentina. Losing to Argentina at football is one of the ultimate blows to a Brazilian's pride and with morale at such an all-time low, Simoes looks resigned to swallowing his pride tomorrow.

'What I have to do in the last four years is nothing compared with what I do last Saturday and Sunday before the game,' continues the coach. 'Normally my team talk is only fifteen minutes but then I spend one hour talking with them. We had a problem, a big one.' His eyes look totally dead behind his glasses and he pauses before the professional in him kicks in again '. . . but it's not the reason we lost the game.'

The Argentinian press are very interested to hear what the Brazilian coach has to say and as the questions continue in Spanish, I grab a word with Alfredo. He says that the JFF were foolish for not demanding the right to see the documentary before it was screened and that the players 'want to kick' Rupert and Todd. He is uncertain as to what his future holds but he thinks he will follow Rene. As Alfredo disappears back into the changing area, the coach is talking in English again. 'The time I have in Jamaica is the most beautiful time I have in my life but now it is finished. My contract is out in October and after World Cup I take three months' holiday because I have no time off in four years. It's over.'

ROBBIE

21 June

After a light breakfast, Simoes calls a meeting to name the team. Peter Cargill, the impressive Onandi Lowe and myself are omitted. I can understand the professor's reasoning but it does not mean that I agree with it. Onandi was one of our best performers in the first match and I am puzzled as to why he has been dropped. I suspect this is a decision that has more to do with personality than football, as the management think Lowe may have stirred the unrest over payment and the way we have been treated in France. He certainly has the physical presence to encourage some of the younger players to fall in behind him. I am a little surprised that Simoes has not made the distinction between footballing and personal matters, however. It is the first time I have really questioned one of his decisions.

Simoes goes on to talk about not letting this opportunity pass us by as in years to come we may regret what has happened but will not be able to do anything about it. In my opinion it is the time to clear the air properly; to discuss all the problems that need to be addressed and then move on. Now, more than ever, the coach needs to show his motivational genius but we leave the hotel to face one of the best teams in the competition feeling less than hyped up.

DANIEL

It is swelteringly hot inside the Parc des Princes and the Argentinian fans have decorated the famous stadium with huge banners proclaiming slogans such as 'Diego es dios'. Music blasts from the PA system and Bob Marley's 'Would You Be Love' gets an enthusiastic reception. The players are out on the pitch warming up and Bibi is in white boots while Boyd, Dean Sewell and Onandi juggle the ball between them near the tunnel. Carl Brown is alone on the centre spot in green tracksuit bottoms, milking in the occasion from behind his dark glasses. Captain Burrell is pacing the touchline, waving to friends in the stands as the stadium MC announces that this is FIFA Fair Play Day. Simoes had berated his team for the low number of fouls against Croatia so everyone is expecting Jamaica to come and play with a bit of fight this afternoon.

In the press box, the Jamaican contingent is looking puzzled by the latest in the series of curious selections. 'This is a strange team,' says Earl Bailey of the *Jamaica Observer*, as he looks at the sheet that has been placed on his desk. 'It reminds me of when we went to Mexico and lost six-love. That was a strange team then.' He has a point, for it barely resembles the side that was cast in stone during qualification. Christopher Dawes has been brought in to replace Lowe, Darryl Powell has succeeded Peter Cargill in midfield and Steve Malcolm has been introduced as a man marker. The only change they agree with is the addition of Powell and most are taking bets on the size of the margin in defeat. Four or five is the short-price favourite.

It takes just 15 seconds for Gabriel Batistuta to carve through the shaky Jamaican defence but his first opportunity is beaten away by Barrett. The Argentinians look much stronger on the ball and more assured in their touch. Darryl Powell is chasing shadows in midfield and picks up his first caution after four minutes for clattering into the back of his tormentor, Ariel Ortega. Roberto Sensini then steals in behind the Jamaican defence but wastes the fifth opportunity to put Argentina a goal to the good. It can only be a matter of time before the floodgates open.

But Jamaica come back into the game, slowing the tempo and finding their range. Bibi makes a promising break but as so often, suffers from stage fright with the goal looming. Suitably encouraged, Fitzroy flights a long pass to his club mate Paul Hall and Almeyda gives away a free kick which comes to nothing. The Jamaicans are seriously outnumbered in the crowd but the familiar whistling floats up from the stands as Argentina show the first signs of being rattled. On the far side, I see 'Tiger', the Jamaican mascot, dancing in the aisles to whip up support for the Reggae Boyz.

Bibi uses his pace to make inroads into the Argentinian half but when Hall finds space on one side of the penalty area, Fitzroy is the only person in the stadium who cannot see him. Burton then has a chance but a whistle from the stand distracts him and he delays his shot too long. Jamaica are at least mixing it with one of the tournament favourites but there is still a feeling of impending doom every time Argentina get the ball.

The harbinger is the tiny Ortega who has feet like precision instruments. He has got the better of a ragged-looking Darryl in midfield and opens the scoring with an exquisite chip over the onrushing Boopie. Jamaican heads drop as scarves are helicoptered above Argentinian heads around the ground. Simoes shrieks for his players to keep going forward but in first-half injury time, the final nail is hammered into the coffin when Darryl Powell commits his second ugly foul and looks up to see a red card being brandished. He does not have far to walk to the bench and rips his shirt off before making it to the touchline. The Jamaican press vent their frustrations during the interval, questioning whether Simoes has lost his mind.

One Love

ROBBIE

It is a deflated dressing room at half-time. Darryl Powell is lying on the floor, blowing hard. He is one of the fittest players in the squad but the challenge of marking the world-class Ortega and the red card have taken their toll. The coach works diligently to revive spirits and calls on Cargill to add a little composure in place of the ineffective Deon Burton. The game plan has flown out of the window with the red card and if it was a tough test before, it is going to be nigh-on impossible with ten men.

DANIEL

Jamaica show their inexperience, inviting wave upon wave of Argentinian attacks by defending deep in their own half. Tempers are getting frayed and arguments break out all over the pitch as Argentina pour through the gaps. A one-two on the edge of the box allows the impish Ortega to make it 2–0; he is enjoying one of his easiest afternoons in an Argentinian shirt.

Simoes looks intent on making it easier still by throwing caution to the wind and putting Walter Boyd on in place of Malcolm. The Reggae Boyz are strung out across the field and on one of their rare break-outs, Tappa scuffs his shot wide. It merely underlines the disparity between the ball striking of the two sides. Walter comes up with a trick that delights the crowd but the third goal is just waiting to go in. As Robbie loiters on the touchline to come on, Ortega (who else) tees up Batistuta in space and the master marksman buries his shot low past Barrett. Eight minutes later he adds a second before completing his hat-trick with his third, and Argentina's fifth, ten minutes from time.

The enduring images of Jamaica's day are the angry exchange between Pepe and Frank after the fourth goal and Rene's rueful smile as he walks down the tunnel after the final whistle. Reality has rushed in and the euphoria of achieving a draw with a Gold Cup Brazil back in February is doused with the cold-water humil-iation of a five-goal defeat at the hands of World Cup-primed Argentina. It was men against boyz.

ROBBIE

We have been dished up with what the Jamaicans call 'five pieces *and* fries'. After 30 minutes we felt that the game was going reasonably well but Argentina were buoyed by the sending off and we folded after the second Ortega goal. I think the decision to introduce Walter Boyd was a little odd when we might have been better suited trying to shore the game up and maintain some respectability. The players are disgruntled that the coach admitted to the press that the documentary hit team morale. Perhaps if outside factors were seen to affect our performance it would then take the heat off.

DANIEL

Rene takes the stage first and has no complaints with the result. 'The team don't recover from their problems in the first game and that is what broke us. Before Croatia, the preparation was wonderful and the team was very strong but I don't want to talk about that too much. Veron, Ortega and Batistuta are killers and we cannot play them with only ten men but I am proud of the team and I think they did well. In the second half time I had two options: close the team and keep it one-zero only, or allow the players to play the game and to express themselves. I took the decision as a coach because to lose the game one-nil was excellent for me as a coach but not good for the players. I thought about the players and I didn't care about my reputation.' It is not entirely convincing.

Two coaches have already been sacked after poor showings at the World Cup and a reporter asks whether Rene fears that he will be the third. 'I know the President of the Federation and he has a plan and he is very sensible,' answers Simoes, 'so I don't think so. When you win everybody win and when you lose, everybody lose. I accept it if the coach, twenty-two players and all the staff no longer have job but not only the coach.' There is a sympathetic murmur of laughter from the floor.

The main attraction, Daniel Passarella, is waiting in the wings and Simoes is ushered from the spotlight and steps over to brave the inquisition of a disgruntled Jamaican press corps.

Coach, is it too early to think about Japan?

'Again, I have to say what I said. We have to lift morale of the team because before Croatia it was down and today it was down again. Is this the reason we lost the match? No, but when your morale is not so good you need to be strong and we did not have that.'

And has today's result finally made up your mind about leaving the job after the tournament?

'Jamaica does not have the culture to accept the salary that the Federation has offered to me. I don't want to break the respect that I have for Jamaica and Jamaica has for me, that is why I cannot stay after the World Cup. This is the start of the road for Jamaica. It is a wonderful country and has fantastic players who will be much, much better at next World Cup.'

The players are saying nothing. Onandi Lowe breezes through first and does not even look round when asked for his thoughts. Walter Boyd and Pepe are equally reticent but Peter Cargill forces a pained smile and stops to give his verdict. 'We have to keep playing. We have been licked before and we will be licked again but we have to just keep going, play one more game.'

'One more game.' The World Cup is now starting to sound like a chore. I had been worried that the team would be exhausted by the time it arrived and now it seems that France '98 has indeed become a tour too far. Too much travelling, not enough rest and being locked in strange hotels for weeks on end has produced a jaded team that bears no relation to the spirited outfit that overturned the odds to qualify.

'It's a big shame,' concedes the shattered-looking Cargill. 'People usually support winners but now we are among the losers. Maybe the people who followed us from the start will stay behind us but right now who cares? It has been a disappointment especially after all the preparation we had done. We just threw that all down the drain but there were things going on behind the scenes that didn't involve the players. It's all bullshit.'

I ask him whether he will be tempted to apply for the vacant position left by Simoes and his answer says a lot about the mood within the camp. 'I have to look at the structure, at what's in place, because I'm not going to take a job just like that. I need to know exactly what I'm getting myself into. I think a lot of mistakes have been made in the last two weeks. Things we have been doing for the last three years, we just change the way we do them. I think this has made an effect on the team. We definitely would have liked to get out more because we are Jamaicans and we are like that. We don't like being cloaked up in one place.'

It makes me think of what Horace Reid said back in his office in Jamaica at the end of Reggae Boyz Week. 'For me, it is absolutely important that the team should never be hampered because of something that should have been done from this office,' he said. 'This has always been my approach in football – that the team should never have to walk from the field and say they lost because of something that happened off the field. We want to ensure that our players will be as comfortable as possible.'

Another reporter hears Cargill talking about internal problems and asks him what is going on. But he is not interested in raking over the coals again and says, 'Look. It's history, y'know. It's just sad. People will be very disappointed back home because there was so much hope after what we did. It's very disappointing to come so far and not do your best. Hopefully if we are in a tournament like this again, we won't make the same mistakes. What I say is that if it ain't broken, you don't fix it.'

I wish him luck for the game against Japan and tell him to lift morale. Peter half smiles and looks back. 'It couldn't get much lower, could it?'

ROBBIE

We are left to mull over an embarrassing, demoralising defeat which has emphatically ended our hopes of qualifying but there is an official function with the Jamaican Prime Minister at the Ritz in the centre of town, the same hotel where Princess Diana enjoyed her last meal with Dodi before the accident. The morning her death was announced in the UK, I left England to join the Jamaican squad for the Shell Cup.

It is strange to be drinking complimentary champagne after such a battering but the evening passes with the visiting Jamaican delegation saying how proud they are of what we have achieved. They remain optimistic that we will come back and learn from the experience. P.J. Patterson addresses the assembled dignitaries, talking of how Caribbean cricket grew steadily to the point where it was the driving force in the sport and how football can follow the same path. He inisists that he will stay loyal to the programme for as long as he is in office.

We round off the evening at the official Reggae Boyz after-match party, which provides much-needed relief after the stifling atmosphere within the camp. It is a massive dancehall event featuring Stone Love, the top sound system on Jamaica. Many supporters from the UK who have travelled over by coach pass on their commiserations, and it is humbling that they are so appreciative of our efforts despite the fact that they have been badly let down. I meet up with Lennox Lewis, very much a Jamaican, and he applauds what we have done for the country and asks why I did not start against Argentina. I am asked this question at least 100 times during the night, mainly by the UK-based fans who know more about me as a player.

Many people seem to know that all is not well within the squad and ask whether the rumours about division between the English-based players and the Jamaican-born lads are true. I state that there are no problems although I don't make too much eye contact while I'm doing it. Now is not the time to tell people what has happened behind the scenes.

We stay until the early hours of the morning and I enjoy a couple of drinks with mates over from England. It is refreshing to break camp and let our hair down and I wonder if things could have worked out differently if we had been given a little more freedom from the outset.

14

Redemption

ROBBIE

22 June

A year as a Jamaican international has taught me to expect the unexpected and true to form, our World Cup approaches its final act in bizarre fashion. Despite the sore heads caused by the 5–0 defeat and night out at the Stone Love party, we are herded to EuroDisney for another function. Unsurprisingly, the players are not particularly keen on the idea but someone from the Federation has set this up and it is imperative for us to show.

We are trailed across the park by a herd of kids and well-wishers which means that we end up standing in the same spot for 30 minutes at a time, posing for pictures and signing bits of paper. Normally we would not mind, but getting spanked by Argentina has not done much for our self-esteem. There isn't much opportunity to try out any of the rides so a number of us retire to the Disney Hotel cafe and sit around drinking coffee and putting the world to rights.

We leave at 7pm, and after another four hours on the bus, everyone falls into bed exhausted from the day's excursion. I am disappointed to hear that England lost 2–1 to Romania.

23 June

If we get beaten in a third straight game there will be ructions back in Jamaica and we all want to put on a show for the last match. Spirits are up because we know we will be going home after Saturday's game – although this is not the way we expected to be feeling at this point in time.

Coach Simoes finally calls a clear the air meeting after breakfast. In a frank and open discussion we are accused of losing our nerve, of being driven by money and of lacking the tactical expertise to cope with football at this level. Perhaps Simoes believes that a good coach never shows any signs of weakness because he does not admit to any mistakes of his own. I think the pressure might be getting to the Professor.

He nevertheless states he is proud of us regardless of the results and would like to be able to look us all in the eye if our paths cross in the future. It is another strong hint that he will not be returning to Jamaica after the World Cup. He hints that the scale of the Argentina defeat might have cost him the Brazilian job, claiming that his decision to abandon the midfield and go for all-out attack was because he wanted to give us a chance to shine rather than enhance his future employment prospects. A fairly amicable meeting, under the circumstances, is closed with Simoes telling us that our previous financial agreement with Burrell will stand. It smacks of shutting the stable door after the horse has bolted.

Coach Brown then stands up and expresses the hope that we can all be friends at the end of the adventure. Carl might not be as well-travelled or as experienced as Simoes but he is hugely respected as a man and has become vital for the harmony of the camp.

We train as normal in the evening and prepare to leave Chaumont for good. There is no sadness about departing.

24 June

Three more hours on the bus brings us to our final base in Lyon and we arrive mid-afternoon in time for a vigorous training session incorporating the customary Simoes v. Brown ten-a-side game. These contests are supposed to be a bit of fun but they never work out that way and disagreements always occur. Fortunately, I am on Simoes' team, which has an inbuilt advantage because he is also the referee!

25 June

We train on the pitch in Lyon in preparation for our final game against Japan. It has become imperative to beat the Japanese because we do not want to finish bottom of the group. A win will also guarantee a spark of optimism which can be taken from a disappointing first World Cup experience. It is a matter of national pride and training reflects that. It feels like the old vibe is returning.

26 June

After a light breakfast we attend our customary pre-match meeting. Simoes realises the importance of getting us psychologically prepared and makes the conversation lighter than usual, saying that this is not a day for tactics, systems or strategies, it is a day for pride in the nation and the chance for the group to reunite and leave the World Cup in a positive frame of mind. He admits that there have been many faults since our arrival in France, but talks of them being in the past. It is now time to look forward.

He recalls an incident in the Argentina match where Pepe made a miraculous recovery to cancel out a mistake by his 'brethren' Bibi. He talks of Pepe's love for Bibi, meaning that he was prepared to commit everything to make sure his friend's mistake did not cost us a goal. This is the feeling we need to rediscover as a group, he says, as it is the very same spirit that got us here in the first place.

The coach announces that he is returning to the 3-5-2 formation, favoured by the players. He says he is disappointed we did not approach him earlier to talk about our dislike of the 4-4-2 system but he explains to the group that he is going to try to give everyone a game. However he says he will also play as many of the Jamaican-based lads as possible because it's their last chance to put on a show that might generate a move abroad. A 33-year-old has-been like me is probably past a move to AC Milan anyway. This seems fair enough, but then Fitzroy and Paul, who played in both previous games and are at an English professional club already, get picked for the third game running. I suspect that Simoes might feel an allegiance to the pair because of the amount of time they have given up to be with Jamaica. It also suggests that team politics and sentiment have affected the coach's policies. Whatever his thinking Simoes is remarkably adept at distancing himself from the blame when things goes wrong, which could be seen as both a strength and a weakness in a coach.

Yet as we head to the final game, the players feel revived, relieved even. One of the most important reasons for this change in spirit is that my good mate Spider Lawrence has been picked to play his first World Cup game. Not only a competent keeper, Spider has the ability to raise the spirits of all around him and his role in the dressing room is as big as that of the coach, captain or physio.

The dressing room is a complex arena, and needs to be carefully balanced. Over the years I have come across many individuals with unique talents that add to the right atmosphere. A few years ago, our 'vibe master' at Wimbledon was a rather inexperienced, ex non-league played named Steve Talboys. He won't mind me saying he wasn't the greatest player God ever put on this world but his humour and outlook meant that he had a massive influence in the dressing room. Steve probably only took part in about 20 first-team games in four years but was almost always a member of the squad because Joe Kinnear recognised his value. When he finally left to join Watford, we lost an integral part of the dressing room atmosphere, which to this day has not been totally replaced. Characters like Talboys and Lawrence are often underestimated and because Spider's enthusiasm is so infectious on the pitch I have a feeling that we will do well today.

There is a sea of Japanese fans in blue jerseys around the Stade de Gerland in Lyon and it looks like the Jamaicans have forgotten the game is on. Luckily, I am used to every game being like an away game after years of playing for Wimbledon. Our fears are confirmed when we run out for the pre-match warm-up – 80 per cent of the ground is filled with Japan's enthusiastic followers, interspersed with splashes of yellow where the Jamaicans are sitting. However, the Reggae Boyz have become big stars thanks to the amount of media coverage they get in Japan so there is a friendly atmosphere inside the stadium. It's a relief, particularly as this is the first game my mother and father have made it to in France.

DANIEL

It is a sombre party that assembles around a table in the press cafeteria in Lyon. The travelling Jamaican press corps is weary and looking forward to going home. After all the hype, Jamaica's first World Cup has been a disappointment and we agree that the players probably feel stale after spending so long together. The story still has a chance for a happy ending and everyone is desperate to see Jamaica play the way we know they can. Lack of ability will always be forgiven if the spirit is willing but in the last two games, the Reggae Boyz have showed little of the steel that saw them through the trials of Toros Neza and the bags of piss that rained on them in El Salvador. It is important for the future of Jamaican football that the team now signs off with a performance that, in the words of Simoes, can 'plant the seed of hope'. A third straight defeat could see the bubble burst back on the island.

It is a game between the two World Cup novices of Group H but there is an air of anticipation inside the ground. Marcus Gayle makes his World Cup debut up front and Onandi Lowe returns to the defence but there is no starting place for Andy Williams, Dean Sewell, Walter Boyd or Durrent Brown. Most reporters have given up trying to second-guess the professor and settle back instead to watch Jamaica start with an urgency that has been sadly lacking so far.

Japan's fans are fantastic, clapping and singing at a pitch that betrays how popular the game has become for women. Hidetoshi Nakata, the pin-up of the J-League, gets a huge squeal of encouragement every time he picks up the ball but for the first 20 minutes Japan lack the killer instinct to round off their attractive passing patterns. Pepe is busy at the back and looks like adding a third impressive performance to win the jeep offered for the best Jamaican player at France '98. In midfield, Bibi and Tappa play with an invigorating freedom but their final ball is still lacking. Marcus is troubling the Japanese defence with his height and at the other end, Spider is a blur of black tracksuit bottoms and flying arms. This is much more like Jamaica.

Six minutes before half-time, Marcus leaps to flick a cross into the path of Steve Malcolm and as Shorty stumbles, Tappa seizes on the loose ball to fire it past Kawaguchi in the Japanese goal. It is a great finish and the Jamaican fans in the upper tier of the stand to my right acclaim the moment as the popular midfielder is engulfed by his team mates. He adds a second ten minutes after the break and despite frantic attacks from Japan, Spider is no mood to let victory slip from his grasp. Masashi Nakayama gives the Japanese fans hope with a goal in the 74th minute but it is not enough. The Jamaican World Cup ends in a victory that was beyond the likes of the USA, Scotland, Bulgaria, South Korea and opponents Japan. It should be noted that none of the Japanese players commited suicide.

ROBBIE

It is a shame that my parents only see three minutes' injury time of their offspring in action but I am delighted at the way the day has gone. Tappa was the first Jamaican player I believed had the ability to play at top level and although his lack of inner belief means he does not impose himself on games the way his talent demands, today was most definitely his day. It may just be the performance that sways one of those foreign club chairmen to write the £2 million cheque for his services.

Along with Theodore, I feel that Pepe, Bibi, Onandi and Spider have shown the talent and maturity to warrant a chance to ply their trade overseas. Warren Barrett will be slightly disappointed with his tournament although he was carrying a couple of restrictive injuries that hampered him. For his dedication and professionalism, I hope Boopie gets another chance to show his true worth.

It is amazing what a win can do and I look across a happy changing room and see Rudi Dixon smiling and joining in the celebrations. Poor Rudi tragically twisted his knee a week before our journey to France and instead of looking forward to the greatest event of his life, he now has to travel the long road to recovery. To his credit, he has remained upbeat and supportive of everyone throughout. He epitomises all that is good about Jamaica and her people and I have every faith that he will be around for a second bite at the cherry in 2002.

My joy at winning is mixed with a feeling of remorse. Simoes has told me to call this my 'first World Cup' but the reality is that my World Cup dream is at an end. I would like to think that I can emulate Roger Milla of Cameroon, who played at the age of 38, but France has been hard work and I need four years off before the next one. Playing for Jamaica has been a wonderful experience but the World Cup, sadly, hasn't quite lived up to expectations.

DANIEL

'I feel proud,' says a happier-looking Simoes in the Mixed Zone, 'although I don't feel anything different to what I did before the game. I keep proud of the players. Always I am saying, I treat the players as I treat my daughters. Always when they make mistake, I punish them but I never lose my love for them. Today, before the game, we discussed what had gone wrong. It's like when you are in families, as everyone is guilty. The coach, the players, the Federation – we all have some problems there and all of us is guilty. It is not time to point fingers, it is a time for learning as a man and as a player.

'I think and I thought that this team has a spirit. When you have a spirit and you are on a mission, it's very difficult to be beaten. But we lost the spirit before the first game and that's what frustrate us. Even with that, I am very proud of the team. There is no reason to be disappointed because with the win today we are twenty-fifth position in this World Cup. We have come for the first time, Jamaica had 2.5 million people only and you have to congratulate the players, everyone involved in sport, the media, the sponsors. Everyone must be congratulated for their tremendous efforts they have put together to come here and perform quite well.'

I ask him for his reflections on the last four years and he gulps. It is hard to put into words – even in his inimitable manner – what it all means and where we go from here. 'This team teach the people of Jamaica how to work together,' he says, 'and it is the best moment I have spent in my life as a human being, as a man. Professionally, I had other great times but as a human being it is the best time I have spent in my entire life.'

It will probably be the last time I see the coach. I will miss his colourful analogies, his passion, the way he chops the ends off his words (always interesting with 'country'), his fiery temper and his contradictions, but this is the way I want to remember him. Smiling and shooting from the lip.

Captain Burrell makes a rare appearance and is mobbed by the Jamaican journalists. 'I just want to build on what has been achieved,' he pronounces, side-stepping the question on what he has learnt and what he might do differently next time. 'Despite the limitations so far as our facilities are concerned, Jamaica has been able to rise above. It shows how greater a people we are and I say that Jamaica is one of the greatest nations on earth in all aspects of life. A Jamaican can do anything that he wants to do and this is really a proud moment for all of us. We are the first English-speaking Caribbean nation to qualify for the World Cup and the nature of our victory today, a hard-fought victory, will mean that the entire world and the Jamaican people all around the world will be very proud.' He has no comment to make on the documentary.

And, Captain, will you be stepping down if Simoes leaves as announced? 'When I made reference to stepping away should Simoes leave, I should have gone further to say, "If Simoes had gone under those circumstances I don't think I would have really wanted to stay."

'The thing is, at this time, I am leaving no stones unturned to make sure that we get the necessary sponsorship from outside Jamaica, as well as inside, with a view to retaining the services of Professor Simoes who I am sure would want to assist our football in this upward mobility.' The World Cup is not even over and The Captain is already tub-thumping for the next campaign. I cannot help but admire the man.

He has not been seen much during the World Cup but it sounds as though he has been busy. He is reported to have attended meetings in London during the tournament. (Or perhaps the shopping was not up to much in Chaumont.) I wanted to know whether The Captain and the bald British agent he had hired had successfully negotiated any transfers for players contracted to the programme. How would the transfer fees be divided up and more specifically, how much would go to the JFF? After discussing a series of tame issues with the Jamaican press, his cheeks deflate when the question flies in from left field. The Captain's nostrils flare and he addresses me with a look of barely concealed disdain.

'That is certainly a private matter for the players, the clubs and the JFF and it is not something I would like to make public.'

I am also anxious that the JFF should actively ensure that players are placed at clubs that are right for them. Despite travelling the world in the last two years, many of the younger prospects in the squad show a frustrating mixture of calculated reserve and small island introspection. It is vital for the future of football in Jamaica that the best of this historic vintage go abroad and do well. Becoming a role model for the youth – an answer that most of them gave when asked what representing their country meant – entails more than languishing in the reserves in a strange country that seems a million miles from home. After six months of following the team, I know that Ian Goodison, Onandi, Tappa and Shorty are fine players, but to make an impact abroad they will have to hit the ground running. Only Bibi has age firmly on his side.

So what has the president been doing? 'The Jamaican Football Federation has been receiving what I would say is maximum respect,' he says beaming, those big cheeks puffed out with pride once more. 'The level of respect meted out to me personally and the people in my organisation is next to none. It shows what good performances can do and after today's performance, I am pretty sure that anybody who wears the Jamaican shirt, in France or any part of the world, will receive even more respect. That, to me, is very important and another major achievement for Jamaica. As it is said, "We liccle bit, but we tallower" – which means that Jamaica is small yet very significant in every aspect of life.' It is nothing less than you would expect from a president.

Marcus Gayle is behind him, pulling faces. He reveals that the victory was down to the haircuts he gave the players this morning, his special role within the squad now being team barber. Peter Cargill looks a whole lot happier too. 'We have something to smile about today and hopefully people will remember the last thing that happened. I'm going to enjoy my family now and take it easy. It's been a long road.'

It's been a long road for Fitzroy too. 'I wanted to score six goals and I genuinely had a dream over and over again that I would,' he says. 'I think I have come out of the tournament with a lot of credit. I have pitted myself against the best in the world and come out and done well.' Evon Hewitt, using his best broadcasting voice, shoves a microphone in front of Fitz and asks about possible contracts. The player made some flippant remarks about English football in the documentary that were picked up by the papers back home. He smiles ruefully. 'I'm still waiting for my phone to ring.'

Fitzroy has had a tough World Cup but I'm pleased that it has ended well for him. He says too much but is entertaining for it.

His commitment to Jamaica can never be questioned and although it would be very easy for him to turn his back on international football after what has happened in the last month, he laughs at the suggestion. 'Fitzroy Simpson is a Jamaican for life and as long as they want me there, I'll be there. I feel very proud that we have left the tournament winning a game and I'm looking to go to 2002. We were playing for the future of Jamaican football today and hopefully we have laid the foundations for young players coming through.' Whatever people say about him, Fitzroy is one of the men that made it happen.

Darryl Powell says he has 'a lovely feeling' but his memories of the World Cup will remain bitter-sweet. Carl Brown, one of the Jamaican success stories of the tournament, admits that the players only understood what it meant to play at the World Cup when it was too late, but is glad that pride shone through in today's performance. Paul Hall is happy to have made it to France and participated and is now looking forward to 'kicking back and taking a holiday'. Portsmouth want him back for training but he says they can wait.

The heroes of the hour come through together. 'Well, it's a great feeling,' laughs Tappa when asked what it's like to be the leading Jamaican scorer in World Cup history. 'The World Cup is a different level of football and although we have not come here and matched people's expectations back home, I think we have given it a fair shot and we can move on from here. A lot of doors have been opened for me and anything can happen. I give God thanks for where we are and where we are going and now we have to leave it up to the Father.'

Did he wake up this morning and know it was going to be Tappa's day? His large features break into the smile that makes Jamaican women wilt. 'Last night I talked to my friend Banky and I told him that I was going to score one and Ricardo Gardener was going to score the other. But because Ricardo can't do it I have to do it for him.' It is a fitting finish for the man with the long red boots.

Spider is next and plays down his heroics although his face is creased into that film-star smile. 'I'm here working, this is my job and this is what I do. I'm always ready to go out there to give my best. This win will help boost the players and give everyone momentum.' He says he's now supporting 'my boys' Brazil all the way to the final.

I do not see Devon – who had promised to give me some pictures – or the unforgettable Evon Hewitt before I pack up my gear and head for Marseilles and the next round. My last sight of the Reggae Boyz is as I stand with a small pocket of fans who have waited in the drizzle to see them off. They have not played the seven games that Rene promised but then again, nothing is ever straightforward with Jamaica. The players stand up and wave through the windows of the bus. They look like they are all friends again.

Captain Burrell travels separately in a limousine.

ROBBIE

It would have been nice to enjoy each other's company before we all scatter. It might be the last time we are all together but in their wisdom, the JFF bring two coachloads of people to the hotel. We have always been too accessible as Reggae Boyz and I think it is time for the JFF to drop the name and concentrate on the players as international footballers rather than as a Harlem Globe Trotter circus act. Instead of the quiet drink and chat we had hoped for, over 100 people cram into a tiny room. My parents come back to the hotel and say thanks to the coach for giving their son the opportunity to represent the country and make them so proud. He is as charming as ever and after everything, we sit down and have a good chat. Whatever went wrong in the final few weeks, I will always have a lot of affection and respect for Simoes. It is unlikely that we would have been in Lyon toasting a maiden World Cup victory without him.

I buy a bottle of champagne and share it with Spider. We drink to what we have done but agree it is not the ending we had wanted. I hardly see Boopie or Cargill during the evening and reflect that we should have been together on this last night. They have both been very good to me and I feel strongly that I don't just want to be friends for a year. I intend to spend more time in Jamaica, a home that up until a year ago I never really knew I had. It would be good to keep in touch with my team mates and see them whenever I go back to the island. We have been through a lot together.

27 June

Everyone has gone their separate ways and I am left with my memories. That historic goal in Lens is the most vivid, epitomising what I have made a name for: the break from midfield, the timing of the run and the contact with the head. The Jamaican boys have always said that my best foot is on my head and that Nike should sponsor my haircuts as well as my boots.

The experiences I have had with Jamaica will stay with me for ever. We might not have 'shaken up the world' on the pitch but Jamaica became the smallest – and probably one of the poorest – countries ever to qualify. Most importantly, we made a nation believe in itself and brought happiness to a lot of people. Respect.

Footnote: Rene Simoes stayed on, although it was Carl Brown who led Jamaica to Shell Cup triumph in August. Ricardo Gardener, who won the jeep for the best Jamaican player at the World Cup, moved to Bolton Wanderers for £1 million.